The EVERYTHING®
Birthing Book

Dear Reader:

When I was writing *The Everything® Pregnancy Book, Second Edition*, it struck me just how brief and fleeting nine months can be to prepare a woman for one of the biggest events of her life—the day she gives birth to her child. Right when you've gotten attuned to your tenant's tumbles and pokes, it's moving day. Suddenly, those few hours of childbirth classes seem woefully insufficient and you're wishing you could have a dress rehearsal.

Although I've been through pregnancy and birth twice myself, I've never quite felt fully "prepared" for what was coming. Case in point—my first daughter, who made her debut ten days late after an induction, twelve hours of heavy labor that stopped progressing at six centimeters, and an eventual C-section. A guide that would have mentally and emotionally prepared us for the possibility of alternate routes through childbirth as well as helping us make informed decisions about our "ideal" birth would have made the experience much easier to handle. *The Everything® Birthing Book* has been written with that need in mind. I think you'll find it a comprehensive source, one that lays out all your options for educated childbirth choices and a fulfilling, healthy birth.

Paula Ford-Martin

The EVERYTHING® Series

Editorial

Publishing Director	Gary M. Krebs
Managing Editor	Kate McBride
Copy Chief	Laura MacLaughlin
Acquisitions Editor	Eric M. Hall
Development Editor	Christina MacDonald
Production Editor	Jamie Wielgus
Technical Reviewer	Elisabeth A. Aron, M.D., F.A.C.O.G.

Production

Production Director	Susan Beale
Production Manager	Michelle Roy Kelly
Series Designers	Colleen Cunningham
	John Paulhus
Cover Design	Paul Beatrice
	Matt LeBlanc
Layout and Graphics	Colleen Cunningham
	Rachael Eiben
	Michelle Roy Kelly
	John Paulhus
	Daria Perreault
	Erin Ring
Series Cover Artist	Barry Littmann
Interior Illustrator	Argosy

Visit the entire Everything® Series at www.everything.com

THE
EVERYTHING®
BIRTHING
BOOK

Know all your options and choose the method that is right for you

Paula Ford-Martin

Technical Review by Elisabeth A. Aron, M.D., F.A.C.O.G.

Adams Media
Avon, Massachusetts

For Mom, whose birth
experience made this book possible.

An Everything® Series Book.
Everything® and everything.com® are registered trademarks of F+W Publications, Inc.

Published by Adams Media, an F+W Publications Company
57 Littlefield Street, Avon, MA 02322 U.S.A.
www.adamsmedia.com

ISBN: 1-59337-141-1
Printed in the United States of America.

J I H G F E D C B A

Library of Congress Cataloging-in-Publication Data
Ford-Martin, Paula.
The everything birthing book / Paula Ford-Martin.
p.   cm.
(Everything series)
ISBN 1-59337-141-1
1. Childbirth--Popular works. 2. Labor (Obstetrics)--Popular works.
3. Delivery (Obstetrics)--Popular works. I. Title. II. Series.

RG652.F674 2004
618.4--dc22
2004013271

This book is available at quantity discounts for bulk purchases.
For information, call 1-800-872-5627.

Contents

Acknowledgments

This book would not have been possible without Eric Hall and Barb Doyen—thanks for your guidance, encouragement, and advocacy. I'd also like to thank my colleague Robin Elise Weiss, B.A., L.C.C.E., I.C.C.E.-C.P.E., C.D. (DONA), childbirth educator, mother of six (yes six), and home birth veteran, for promptly answering my queries and sharing her expertise. I'm grateful to Erin Dugan, M.P.H., Breastfeeding Coordinator for the Rhode Island Department of Health, for offering her birth and breastfeeding knowledge and many clinical references (as well as being an outstanding playgroup host), and to both Barbara Harper of Waterbirth International and Mickey Mongan of HypnoBirthing International for their assistance. Finally, a very special thanks to my family for their tremendous support and love during the birth of this book.

Top Ten Things You Should Know
About Birth

1. Birth is a normal, natural physiological process, not an illness that inevitably requires medical intervention.

2. No two births are exactly the same—even for the same woman.

3. Exercise in pregnancy can help make labor and birth easier.

4. Childbirth classes come in all flavors. Shop around for the one that fits your tastes and birth expectations.

5. Lamaze isn't just about funny breathing, and HypnoBirthing isn't a cabaret act.

6. A birth plan provides a basic script for your birth attendants and care providers to stage the birth you want, although you may have to improvise along the way.

7. The best person to have with you during birth is the one you feel most comfortable with and can trust—and that goes for support partners as well as care providers.

8. You give birth with your mind as well as your body, and stress, fear, and anxiety can all make labor and birth more painful and less fulfilling.

9. "Once a cesarean, always a cesarean" is an outdated notion.

10. Your body is designed to give you natural cues and instincts to guide you through the birthing process. Trust yourself, and realize that you own your birth.

Introduction

▶ Birth is the culmination of nine months of careful planning, anticipation, anxiety, and fears. It is guaranteed to be one of the most unforgettable experiences of your life, the event that marks your entrance into the lifelong journey of motherhood. Your baby's safe passage into this world is a one-night-only performance, so it is important to carefully contemplate the kind of birth experience you and your significant other would like to have.

As you'll be hearing ad nauseum throughout your pregnancy, women have been giving birth since the beginning of time, so in that sense you know that a) you can do it too, and b) this baby is coming, ready or not. However, that doesn't mean that you are forced into choosing childbirth techniques that are antiquated. Never before have there been so many choices for women giving birth. From natural and synthetic pain relief methods, to schools of preparation such as Lamaze and Bradley, to methods of intervention, there's lots of information to absorb before the big day arrives.

Learning about your childbirth options ahead of time and compiling a written birth plan that lays out your particular "blueprint for birth" will help ease any anxieties about labor and delivery and will make the event itself a more fulfilling one. It will also get you and your health-care team on the same page as far as your expectations and medical requirements are concerned. Having an open and honest discussion with your health-care provider about your birth plan well before your due date will prevent any misunderstandings later.

Birth is a highly emotional experience as well as a physical one, and along with your medical care providers you'll need a companion to provide adequate support for you during the hard work of labor and delivery. Who will attend this momentous event—whether it be a professional doula, a spouse or significant other, a close friend, or a family member—and the role that person will play in the birth are issues you should start thinking about now.

Finally, keep in mind that that you're giving birth to a brand new family as well as a baby. Whether you're a single first-time mom or married with two children already, your family will take on entirely new dimensions with the arrival of your child. Your family unit may play a role in some of your birth decisions. Some women make the choice of a home birth so their other children can take part in the birth, while others may feel more comfortable first bonding with their new addition in the hospital without any distractions of home responsibilities.

It's easy for the needs of doctors, health insurers, hospitals, and well-meaning friends and family to overshadow what the parents themselves would like to get out of the birth experience. Remember that while these other factors are certainly important and should bear some weight, in the end this is your body, your baby, and your show. Own it and enjoy it!

Chapter 1

Modern Childbirth: A Short History

A journey into motherhood, the emergence of a fresh and promising life, a physical and emotional transformation imbued with both spiritual and mystical power—childbirth is the everyday miracle of our existence, proof that we are indeed here for a reason. Although women have been giving birth since the beginning of time, it's only been over the past several hundred years that major developments in obstetric care and technology have radically changed the childbirth experience.

In the Beginning

Throughout time, childbirth has symbolized many different things across societies and generations. Many ancient cultures invoked mysticism and religion into the birth ritual. The Egyptians, for example, used mud "birthing bricks" that a woman would squat on to deliver her child. The birthing bricks were adorned with Egyptian gods and goddesses charged with the protection of both mother and child.

Other cultures had rituals that seem far before their time. An 1879 account of a Ugandan healer performing a cesarean section describes the use of wine to disinfect both the abdomen and his hands, and the technique of cauterization to minimize bleeding of the wound—two effective techniques that were not widely practiced among Western practitioners at the time.

Hospitals and Surgical Intervention

Before the eighteenth century, obstructed labor was a major cause of infant mortality in Great Britain. Delivery by cesarean section was not an option; at the time, a C-section was generally only attempted in cases where women had died or were close to it. If obstruction didn't resolve itself with version (turning) of the fetus or other techniques, the only other available option that would preserve the mother's life was surgical destruction of the infant in the womb.

While puerperal fever, caused by streptococcal bacteria, claimed countless lives in European "lying-in" hospitals, American women, who rarely gave birth in hospitals, largely escaped the epidemic. Midwife-attended home births on both sides of the Atlantic were also known to have lower rates of puerperal fever, possibly because most midwives were known for their cleanliness.

Most women avoided hospitals like the plague because, in fact, they were rampant with something almost as bad—puerperal fever, a postpartum infection also known as childbirth fever—not to mention other infections. Unless a woman was without any means or shelter, the vast majority gave birth in their own homes with the help of a midwife and/or female friends, neighbors, and family, who would stay through the birth into the postpartum period to help with the infant and household.

Scottish physician William Smellie is credited with the first scientific and effective use of the obstetrical forceps in the mid-eighteenth century, giving women renewed hope for delivering healthy infants. Still, nonsterile techniques and the widespread incidence of puerperal fever made infant and maternal mortality rates high throughout Europe. Until Joseph Lister and Ignaz Philip Semmelweiss independently introduced the concept of antiseptic techniques in surgery and medical practice in 1865, and hospitals chose to adopt them a mere thirty years later, babies were delivered both vaginally and through C-section by doctors and attendants in street clothes who may or may not have bothered to wash their hands.

By the 1900s, hospitals were safer, antiseptic places, and women began moving from the bedroom to the delivery room. The new and improved hospitals began to attract middle- and upper-class clientele.

Regional anesthetic blocks also first made their debut in the early twentieth century and became another factor in the growing popularity of hospital birth. By 1950, almost ninety percent of births in the United States took place in a hospital setting. Fifty years earlier, ninety percent of women giving birth did so at home, and midwives attended almost half of all births.

Midwifery Traditions

Midwives have been around for thousands of years. Ancient Greek texts from the second century A.D. tell the stories of these women, who were respected for their knowledge of medicine and cited by prominent physicians of the day. During the Middle Ages, there are historical accounts of midwives accused of witchcraft, even burned at the stake because of their knowledge of herbal remedies such as belladonna and ergot, and the mysticism surrounding "woman healers."

The word midwife translates to "with woman." This applied to training as well as to practice. Early midwives gained their skills through apprenticeships with an older, experienced midwife, often a friend or relative. In nineteenth- and twentieth-century America, they weren't licensed practitioners, but this was not uncommon given that registration and licensing requirements for physicians were very lax at the time.

Obstetricians Versus Midwives

By the mid-nineteenth century, the introduction of the forceps helped give physicians the edge in the childbirth arena. At that time, the term "physician" implicitly referred to someone of the male gender; the first woman to enter medical school, Elizabeth Blackwell, would not graduate until 1849. Doctors began to lobby hard to push midwives out of the lucrative middle- and upper-class birthing business. Physician-published pamphlets of the day claimed that female birth-attendants made hormonally charged irrational decisions and heavily promoted the class status of having a physician-attended birth. As the decades passed, American families began to migrate toward male physicians—who soon acquired the name of obstetricians—for the delivery of their children, and the midwife became relegated to poor and rural clients. The move toward obstetricians and hospital birth marked another important passage in the American social perception of birth itself. Once considered a natural, normal physiological process that required minimal outside assistance, childbirth began to be perceived as a medical condition or pathological process that mandated physician guidance and interventions.

The Nurse-Midwife Is Born

The resurgence of the art of midwifery began in the 1920s, when public-health pioneer and nurse Mary Breckenridge established the Frontier Nursing Service (FNS), a mobile family health-care service for families in the remote Kentucky mountains. The FNS introduced the concept of nurse-midwife to America and started a new model for midwifery services. Educational programs for nurse-midwives were established at universities, and by 1955 the first professional organization for the advancement of midwifery—the American College of Nurse-Midwifery (ACNM)—was established.

Yet midwives who had learned their craft the traditional way—through apprenticeship and birth attendance—were still faced with the challenge of gaining medical and governmental legitimacy. These "direct entry" midwives formed their own professional organization, the Midwives' Alliance of North America (MANA) in 1982, and eventually created educational and accreditation standards that gave them renewed legitimacy.

Today, MANA is one of the two major certifying organizations of midwives in the United States, the other being the American College of Nurse-Midwives (ACNM). A CPM, or certified professional midwife, has met education and clinical standards set forth by MANA. For more on midwives and their role in birth and prenatal care, see Chapter 3.

QUESTION?

What kind of educational standards do midwives have to meet to be licensed?
Nurse-midwives are currently the only type of midwife licensed in all fifty states. The designations CM and CNM stand for "certified midwife" and "certified nurse-midwife," respectively. A midwife with these credentials has met clinical board certification standards established by the American College of Nurse-Midwives (ACNM) and has completed an ACNM accredited midwifery program.

Advent of Anesthesia and Analgesia

Even though anesthesia for surgical procedures was introduced in the 1840s and soon became commonplace, childbirth remained a forbidden arena for its use, no matter what the circumstances. Most obstetricians and medical professionals of the day viewed the idea of anesthetizing women in labor as unacceptable on moral grounds, saying that the pain associated with childbirth was biblically mandated.

And then along came Sir James Young Simpson, a Scottish obstetrician who was professor of midwifery at the University of Edinburgh. In January of 1847, Simpson administered diethyl ether to a laboring patient with a deformed pelvis, a procedure that would be the first use of an anesthetic in labor and delivery.

Simpson was criticized severely by both colleagues and laypeople for advocating the use of anesthesia in childbirth. In a largely Catholic United Kingdom, many objected on the theological grounds that "the sins of Eve" had destined all women to endure the pain of childbirth, no matter what the circumstances.

Simpson always replied with a biblical quote from the Book of Genesis, which stated that God "put Adam in a deep sleep" to remove his rib in order to create Eve, implying anesthesia was a natural gift from God. So widespread was this conviction that in 1847, Simpson felt compelled to publish a paper on the subject entitled "Answer to the Religious Objections Advanced Against the Employment of Anaesthetic Agents in Midwifery and Surgery."

FACT

Several months after Simpson's debut of ether in obstetrics, the first American childbirth utilizing ether as a pain-relief agent would occur in Cambridge, Massachusetts. Fanny Longfellow, wife of poet Henry Wadsworth Longfellow, had her third child with the help of ether administered by Dr. Nathan Keep, the dean of dentistry at Harvard.

Chloroform: Fit for a Queen

The debate continued until April 7, 1853, when John Snow, a physician who had worked to refine Simpson's anesthetic methods, administered chloroform at the request of none other than Queen Victoria. Victoria, who was giving birth to Prince Leopold, her eighth child, legitimized the use of chloroform in childbirth once and for all.

Because of his contributions to the field of anesthesiology, many consider Snow the first official obstetric anesthesiologist. Throughout his career, Snow used chloroform on 4,000 women in childbirth, including the daughter of the archbishop of Canterbury—proof that the old Adam and Eve argument no longer held any weight. He refined the techniques of administration so well that he was able to accurately dose for both analgesia (relieving pain but not consciousness) and anesthesia.

Chloroform remained in favorable use both in the United Kingdom and United States for approximately seventy-five years, or until the introduction of the next big thing in obstetric anesthesia—twilight sleep.

Twilight Time and Laughing Gas

Arriving on the obstetric scene in Germany in the early 1900s, twilight sleep—a mixture of scopolamine and morphine—caught the attention of American women when it was the subject of an article in *McClure's,* a popular magazine of the day.

Although morphine and scopolamine had been used as anesthetic agents previously, University of Freiburg physicians led by Carl Joseph Gauss are credited with creating the formulation that became known as "twilight sleep." The scopolamine in twilight sleep acted as an amnesic, meaning that women who took it had little to no memory of the birth experience, while the morphine acted as an analgesic, or pain reliever.

Representatives from the University of Freiburg presented their findings on the anesthetic/amnesiac at a 1909 meeting of the American Association of Obstetricians and Gynecologists in the United States, which also heightened the profile of twilight sleep. Its use spread rapidly in the States thereafter.

FACT

Another pain-relief gas no longer in use today is Trilene (trichloroethylene). Trilene, popular in the 1970s, was self-administered through either a face-mask or specially designed inhaler that was strapped to the patient's hand.

By 1945, there was a backlash against twilight sleep and its capacity to completely remove a woman from her own birth experience. In addition, the narcotic morphine, given as an analgesic, was also known to cause depression in newborns (neonatal depression).

Nitrous oxide, more commonly known as laughing gas, was first used as an obstetric analgesic in the early 1800s, when Polish-Russian physician Stanislav Klikovich tried out the self-manufactured anesthetic gas on twenty-five of his patients. Klikovich found that nitrous was most effective when administered thirty seconds to a minute before the start of a contraction.

Laughing gas was commonly used in U.S. delivery rooms up until the 1970s, and it is still used quite broadly in England (under the trade name Entonox) as a labor pain-relief option today. Because it is self-administered by the mother in labor, who uses the mask at will to breathe in the gas, many women feel that nitrous oxide gives them more control over their own labor.

Regional Anesthetics/Analgesics: Blocking the Pain

Perhaps one of the most important developments in modern obstetrical anesthetics was the development of regional anesthetic blocks that numbed part or all of the cervical, vaginal, and perineal areas. These regional blocks managed to provide considerable pain relief while keeping the laboring woman fully alert and awake—an accomplishment that was unattainable with those earlier pain-relief medications that either knocked a woman out, wiped her memory, or altered her consciousness.

ALERT!

Spinal blocks, which are frequently used for cesarean section, have the potential to cause a rare but severe form of postoperative head pain known as a postdural puncture headache (PDPH). The headache is thought to be caused by a slow leak of cerebrospinal fluid and/or a change of pressure in the spinal fluid during the block procedure. In some cases, an epidural blood patch, which effectively "patches" the puncture hole with the patient's own blood to stop any cerebrospinal fluid leaks, is required to bring relief.

The earliest use of regional blocks involved injections of cocaine solutions into the spinal column through tubing connected to a needle inserted between the vertebrae of the lumbar spine. Cocaine was soon replaced by Novocain (procaine), which would eventually be succeeded by anesthetics such as Xylocaine (lidocaine), Marcaine (bupivacaine), and Carbocaine (mepivacaine), sometimes combined with a narcotic.

In 1942, physicians at Philadelphia General Hospital developed the first continuous regional anesthetic blocks. Once the needle was placed in the epidural space of the spine, anesthetic and/or analgesic drugs could be administered at any point in labor (rather than in just a single shot). For more on today's regional anesthetic blocks and epidurals, see Chapter 14.

A Father's Place

Advances in pain-relief methods also paved the way for men to start doing more during labor and delivery than pacing the waiting room. When women became conscious participants in their birth experience, the emotional and physical support roles for fathers naturally opened up (with the help of childbirth advocates like Robert Bradley and Fernand Lamaze). In the 1960s, hospitals grudgingly admitted fathers into the labor room only, and by the 1970s, dad had finally gained entrance into the delivery room as well.

FACT

When the United States was first founded, the only fathers who attended their wives during birth were those who were isolated on the frontier and had little choice in the matter. Birth was very much a woman-centered event, attended by female family and neighbors who would extend their stay to care for mother and child during the traditional "lying-in" period after birth.

The natural childbirth movement also helped to move men into a more active role in labor and birth. In 1965, Denver obstetrician Robert Bradley published *Husband-Coached Childbirth*, a new approach to labor and delivery that advocated a father's role as coach to the mother-to-be and emphasized education and preparation well before the due date. Bradley also promoted avoidance of anesthetic or analgesic drugs during childbirth if possible, teaching couples to rely on relaxation and breathing techniques instead.

Back to Natural

Well before Bradley became a household name, English physician Grantly Dick-Read had set forth his views on childbirth with minimal medical interventions in his pioneering works *Natural Childbirth* (1930) and *Childbirth Without Fear* (1944). Dick-Read believed that the pain of labor and birth was greatly magnified by fear and anxiety. Dick-Read was ostracized by the medical establishment in Great Britain, and it wasn't until several decades later that his views became widely embraced. (For more on Dick-Read, see Chapter 8.)

Prepared Childbirth

While Dick-Read introduced the natural childbirth concept, Dr. Ferdinand Lamaze popularized it to a point that it sparked a virtual childbirth revolution in America. Lamaze's technique, known alternately as psychoprophylaxis, painless childbirth, and the Lamaze method, was described in detail in his first book, *Painless Childbirth: The Lamaze Method* (1965).

Built on some of the same ideals that Dick-Read had pioneered, psychoprophylaxis was based on the concept that fear and anxiety in childbirth beget pain, and this pain could be diminished through conditioning techniques such as rhythmic breathing and relaxation exercises.

Ferdinand Lamaze attended early lectures of Dr. Grantly Dick-Read, but Lamaze based most of his theories about painless prepared childbirth on the work of Ivan Pavlov. Pavlov was the Nobel-winning Russian scientist who is best known for his work on behavioral conditioning.

Lamaze was still a little-known method in the United States until 1959, when Marjorie Karmel wrote *Thank You, Dr. Lamaze,* a book that introduced a whole generation of American women (and men) to natural childbirth. Karmel, who had been a patient of Dr. Lamaze's in France, tells the story of her two births—one in France and one in New York—using psychoprophylaxis (or the Pavlovian method).

Karmel's tale, infused with wit, offers a revealing look at the stark contrast between European and American perspectives on interventions in childbirth. Her book quickly became the force behind what is today the most well-known childbirth method in America. Each year, more than 2 million parents-to-be attend childbirth classes taught by certified Lamaze instructors.

The Rise of the Cesarean Section

Originally, cesarean sections were performed only in dire circumstances in an attempt to save the life of the infant, and there were few reports of women surviving the operation. With the advent of anesthesia and antibiotics in obstetrics, doctors were able to practice cesarean section with much better outcomes. The introduction of the regional spinal anesthetic blocks allowed women to be alert, yet anesthetized, during C-section for the first time.

Today, the United States has one of the highest cesarean rates in the world—an astounding 26.1 percent of all live births in 2002 were delivered by C-section. And of women who had a previous C-section, only 12.7 percent had a successful vaginal birth after cesarean (VBAC). The reasons behind this are complex, but the numbers could be due to factors as diverse as advanced maternal age, medical liability issues faced by American physicians, and a resurgence of the so-called "medicalization" of childbirth.

Freedom of Choice

Today, there are more childbirth options than ever for a pregnant woman. She can welcome her child into the world in the comfort and security of her own home or labor with ease in a birthing center with amenities like birthing pools and massage. Or she can opt for a hospital birth in a labor and delivery room and "room in" with her baby during her stay. While unforeseen circumstances and issues like health insurance may play some role in your "ideal birth experience," the more you learn about your birth options early in your pregnancy, the more likely you are to have the experience you and your partner want.

Labor-Delivery-Recovery Rooms

Before the natural childbirth movement shook many of the old-school maternity methods, a hospital birth meant laboring in one room, then being swept into a sterile delivery room for the actual birth itself. A third recovery room would allow mothers to recoup from any effects of anesthesia. Today, a large percentage of hospitals have labor/delivery/recovery (LDR) rooms where women can spend their entire birth experience, from contractions to cuddling with their newborns.

In addition, many hospitals have taken a hint from birth centers and turned once-sterile hospital rooms into a more inviting environment for childbirth. Larger beds, reclining chairs, music, window treatments, and private showers to ease labor pain can make the hospital environment seem more like home.

FACT

Postpartum restaurant room-service for the new parents, complete with champagne or sparkling juice, is offered at one Rhode Island hospital. This five-star treatment can be just the ticket for women who feel more at ease with a hospital birth but still want the comforts of home.

Birthing Centers

Birthing centers are often called the middle ground between home birth and hospital birth. While equipped with essential items like emergency resuscitation equipment, you won't find epidurals, episiotomies, or other major medical interventions. Birthing center staff members are usually primarily midwives, and they are well-versed in the art of nonmedicated pain relief. Showers, soaking tubs, and birthing balls and stools are usual options.

That's not to say that prescription pain relief is banned from birthing centers; many nurse-midwives have prescribing privileges, and a midwife will discuss your pain relief options in detail well before your due date. However, women typically choose birth centers because of their noninterventional philosophy, and that often means natural childbirth.

At a birthing center, your entire family is welcome to participate in the birth experience as much, or as little, as you prefer. The environment is typically warm and inviting—large family-sized beds, comfortable furniture, and access to food and drink.

However, because a birthing center has no surgical facilities and may have limited medical capabilities, each one has guidelines on what types of patients they will accept. If complications arise during a birth, and interventions are required that the center is not set up for, they will transfer you to a nearby hospital. All accredited birthing centers have a written emergency transport plan in place for such situations.

Home Birth

Having a home birth is very similar to a birth center experience except that you are on your own turf. Many women find that giving birth in the familiar comfort of their home provides a level of relaxation and ease that decreases pain and enhances the childbirth experience. Midwives, often with the assistance of a doula, oversee the vast majority of home births in the United States.

ALERT!

Some women choose to give birth at home without the assistance of any health-care provider. Unassisted childbirth is a valid decision for many women with uncomplicated pregnancies, but it's one that should be thought out carefully and completely, with a backup plan in place should an emergency arise. If yours is considered a high-risk pregnancy for any reason, having a midwife or physician in attendance could be a life-saving choice.

Today's Comforts and Challenges

Today's woman has the comforts and the challenges of a wide array of advanced obstetric techniques and equipment and pain relief options. These have become a double-edged sword for many women—tools that can increase their comfort level on one hand while potentially alienating them from full participation in birth on the other.

There is no one-size-fits-all "right" answer to childbirth today. Whether it be a hospital birth with planned pain relief that you choose, a natural home birth with no interventions, or something in between, you need to make the choices that are right for you, your partner, and your baby. Educating yourself about the available options equips you to make a decision that takes into account your particular needs for comfort, safety, and fulfillment.

Trust yourself, and remember that the physiological responses and instincts that drive the childbirth experience are already within you—that miraculous innate ability to bring forth life.

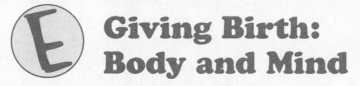

Chapter 2

Giving Birth: Body and Mind

Birth is perhaps the most profound event you'll experience in your lifetime. It involves not just a transformation of your body and the launch of a new life but an evolution of the self. In childbirth, you will find emotional and physical strength within you that you didn't think possible. Preparing your body and clearing your mind of any anxieties and preconceptions about the birth process are the best ways to get ready for a wonderful birth experience.

Training for Birth

Because the birth process is physically and emotionally taxing, training for it, as you would for any strenuous event or mental challenge, is only natural. Regular prenatal exercise enables you to become more aware of your body and the signals it sends. The more attuned you become to your body now, the better you can use that ability to manage your labor more effectively at birth.

Your state of mind contributes as much to a successful birth as the state of your body does. Negative emotions like fear and anxiety trigger the release of stress-related hormones that can work against you and your baby in labor. If you perceive childbirth as a frightening and painful experience, your body instinctively reacts with a "fight or flight" response, releasing epinephrine and norepinephrine, catecholamine stress hormones that can reduce uterine blood flow, increase blood pressure, slow the progress of labor, and actually heighten your pain perception in labor and birth.

Clinical studies have linked corticotropin-releasing hormone (CRH), a stress-related substance secreted by the brain and placenta, to both pre-term labor and low birth weight. Stress during birth itself has also been associated with delayed lactation and lower breast-milk volume.

Physically Fit

Just thirty minutes of moderate exercise daily can pay off in big benefits once birth day arrives. Exercise increases your stamina and energy, improves flexibility, and can tone the muscles that will be working hard in childbirth. It also helps promote mental fitness by calming the mind and improving your self-image.

To stay safe while exercising, keep well hydrated and slow down if you feel yourself getting overheated or you experience vaginal bleeding, dizziness, chest pain, or other unusual side effects. You're overexerting yourself if you can't talk normally while exercising. Women who exercise regularly can usually continue to do so, but all pregnant women should run both new and old exercise routines past their health-care provider to get the green light for continuing.

Here are some good ways a pregnant body can stay in shape:

- **Swimming.** A pool provides the perfect low-impact environment for exercise. The buoyancy it gives your belly can also help ease back strain and other hazards of prenatal exercise. Try a prenatal aquatic exercise class, or simply swim or walk a few laps in the pool.
- **Walking.** The cheapest and most readily available exercise is simply heading outside for a walk. If weather or traffic makes walking hazardous in your area, try pounding the pavement at the local mall. Walking is also a great social pastime, so recruit some friends (pregnant or otherwise) and make it an event to look forward to.
- **Modified yoga.** Prenatal yoga is an excellent way to facilitate fitness of both body and mind. Yoga increases flexibility and strength, and it also teaches important relaxation and meditative skills that can be great tools during labor. If you sign up for yoga, make sure it's a class designed for prenatal needs—some yoga poses (or asanas) may be too strenuous for pregnancy.
- **Prenatal fitness classes.** Many hospitals, health clubs, community centers, and YMCAs offer prenatal exercise classes geared especially for the special needs of pregnant moms. Your doctor's blessing, in the form of a note of approval, is usually required to enroll.

Some high-impact exercises can be risky in pregnancy, particularly in the later months. If you're active in sports like tennis, racquetball, or basketball, talk to your health-care provider about the potential need to scale back or modify your routine. Certain activities, such as contact sports, scuba diving, and water skiing, pose too great a risk to a developing fetus and should be suspended until after your pregnancy.

Prenatal exercise tapes are a good alternative if you prefer to work out at home. An excellent resource for learning more about effective exercises for staying flexible, fit, and healthy in pregnancy is *The Everything® Pregnancy Fitness Book* (Adams Media, 2003) by Robin Elise Weiss, L.C.C.E., I.C.C.E.-C.P.E., C.D. (DONA). Always check with your health-care provider before starting an exercise program in pregnancy. Depending on your particular health history, your fitness plan may require certain restrictions or modifications.

Mentally Fit

Just as physical fitness can help prepare your body for birth, relaxation and visualization exercises can help clear and center your mind for the task ahead. Take a half hour or so each day to rest in a soothing environment and picture your successful birth. Wear comfortable clothing, dim the lights, and put on some soothing background music. If pregnancy hasn't left you hypersensitive to smell, an aromatherapy candle or essential oils may also be helpful. Let the rest of your household know this is your time and you shouldn't be interrupted.

Don't lie flat on your back, but do get comfortable by reclining in a chair or propping yourself up with pillows on a bed or couch. During this quiet time, clear your thoughts by focusing on the sensations of your body breathing in and out, and the feeling of your child in your womb. Once you're completely relaxed, visualize the safe and joyous birth of your child in the circumstances and environment you have chosen.

There are a number of good relaxation and visualization tapes available that can guide you through this type of prenatal exercise. Appendix B lists some resources for further information on these techniques, and Chapter 14 discusses the use of relaxation and visualization exercises for childbirth in more detail.

Emotional Barriers

"I don't know if I can do this" is a common refrain among first-time moms. Yes, childbirth is a challenge, but so is every other goal worth achieving in life. There will be pain, but it's positive pain—pain that is bringing your baby to the outside world. And don't forget that you have many tools at your disposal to work through that pain in your own way. It may sound clichéd, but the best way to ensure a good birth experience is to believe in yourself and your abilities. If you open your mind to your own potential and jettison any preconceived notions of birth, you'll realize you can do it—and do it quite well.

Preconceptions

Anxiety, stress, and fear are all natural emotional reactions to the unknown. If you're a first-time mom, most of what you believe you know about childbirth has probably been gleaned from friends, family, and media representations—not always the most accurate portrayals of the birth experience. You may be paralyzed with fear by horror stories about marathon labor sessions, unbearable pain, and babies born in taxicabs. Remember that birth as portrayed in television, movies, and even the stories of friends and acquaintances is usually treated with a liberal dose of drama. Don't base your expectations on these overly embellished accounts.

For every "three days of grueling labor and I had the baby in the hospital elevator" story, there is an equally compelling birth story of joy and empowerment. Don't let the perceptions of others cloud your mental outlook toward a positive birth experience.

Overcoming Fear and Anxiety

One of the best ways to prevent negative emotions from hampering your birth experience is to learn all you can about the birth process. Knowledge is a great weapon against fear and anxiety. Having a birth plan—a blueprint for your ideal birth experience—can help you and your partner determine the specifics surrounding your personal childbirth experience. A birth plan also gives you the opportunity to make educated choices about possible interventions early on in your pregnancy so you won't have to deal with the stress of those decisions during childbirth itself. (See Chapter 5 for more on creating your birth plan.)

Keep the following tips in mind to help you mentally prepare for a positive birth experience:

- **Go to the head of the class.** Sign up for childbirth education classes, and be an active participant in them.
- **Ask questions.** Keep a running list of questions, and bring them to your provider at each visit.
- **Remember that every birth is unique.** You'll hear a lot of birth stories during your pregnancy, from the grueling to the effortless. Take them with a grain of salt, and don't base your own birth expectations on them.
- **Talk to a professional.** Consider hiring a doula for some prenatal guidance. She can be an invaluable source of information and support. (For more on doulas, see Chapter 3.)
- **Keep an open mind.** Don't dwell on what could go wrong, but do take the time to consider what choices you may face—and how you will address them—should your birth not go exactly according to plan.
- **Realize that your baby is calling the shots.** Babies don't follow calendars or timetables. Don't let a missed due date or a long labor get you down or anxious. As long as your baby is doing well, everything is fine.

FACT

Don't be disappointed if your due date comes and goes without so much as a muscle spasm. Because date of conception is sometimes difficult to pinpoint, and cycle lengths vary, your estimated date of delivery (EDD) is an educated guess at best. In fact, only five percent of babies are actually born on their due dates. Women who have given birth previously, however, are more likely to deliver on or near their EDD.

Empowerment: Owning Your Labor and Birth

While a good doctor or midwife is an important part of your birth team, your provider isn't in the driver's seat—you are. Many women become passive in the presence of a doctor, assuming they should automatically submit to whatever is suggested. While carefully considering the recommendations of your provider is important (after all, in most cases those recommendations are based on years of education and experience), you shouldn't forget that this is your birth and your baby. Although you may not believe it yet, your knowledge of your own body and the instincts that have guided you this far give you considerable expertise on what's best for the two of you.

Of course there are situations in which your medical history will require that certain interventions, such as a C-section, be performed for the sake of your or your child's health. These will also be circumstances in which you'll rely on your provider's medical expertise for a safe outcome. But even in the case of a cesarean, you still have choices—such as who will be there and how your baby will be handled after birth. Birth is never something that is just "done to you"; you created and nurtured the life inside you, and now you—not the masked figure behind the curtain—are delivering that life into the world.

Your provider should always a) be respectful of you as both a paying customer and as the mother of this baby, b) answer all of your questions, and c) make sure you are given all the information you need on any intervention or procedure he proposes. In turn, you have the responsibility to communicate your needs and carefully consider the information he provides. Chapter 3 has more information on finding a good health-care provider who will work with you to achieve the kind of birth you want.

Your Body in Labor

The preparation for your child's birth may start weeks before labor begins as your baby moves into position for birth by dropping, or engaging, into the pelvis. Although more common with women who are in their first pregnancy, this "lightening" is usually noticeable by a change in your pregnant profile and greater ease in breathing as baby lets up on your diaphragm. While you may be able to breathe better, you will probably be taking more frequent trips to the bathroom as the pressure on your bladder increases. The pressure caused by the baby's head against the cervix may help begin the process of cervical effacement—the thinning of the cervix in preparation for your baby's birth.

Dilation and Effacement

Throughout your pregnancy, the cervix is long and thick, and sealed tight by a mucous plug. It will start to ripen, which means it will start to thin (efface) and open (dilate), as early labor begins and your uterine muscles begin contractions. Effacement is measured in percentages. A cervix that is 100-percent effaced is wafer thin, while a 50-percent effaced cervix still has quite a way to go. Dilation usually does not start until the cervix is significantly effaced, at least in first pregnancies. The dilated opening of the cervix is measured in centimeters, with full dilation (the point at which you can begin pushing) being ten centimeters, or about four inches.

At some point during cervical ripening, the mucous plug will come loose and be expelled. The amniotic sac (the membrane that holds the amniotic fluid surrounding your baby) may also break, although this often doesn't happen until well into labor and sometimes will be done manually in an effort to speed labor.

QUESTION?

How will I know if I'm really in labor?

If your contractions (periodic cramping pain in the abdomen and/or back) are coming in semiregular intervals, do not subside with movement, and increase in intensity as time progresses or with activity, chances are it's the real thing. Sudden diarrhea, expulsion of the mucous plug, and breaking of the amniotic sac ("water breaking" in either a gush or a trickle), are also signs that labor is here or imminent—although some of these won't occur until well into labor.

Anatomy of a Contraction

Your uterus is comprised of four layers of smooth muscle known as the myometrium, which are covered by a sheath of connective tissue called the serosa that holds the organ in place. Lining the uterine cavity is the endometrium, the vascular inner layer that first nourished your fertilized egg and then your placenta. At the low end of your uterus lies the cervix, your baby's doorway to the outside world.

During a labor contraction, the myometrium of the uterus tightens, or contracts, in an effort to move your baby out of the womb and into the birth canal. This squeezing action also helps to shorten the cervix and widen its opening for her departure. Contractions will feel like abdominal cramping and/or lower back pain that doesn't go away when you change positions.

Contractions start out slow and far apart, but by the time active labor begins you will probably be having three to five contractions every ten minutes. To be defined as "real labor," they must come at roughly regular intervals and cause cervical dilation.

FACT

Although the exact mechanisms that start labor aren't completely understood, it is known that the pregnancy hormones oxytocin and prostaglandin initiate contractions. Oxytocin is released by the pituitary gland in the brain, while prostaglandins are produced by cortisol that is secreted by the fetal adrenal glands.

Three Stages of Labor

On average, labor lasts between twelve and fourteen hours—a bit longer for some first-time moms and somewhat shorter for women having second or subsequent children. Keep in mind that there is no hard-and-fast time-frame for any labor; some women may labor for days and others for hours. In addition, circumstances such as the position of your baby can have an impact on how quickly labor progresses.

The bulk of laboring time is spent in the first stage, with the second "pushing" stage where the baby actually arrives lasting anywhere from a few minutes to several hours for women having their first baby. The final stage—the delivery of the placenta—usually lasts no longer than a half-hour.

- **First stage.** Lasts from early contractions until your baby has descended into the birth canal. The first stage is a three-part process itself, consisting of early (latent) labor, active labor, and transition (descent) labor.

- **Second stage.** The pushing part. This is the actual delivery of your baby.
- **Third stage.** Delivery of the placenta.

Chapter 13 discusses strategies for effective laboring in detail.

I had a long, hard labor with my first child. Should I expect the same this time?
Second and subsequent labors tend to be shorter, and you may be much more relaxed this time around since you've done it before, which can also make your labor progress more quickly. You have the benefit of experience behind you, so use it to your advantage to enjoy your birth.

Second or Subsequent Births

Women who have already been through childbirth have the advantage of experience on their side, but they can also feel locked into certain expectations based on those experiences. Remember that no two births are exactly alike. Just because you were induced or ended up with a cesarean delivery last time doesn't mean that you are destined to repeat the same birth experience with this baby.

If you've been through childbirth before and you've picked up this book, chances are there was at least one aspect of your previous birth experience you'd like to improve on this time around.

Think about what you liked, and didn't like, about childbirth the first time. Could you have had better emotional support? Was your pain relief inadequate? Did you feel overmedicated? Was your provider a help or a hindrance? Use this information to build a birth plan that will address those shortcomings. (See Chapter 5 for more on birth plans.)

Remember that your family dynamic is different this time out, too—your baby-to-be has a sibling (or siblings), so there is at least one more person whose needs must be considered. Keep in mind that older brothers and sisters of the baby-to-be may want to get involved in the birth too, maybe even to the point of witnessing the birth itself. If you and your child are comfortable with the prospect, prepare for the event early by reading age-appropriate books on pregnancy and birth, and discuss just what will happen at the birth. (Chapter 12 includes information on classes that will help older siblings prepare for the new baby's arrival, whether they are present during labor or not.) You may decide that having your children present at the birth will be too overwhelming for them or distracting for you, and that's fine too. Make appropriate child-care arrangements until they can meet their new brother or sister so your mind will be free from parental worries and you can focus on the task at hand.

Chapter 3

Selecting Birth Partners

Who will help guide you in your birth journey? It's an important decision that you shouldn't leave up to the Yellow Pages. Ask yourself where your comfort zone lies. Does having an obstetrician in attendance give you additional peace of mind? Do you feel more at ease with an experienced midwife and doula on your team? Or is an intimate birth experience with one-on-one midwife care more your style?

Your Team

Choosing the people that will attend your birth—both health-care practitioners and support attendants—is one of the most important and far-reaching decisions you'll make about your birth experience. Having a clinically competent and empathetic team in your corner can make even the most difficult birth a positive experience.

Consider the three essential Cs—communication, comfort, and connection. Your birth partner needs to be someone you can talk to openly and frankly and who won't be afraid to be candid with you as well. A fourth "C"—convenience—may also be an issue for you, but in many ways it will be easier on you to drive a few extra miles to a provider you love than to be stuck with Nurse (midwife) Ratchet right down the street.

ALERT!

Check with your health insurer before selecting your care providers for your birth. Some insurers may have restrictions on coverage for midwives who are not certified nurse-midwives (CNMs). They may also limit coverage on doula services. Many midwives and doulas will offer sliding scale fees to offset costs if coverage is a problem.

If you already see a gynecologist or family-practice doctor with an obstetric practice and have forged a good patient-doctor relationship with him or her, your search may be already over. If you're looking for a new provider, your options include these:

- **A midwife.** Midwives may be either certified nurse-midwives (CNM), direct entry midwives (DEM), or licensed midwives (LM). Their focus is on patient-directed care in pregnancy, labor, and delivery.
- **An ob/gyn.** An obstetrician and gynecologist is an M.D. who has completed training in women's health and reproductive medicine.
- **A doula.** Unlike a midwife or ob/gyn, a doula's sole purpose is for emotional support during delivery.

Many of today's obstetrical practices are combined, employing midwives, nurse-practitioners, and ob/gyns. Sometimes you will have a choice of seeing one or more different types of providers throughout your pregnancy.

It's never too late to change health-care providers. If you've been seeing someone for prenatal care and have found that you have irreconcilable philosophical differences about your impending birth, do not hesitate to start looking for someone you can work with. Other mothers are great sources of information on midwives, obstetricians, and doulas.

Choosing Wisely

Remember that some of your wishes for your baby's birth may already narrow down the playing field for choosing a practitioner. For example, if you want a home birth, you will probably be choosing a midwife, since there are virtually no physicians who will attend a home birth because of liability issues.

Don't be afraid to interview your potential candidates before committing to a decision. Here are some things to ask your interviewees:

- **Who will deliver my baby?** Will the doctor or midwife you choose deliver your child, or is there a possibility it will be another provider within their practice? Who provides backup care for them during downtime and emergencies, and will you have the opportunity to meet that person before the birth?

- **What hospital or birthing center are you affiliated with?** Where your birth will take place will be an important part of the birth experience. (For more on birth places, see Chapter 4.)

- **Do you encourage birth plans?** Will the provider honor your wishes as outlined in a birth plan and work with you to explore options should things veer off course? Will the plan be submitted into your chart so those in attendance at your birth will have access to it? (Chapter 5 has more information on birth plans.)

- **What is your philosophy on pain relief and birth interventions?** If you have strong feelings about pain-relief choices and interventions like episiotomy, here's your chance to find out if your provider will work with you toward the birth you want.

- **How can I reach you in an emergency?** Find out the triage procedure for calls to the office and whether the provider is available by pager or cell phone.

If you are planning a home birth, there are additional questions you should ask of your potential providers. See Chapter 11 for more details.

It's Your Ball Game

Now here's the tricky part, one that some women fail to understand until birth is well over. Too often, health-care providers of any stripe—physician, midwife, or nurse—are perceived as superhuman figures, unquestionable and absolute in power; as someone who is delivering your child rather than empowering you to give birth to it. Sometimes that's due to a passive patient who doesn't speak up, ask questions, and let her needs be known. Other times it's attributable to a practitioner who has the proverbial "God complex." Most providers probably don't enjoy it much when their patients have such lofty perceptions. Living up to that kind of reputation is a tall order to fill.

It's important to remember that birth is a natural process. In the vast majority of uncomplicated, low-risk pregnancies, interventions are not necessary and medical oversight is more for emotional comfort than physical need. This is your ball game, your show, your big production. While you should consider the input of your provider carefully, it's ultimately up to you to make the final decisions surrounding your birth. Now that you have the picture, here are four things to remember about the provider/patient relationship:

- **Doctors are not infallible.** You do not have to agree with all of your provider's suggestions, just take the time to listen and consider them.
- **Your physician is not a mind-reader.** Make your needs known, both before and during the birth.
- **Your health-care provider works for you, not the other way around.** If you feel that your provider is not listening to you or doesn't respect you, find a replacement.
- **You need to ask questions to get answers.** If you don't understand something fully, it's your right and your duty to ask for an explanation.

The Role of a Midwife

The occupation of midwife is as old as recorded history, and the name itself invokes a certain mystical and almost antiquated quality. Don't infer more from the name than you should. In the vast majority of cases (depending on where you live), a midwife (meaning "with woman") is a licensed health-care practitioner with extensive education and experience attending births. Because a midwife or nurse-midwife (a midwife who is also an RN) views her role in the birth process as a holistic one, many women see the midwife as a lifeline to woman-centered care, someone who will put just as much emphasis on the emotional and spiritual needs of mother and child at birth as she will on medical requirements.

That doesn't mean doctors are less caring or concerned about the women they see, but midwives consider the job of providing emotional and social support to a woman in labor to be just as important as clinical care. Midwives look at birth from a different philosophical viewpoint than most physicians—as a natural physiological goal that they are supporting a mother to achieve—not as something to be choreographed, intervened in, or interfered with, and certainly not to be treated as an infirmity. A midwife is a mentor, someone there with suggestions, emotional encouragement, and, when necessary, the ability to recognize clinical problems when they occur.

FACT

What midwives can and can't do in clinical practice, and the type of licensing they require, is governed at a state level. Appendix B has contact information to help you find out more about the licensing and operational aspects of midwifery care in your state.

That's not to say that all midwives are the perfect balance of patience and unwavering emotional support. As with any profession, you are only as good as your training, experience, and innate abilities for the task at hand. And personality conflicts can occur between a "customer" and service provider in virtually any profession. But the basic philosophical viewpoint of midwives—to be a partner, support system, and advocate for a woman's birth choices—stay the same.

Depending on where you live and on your insurer, legislative and economic conditions can have an impact on the ways midwives operate. Midwives cannot perform surgical interventions like cesarean sections no matter where they work, and, in some areas, regulations prohibit them from attending births considered high-risk (although what high-risk actually is defined as can vary by state). In many areas, midwives have had to move into larger practices and hospital groups to survive, and as such, have had to change some of their traditional ways of working. Covering births by shifts, being barred from attending home births, and having to refer patients to a group physician under specific medical circumstances are a few of the ways that traditional midwifery care has been affected by these outside forces in some areas.

A 1998 U.S. Centers for Disease Control study found that infants delivered by certified nurse-midwives had a 19-percent lower mortality rate than those delivered by physicians. In addition, CNMs were 31 percent less likely to deliver low birth-weight babies than licensed physicians. The study authors theorized that the continuity of care and emotional support CNMs provide their patients could have been one factor in their success rates.

A Physician's Assistance

Most American women—93 percent in the past decade—choose a traditional physician to oversee their birth. Why choose a doctor over a midwife? Availability, insurance requirements, comfort level, or complications with the pregnancy and/or birth are just some of the reasons women may prefer a physician as their partner in prenatal and delivery care. If you opt for a doctor, there are several choices available—an obstetrician (OB or ob/gyn), family doctor, or a perinatologist.

Family Medicine Doctors

Family medicine doctors, either medical doctors (M.D.s) or doctors of osteopathy (D.O.s), are more than capable of handling most uncomplicated births. If you're already seeing a physician with whom you're comfortable and who takes obstetric patients, there's no reason not to stay on that course.

OB or Ob/Gyn

An obstetrician/gynecologist is a medical doctor who has received specific training and practical experience (that is, residency and internship) in women's health and reproductive medicine. Those who are board-certified have passed rigorous written and oral competency examinations. Many women already see a gynecologist for regular preventative care and annual pap smears, so it is common for that patient/physician relationship to continue through pregnancy and birth.

Perinatologist

Women who have a chronic health condition or who have complications develop in pregnancy may want to see a perinatologist—an ob/gyn who specializes in high-risk pregnancies. Perinatologists, also called maternal-fetal medicine specialists, have the same training and education as traditional ob/gyns, plus an additional two to three years of training in high-risk obstetrical care.

Often, perinatologists will provide care in consultation with a regular ob/gyn, but depending on your and your baby's needs, may attend and deliver in high-risk birth situations.

Support from a Doula

Women have been serving as birth attendants for thousands of years. It's only been since the early 1970s that the name "doula" (Greek for "women's servant") has come into use in childbirth circles as a synonym for birth attendant and postpartum care provider. The childbirth organizations that govern doula certification in the United States are even younger, emerging in the early nineties to provide a framework for professional certification and training for this growing profession.

The doula's sole job is to provide continuous emotional assistance and support to a woman and her family during birth. While the majority of doulas are engaged for childbirth itself, doulas can actually provide support and assistance during pregnancy and postpartum as well. Doulas may be trained specifically as birth assistants and/or as postpartum care providers.

One of the key benefits a doula provides is continuity of care. In most hospital births, factors beyond your control, like shift changes and the number of patients in labor at any given time, mean that you may see a variety of nurses and perhaps only glimpses of your provider. A doula works specifically for you, meaning that she will be there for you to lean on throughout both your labor and delivery, regardless of when or where they occur.

There are several major certifying U.S. organizations for doulas that require these practitioners to meet specific educational and practical experience guidelines and subscribe to a standard code of practice and ethics. Doulas who have been certified by the International Childbirth Education Association (ICEA) have the designation "ICD" after their names. Those who have completed certification requirements outlined by Doulas of North America (DONA) have the designation "CD (DONA)." Doulas certified by the Childbirth and Postpartum Professional Association (CAPPA) for labor assistance earn the designation "CLD."

Finally, the Association of Labor Assistants and Childbirth Educators (ALACE) offers certification for labor assistants that perform the same functions as a doula. ALACE certification is indicated by the acronym CLA (Certified Labor Assistant). Contact information for all of these organizations can be found in Appendix B.

You can locate doula candidates via personal referrals, professional organizations, and your local birth facility. Interview a doula the same way you would any other health-care provider you are considering. Because a doula's expertise lies in her ability to comfort, to reassure, and to empower you during birth, it's important that you have a good rapport with her so your relationship will be a beneficial one. In addition to checking a doula's certification, it's also a good idea to ask for references.

Doulas are an excellent resource for single mothers-to-be who may not have a family member or close friend nearby to provide labor support. But they're also powerful allies even when a father-to-be is present, lightening the burden for a male partner who may be feeling the weight of the world on his shoulders and whose sole birth experience is a six-session crash course on childbirth education.

Still, some fathers or significant others may feel slightly displaced by the concept of a doula. After all, shouldn't they be the shoulder to lean on? The fact is that a doula is a great source of support for both mom and dad. They can assist the father-to-be with tips for comforting and assisting a laboring woman, and can help him advocate for his significant other. In addition, many doulas will start working before you even hit the hospital or birthing center, providing early labor support at home.

Dad's Place: A Note to Guys

Fifty years ago, it would have been a considerable shock to hear that a father was present during labor and delivery, much less active in the birth process. Today, it would be a surprise to hear that any able-bodied dad opted out of the labor and delivery room. In the end, just what part you play is an individual decision to be made by you and your partner.

Couples should not feel pressured to conform to any preconceived role in terms of coaching and support. Dad's place is where the two of you decide it is.

The Art of Support

As a father, your one and only focus during childbirth should be to support the mother. Her attention will be completely and utterly focused on the task at hand—giving birth to your child. Support takes many forms, from massage and hand-holding to making her needs loud and clear to the health-care providers present. You need to be her eyes, ears, mouth, and legs, monitoring what the hospital or birth-center staff is doing in relationship to her care, communicating for her when she is focused elsewhere, and retrieving ice chips, blankets, and other comforts as needed.

Coaching Versus Comforting

Now that you know what's expected of you, let's cover what's not. Don't take the idea of "coach" too literally. You do not call the plays here. The contraction timing, breathing, and other things you learned in childbirth class may or may not come in handy during the real deal. They are suggestions, not hard-and-fast rules. Women will find what works for them in labor and gravitate toward it. It's great to make helpful suggestions (such as, "Would you like to try a shower?"), but if she isn't breathing like Dr. Lamaze suggests, don't bark orders like a drill sergeant. Follow her lead, and help make the journey comfortable by meeting her needs.

QUESTION?

Hospitals make me queasy, and I'm afraid I may pass out in the delivery room. Should I just suck it up and be there anyway?
If it's the hospital that's getting to you, you and your partner might consider a less sterile setting, such as a birth center or your home. If you're already committed to a hospital birth, think about having a doula or alternate support stand-in ready. Many hospital-shy people find the birth experience so awe-inspiring that they quickly forget any anxieties, but if queasiness does set in, you can take your leave, and your significant other will have a backup.

Working Together

Both prenatal care and birth require a lot of coordination and communication. During birth, your advocates need to be able to communicate your wishes without being combative. The health-care professionals around you need to respect you enough to keep you informed on both your progress and any interventions they might be considering. When you've made good choices about the people who care for and support you during birth, most negative situations can be avoided, but miscommunications can sometimes still occur.

One of the best ways to ensure that you get the birth experience you want is for everyone on both your clinical care and support teams have access to your birth plan. A birth plan outlines all of your wishes—from the music being played during labor to the pain interventions you do or don't want—in black and white. Chapter 5 has more details on building a birth plan.

Should You Invite Your Family?

Once you've chosen your care and support providers, it's time to decide whether there are other close family members or friends you want to witness this momentous occasion. Before issuing an invitation to someone, make sure you've carefully considered the implications of having him or her at the birth. Will this person be a positive influence? Can he or she support you and your choices? Consider whether each person is more likely to be a comfort or a distraction to you.

Making Birth a Family Affair

If this is a second or subsequent pregnancy, you may be thinking about getting your other kids in on the birth. Meeting a new sibling as he or she literally meets the world is an unforgettable experience and a wonderful way to show your older children that they are an essential part of your modified family unit.

However, having your child witness the birth is not an ideal situation for all families. Here are some things to consider when deciding what's right for you:

- **Comfort zone.** Will your children feel comfortable witnessing the birth and, just as importantly, will you be comfortable with their presence?
- **Attention span.** If the sibling-to-be is a toddler and will be bouncing off the walls rather than watching the birth, you may be better off finding a caretaker for the child until a proper introduction can be made.
- **Free choice.** If your children are old enough to do so, let them choose whether they wish to attend the birth or not, and make arrangements for any last-minute changes of heart in either direction.
- **Rules and regulations.** Depending on where you are planning your birth and who is attending it, having children present may not be allowed. Talk to your provider and to the birth facility well in advance of your due date about these issues if having your child present is important to you.
- **Encore performance.** For children who really want to be at a birth but can't attend due to provider policy, illness, or other circumstances, a videotape of the event can help ease hurt feelings. Check with your health-care provider and birth facility about their policy on cameras during labor and delivery.

Creating a Positive Environment

Whomever you ask to attend your birth, make sure they are aware of your desires regarding labor and delivery care and are willing to advocate for those convictions should you be unable to. If they disagree with your choices, tell them point blank that they need to either put aside their feelings during the birth or not attend at all. Negativity in labor and delivery will only increase your anxiety level and hamper your efforts. You need cheerleaders, not naysayers.

Once you've faced the daunting task of selecting the cast of characters for your birth, you'll need to make some decisions on the scenery. Chapter 4 covers choosing a birth place and making it comfortable and conducive to the task before you—delivering your child.

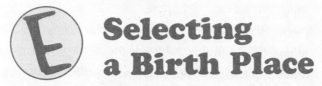

Selecting a Birth Place

Giving birth in an environment where you are comfortable and relaxed can make all the difference between a joyous and fulfilling birth and an experience you will vow never to repeat. While factors such as insurance coverage, medical history, and logistics can limit your choice of birth place, you may have more options than you think. Be sure to check out all the alternatives outlined in this chapter before committing to something less than perfect.

Choosing the Birth Place That's Right for You

First and foremost, you want to be at ease in the place you choose to labor and give birth. Studies have shown that high anxiety levels in laboring women result in increased pain perception. The stress hormone cortisol can also delay lactation and lengthen labor.

Comfort is of course, subjective—some women feel reassured by a hospital setting, knowing that care for any potential medical problems is nearby. Others feel tense in such sterile surroundings and prefer the warmth of a birthing center or their own homes.

Considering Rules and Policies

In addition to personal perceptions of your environment, you also need to choose a place your provider can and will work in. You may have an ob/gyn you really like and trust, but if you want this person to deliver your baby, chances are you won't be able to have a home birth (unless he or she is one of the few rare physicians that will attend one). And depending on state and hospital regulations where you live, a midwife may not be able to be the sole health-care professional overseeing your birth at the hospital. As a starting point, ask your provider about where he or she has privileges to work. You may end up deciding that the person is more important than the place, or vice versa.

FACT

According to the U.S. Centers for Disease Control's National Center for Health Statistics (NCHS), of the more than 4 million births in the United States in 2001, 99 percent took place in a hospital setting. Of all out-of-hospital births in 2001, 28 percent took place in a freestanding birthing center, and 65 percent took place at home.

There are also facility rules and regulations to deal with when you choose a birth place. If you have certain expectations regarding how you will be allowed to labor and manage your pain, and they go against hospital guidelines, it could be a deal-breaker for you. On the other hand, some hospitals and birthing centers may be more flexible on these issues than others, so don't assume out of hand that your needs won't be met—ask questions first.

What's Right for the Baby

Finally, think about your baby's critical, and unforgettable, first introduction to the world. Will the place you select for this grand entrance allow you to spend one-on-one time with your little one immediately following the birth? Will the people you want her to meet first be allowed to attend? What about newborn tests and procedures mandated by the facility? Can cord-cutting be delayed? Will the family be allowed to bond with the baby for an adequate amount of time before any room changes or other interruptions are made? Talk to your provider about his or her personal policies regarding your newborn, and check with your birth facility as well.

Birth in a Hospital

Once upon a time, having a baby hospital-style meant laboring in one room, then being unceremoniously whisked into a second one as you reached the final stages of labor. When the baby emerged, there would be a quick maternal peek, after which he or she would be taken into an adjoining room or area for cleaning, pokes, prods, and incubation. Then, once the placenta was delivered, mom (and if she was lucky, child as well) would be moved into yet a third room for "recovery" from the birth.

Today, many hospitals have smartened up about the musical-chairs routine and introduced more family-friendly labor-delivery-recovery (LDR) rooms so women are able to spend their entire birth experience—labor, birth, and mother-baby bonding time—in the same room.

Again, your experience may vary, and your access to hospital amenities may be limited by your health plan and by where you live. If you think you want a hospital birth, call around and learn more about specific facilities and policies. Ask other women about their experiences delivering, and call up the patient advocate at each facility to ask more questions about what's expected of and offered to maternity patients. Take the time to investigate your options fully before the big day.

What's a patient advocate?

As the name implies, a patient advocate is an individual at the hospital charged with representing patient interests and bringing patient concerns to hospital administrators. They act as liaisons between the patients and the hospital staff. Not all hospitals employ patient advocates, but if the one you're considering does, these representatives can be a valuable resource for answering your questions. If you're planning a hospital birth, call the patient advocate now to introduce yourself in case his or her assistance is needed during your stay.

Labor-Delivery-Recovery Room

The advent of the LDR room on hospital maternity wards has brought many of the appealing characteristics of a birthing center into the hospital. An LDR room has a warm and inviting atmosphere that resembles a bedroom more than a hospital room. Showers, whirlpool tubs, and other nontraditional pain relief amenities, as well as soft lighting and music, are just a few of the perks you might find in today's LDR rooms.

Some facilities have taken the "one-stop" approach even further, offering women LDRP rooms in which they can also spend their postpartum stay. LDRP rooms may feature a pullout bed or other place for the new dad to bunk down, plus comfortable furniture for visiting family and friends. Some even offer special meal catering to the new parents as an alternative to typical hospital-cafeteria fare.

ALERT!

Although HIPPA guarantees a hospital stay of at least forty-eight hours for new mothers giving vaginal birth, you may be able to be discharged earlier if you just can't wait to get your new baby home and your physician agrees that you're physically ready. Some insurers will offer a follow-up home visit from a nurse for women who choose to leave the hospital early.

For those hospitals with LDR rooms, the mother is typically moved into a postpartum room for the duration of her hospital stay. How long that is depends on medical condition, physician assessment, insurance coverage, and state regulations, but in a typical uncomplicated birth, an inpatient stay usually won't exceed forty-eight to seventy-two hours. Under the federal Health Insurance Portability and Accountability Act (HIPPA), health insurers who offer maternity coverage cannot restrict coverage to less than forty-eight hours in a vaginal birth, or ninety-six hours in a C-section birth.

Rooming In

Another thing most hospitals have changed their ways about is keeping the new baby nursery-bound. Barring any neonatal complications, most new mothers are encouraged to have their infant "room-in" with them, going to the nursery only for checkups, weigh-ins, or when requested by mom. In addition to giving new mothers the opportunity to practice new baby care, rooming in promotes breastfeeding and mother-baby bonding.

A variation on rooming in, known as "couplet care," keeps mother and child together as a family for the length of any hospital stay. Both are kept under the care of a single nurse cross-trained in postpartum and neonatal care. If you choose couplet care, your baby remains at your side, along with your partner if you choose, and your nurse can provide breastfeeding guidance, tips on baby care, and other support critical to your new role as mother.

If you choose a hospital birth, take advantage of your time as an inpatient to rest and replenish your strength after birth. Rooming-in is wonderful, but if you need some uninterrupted sleep (something you won't be getting much of after you return home), the nursery is there for your baby. Just be sure to let the nursing staff know your feeding preferences so they will wake you to breastfeed baby if necessary.

A Birthing-Center Birth Experience

So if most hospitals have moved into the age of enlightenment in terms of family-center birth and postpartum care, why choose a birthing center? Hospitals may be revising procedures to emulate the nurturing environment of birthing centers, which are considered by many to be the ground zero of woman-centered care, but there are still significant differences between birthing centers and hospitals.

In addition to their "almost-home" atmosphere, studies have found that birth centers have lower C-section rates and higher reported maternal satisfaction than their hospital counterparts. According to The National Birth Center Study, an analysis of more than 11,800 births taking place in eighty-four freestanding birth centers nationwide, the cesarean section rate for women receiving care in birth centers was approximately half that of women in low-risk, in-hospital births.

FACT

According to the National Association of Childbearing Centers (NACC), thirty-seven states currently license freestanding birthing centers. Some states require accreditation to grant licensure. Birth centers are accredited by the Commission for the Accreditation of Birth Centers (CABC), the accrediting arm of the NACC, and must meet certain quality-of-care, facility, and personnel guidelines as outlined by the CABC.

Why Choose a Birthing Center?

Birthing centers are usually primarily midwife- and nurse-midwife–staffed, and as such maintain a noninterventional philosophy toward birth. Things like continuous fetal monitoring, epidurals, and surgical interventions (including C-section or episiotomy) are not routinely practiced. As such, many centers will only take low-risk, uncomplicated births. Physicians are often on staff on a consultant basis should the need arise for specialized medical advice or care. Because complications can occur during even a low-risk birth, birthing centers have a transport protocol in place to move women who develop labor complications to a nearby hospital.

Many birthing centers also offer onsite prenatal and postpartum care, allowing you to develop a relationship with your midwife and become familiar with the center facilities well before the birth itself.

Some of the other benefits of birthing centers include the following:

- **Freedom.** Women can labor in whatever position they want, not tethered to a monitor or IV line.
- **Peace.** A birth center is typically a quiet place, where the pings, beeps, and persistent PA-system paging of hospitals are not heard.
- **Solitude.** While a maternity ward in an urban hospital may have up to several dozen women laboring at once, the birth center typically has one or two births simultaneously.
- **Continuity.** In most cases, the same midwife will stay with a woman throughout the birth instead of leaving with shift changes.
- **Brevity.** Most women are discharged between four and nine hours postpartum, versus the forty-eight- to seventy-two-hour hospital stay for inpatient births.
- **Cost-efficiency.** In addition to the cost saving from a shorter stay, birthing-center births save money by minimizing costly technological interventions.
- **Strength.** Birthing centers tend to focus on preventative care and instilling a sense of self-sufficiency and self-awareness in women regarding their own health and abilities.
- **Balance.** For many women, the birth center offers a good middle ground between hospital and home.

ALERT!

When interviewing birth centers, be sure to ask what their transfer protocol is, should complications arise, and what sort of complications would mandate a transfer to a hospital. You may or may not be able to stay under the care of your midwife if a transfer occurs, so be sure to inquire if she will continue your care at the hospital.

Is It Really a Birthing Center?

In the move toward creating and marketing more woman-centered, family-friendly birthing environments, many hospitals have adopted the name "birth center" for their inpatient maternity wards. While there are some freestanding birthing centers that are affiliated with hospitals, an in-hospital "birth center" that offers epidurals, has restrictions on family attendance, requires continuous fetal monitoring, or insists on other interventions is not a birthing center in the true sense of the term.

Home Birth

What better place to welcome your child into the world than the cradle of your family—your home? This is the one place where you can completely relax, be yourself, and labor in any way, shape, or form.

Home birth offers all the comforts and many of the perks of the birthing center. And for women who don't want a hospital birth, but may be excluded by a birthing center's "low-risk" selection protocols because they are having twins or because they have had a previous C-section, an attended home birth may provide them the birth experience they want. However, home birth is not without risks. A woman who is already in a "high-risk" situation should have a careful discussion with her health-care provider to go over the options available based on her particular situation and health history.

FACT

If you choose home birth, talk to your midwife about the supplies you should have on hand. Home birth "kits"—which include such essential items as plastic sheeting, cotton balls, and compresses—are available for purchase from childbirth retailers. You can also assemble the components from a list your midwife provides. Finally, if you don't have a big bathtub but would love to labor in a Jacuzzi, rental birthing-tubs are an option. Your midwife or doula can provide more information.

If you live in a rural or isolated area and an emergency situation arises, you won't have the benefits of immediate medical care that a hospital can provide. A good midwife who carries resuscitation equipment and has a transport plan and protocol in place can help minimize some of the risks related to complications.

The American Medical Association (AMA) and the American College of Obstetricians and Gynecologists (ACOG) are squarely against home births, citing safety as a concern. In response, home-birth advocates point to research that backs up both the safety and effectiveness of the home setting for planned term low-risk births.

What to Ask

The best way to avoid any stressful misunderstandings during the birth itself is to clarify all the rules and regulations well in advance. Talk to the hospital or birthing center staff (or in the case of home birth, your provider), and find out what the guidelines are.

If you're planning a birthing center or hospital birth and are will also be attending childbirth preparation classes at the same facility, you'll have an opportunity to ask questions in class. Many centers or hospitals will provide printed information in class that details facility guidelines and may answer many of your questions for you. In addition, facility tours are usually an integral part of childbirth preparation classes.

One advantage of many birthing centers is that you have plenty of opportunities for follow-up questions during routine prenatal care visits, since your provider will typically take appointments at the center. But wherever you plan your birth, don't hesitate to pick up the phone and call the facility with any concerns or questions.

For the Hospital and Birthing Center

If you are planning to check in to a hospital or birthing center, it's important that you know what to expect when the big day arrives. If you have any specific personal requirements—for example, videotaping the birth or having access to certain pain relief options—asking questions early will help you find a facility that will accommodate you. Here are some questions to ask:

- Can I wear my own clothes to labor in?
- What is your fetal monitoring policy?
- Can I eat and/or drink at will during labor?

- Are there limitations on whom I have present during the birth?
- Can I walk and choose my own positions to labor in?
- If I want pharmaceutical pain relief, what are my options?
- Are there any mandatory interventions, such as an intravenous line?
- Can my partner film the birth?
- May I labor in a tub or shower?
- May I give birth in the tub/underwater should I choose to do so?
- What is your emergency transport procedure?
- Do you accept and honor birth plans?
- What is the cesarean rate of the hospital? (Note: It's also important to find out what your provider's individual C-section rate is.)
- Is the birth center licensed by the state? Is it accredited by the National Association for Childbearing Centers (NACC)?
- Will I be consulted about and be the primary decision maker regarding birth interventions?

Questions for Home–Birth Care Providers

Most home births are performed by midwives. Although some physicians will attend a home birth, liability and malpractice issues prevent many from doing so. Some questions to ask your provider if you're considering home birth are the following:

- How early in labor will you arrive for the birth?
- What emergency and resuscitation equipment do you have available?
- If complications occur, what is your procedure for handling them?
- Do I need to assemble home birth supplies or are they supplied by you and included in your fee?
- How many births have you attended?
- What pain relief techniques do you use?
- If I want pharmaceutical pain relief, what are my options?
- Do you place a limit on the number of support people present during the birth itself?
- What is your episiotomy rate?
- What tasks will you perform after the birth in terms of cleanup?
- What is your procedure for examining and disposing of the placenta?

Provider and Insurance Issues

It probably goes without saying that you should check your insurance coverage for participating providers and facilities when deciding on your birth place. If you'd like to have a home birth, there's a good chance it may not be covered by your health-insurance provider. That doesn't mean that you automatically need to take no for an answer.

First of all, leave a paper trail. Remember that any assurances or denials you get on coverage should be in black and white. If you don't see home-birth coverage in your policy, but during a phone consultation an insurance representative assures you that you're covered, ask for written confirmation of coverage to be mailed to you on company letterhead. The same goes for a denial of coverage.

If your insurer does deny home-birth coverage, call your state department of insurance or business regulation and ask what the regulatory guidelines are regarding midwife and home-birth coverage and insurance restrictions so you know your rights. Again, ask for a hard copy of the specific legislation, or at least get a citation so you can look it up for yourself.

Find out what the appeals process is for your health insurer and file a written appeal. It may help to include citations of published clinical studies that have demonstrated the safety and cost-savings of home birth. Your midwife or health-care provider should be able to help you with specific references. Send a copy of your appeal to the state regulatory agency.

QUESTION?

I've had a previous cesarean section, but I'd like to try this birth naturally at home. Is that an option?

While most health-care providers will only oversee "low-risk" home births, many have differing opinions on what actually constitutes low risk. Some may have blanket policies on not attending vaginal birth after cesarean (VBAC) home births, while others look at each request on a case-by-case basis, taking into account a woman's unique health history. The American College of Obstetricians and Gynecologists recommends that all VBACs take place in a hospital setting.

If your insurer still denies your claim, find out the process for filing a complaint with your state insurance regulatory body, and do so. Make sure you send your insurer a copy. Finally, if your health insurance plan is through your employer, talk to your human resources contact about the issue. He or she may be able to assist you in your appeal. At the least, if your human resources department is aware of the denial and you make them aware of the financial and medical benefits of home birth, they may reconsider doing business with the insurer when it's time to renew plan contracts.

If you do end up paying out of pocket, talk to your midwife well in advance of your due date to discuss your payment options. An installment agreement or sliding scale fees (if your provider offers them) may make the cost more affordable.

Making It Your Own

If financial or insurance considerations are dictating the location of your birth, you still have some flexibility in making the birth environment yours. First and foremost, surround yourself with people who will support you and put you at ease. The human interaction of the day will be one of the most important aspects of your birth.

Things like music, flowers, pictures, and other familiar items from home can also help you relax and enjoy the experience. Even having the opportunity to wear your favorite slippers or soft loungewear while you labor will make a difference. Think about what might be on your particular wish list for the perfect birth, and incorporate it into your birth plan. What's a birth plan, you ask? Read on.

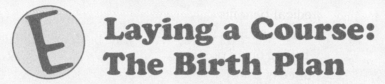 Laying a Course: The Birth Plan

You've picked a provider, scouted out a birth place, and surrounded yourself with the perfect support team. Don't forget your birth plan—your script for staging the best birth experience possible. Planning ahead and getting your expectations down on paper will not only help you get organized, it will give you a chance to discuss your wishes with your provider in advance and avoid unpleasant surprises on the big day.

Why Have a Birth Plan?

Like everything in life, labor and birth are unpredictable. No two occasions are alike, even with the same woman. So why even develop a birth plan? First of all, putting your expectations and wishes on paper gets everyone on your birth team, from your provider to any friends and family who may be present, on the same page.

Also, the very process of creating your birth plan enables you and your partner to discover what you want to get out of your birth experience, to prioritize your needs and wishes, and to resolve any potential disagreements now rather than during labor.

Finally, a birth plan allows you to express your wishes about interventions (such as use of forceps, anesthesia and analgesia use, or episiotomy) should the issue arise. Making informed decisions ahead of time can save you the stress of making difficult choices during the birth.

When your birth plan is finalized, ask your provider to place a copy of it both in your chart and hospital record. Any support people (such as your partner or doula) who will be attending the birth should also be given a copy to familiarize themselves with.

What It Is . . . and Isn't

In simplest form, your birth plan is an outline of what you and your partner want, and don't want, during labor and birth. To be most effective, a birth plan should be brief; anything over five pages is probably too much. It should use cooperative language ("would like" and "prefer" rather than "must have" and "demand") and leave room for alternatives in case complications arise.

In short, a birth plan IS:

- A checklist that can help remind your support team of your wishes when you are focused on labor
- More descriptive than prescriptive

- A place to align common goals and set expectations
- A tool to plan for alternative outcomes should your birth drift off course

A birth plan IS NOT:

- An attempt to thwart your health-care provider
- A legally binding document
- A list of demands
- A guarantee of your ideal birth

Staging Your Birth

Your comfort level and peace of mind on the big birth day will have a direct impact on how your labor progresses. Working out what may seem like minor details now and clearing possible points of contention with your provider will make the birth itself that much easier and anxiety-free.

Atmosphere

So what's the ambiance of your chosen birth place? Is it a four-poster bed and sunshine through cheery floral curtains, or white tile and chrome with an antiseptic scent?

You won't always have control over the total environment of the room, but even if the hospital you've chosen to give birth at is too sterile for your tastes, you can still make small changes that can add significant warmth and welcome to the room. Your birth plan can include a list of items from home to bring to the hospital, such as a quilt and/or pillow, photos of loved ones, and a bouquet of fresh flowers. And remember those hospital-issue foam slippers are no replacement for your own fuzzy favorites.

Music is also a great tool for relaxation, lifting your mood, providing focus, and getting the adrenaline going when it's time to push. Stick with a play list you can control—you don't want to be perpetually dialing past farm reports to get in a station or stuck in a place with bad reception. Creating your own CD or tape with a varied repertoire is a good idea. For example, include selections of classical music to relax you, along with something more up-tempo to motivate you in active labor.

If you want to listen to music during labor and delivery, make sure your birth facility allows the use of a portable stereo, and do keep in mind that depending on where your birth is planned, there may be other women laboring who would appreciate some volume control. Worse case scenario, you have to wear headphones, so it's a good idea to prepare for this by having a pair available. You may want to invest in an extra-long cord as well.

The lighting can also make a big difference in your mood and comfort. The harsh fluorescent fixtures that are common in many hospitals may not create a very restful environment.

Your birth plan can include a request that the lights be dimmed and the curtains drawn if lower light helps relax you during labor and birth. Remember that your baby is coming out of your dark womb, so a darkened environment might help ease her transition into this strange, new world as well.

Cast and Crew

You've already made decisions about the health-care professional who will be attending your birth. (If you haven't, see Chapter 3 for some tips on finding a provider you can work with effectively.) You've also decided on a primary support person, or two, to have on your team. Depending on your personal situation and preferences, these may be the only attendees you will have onboard for this performance.

If your young children are going to be present at the birth of their sibling, be sure to arrange to have a caregiver there to provide supervision and support, even if you're giving birth at home. You and your partner will have your hands full with other things.

However, you may have a bigger cast in mind. Are you thinking about having your children participate in the birth in some capacity? Do you want family and close friends present at the birth, or waiting in the wings nearby? Your birth plan should spell out your expectations in this respect. And if there are people that you wish to meet the baby shortly after birth, but don't necessarily need at the birth itself, include that as well.

Props

Beyond comfort objects to "warm up" your labor and birth room, what kind of items do you want to have access to for pain relief and/or labor assistance? Some items may be supplied by your birth place, while others may have to be brought in. Objects to consider include these:

- **Shower or whirlpool.** Most birth centers and many hospitals now offer a whirlpool tub and/or shower to ease labor pain.
- **A birth ball.** Sitting and/or rocking on this large inflatable rubber ball encourages perineal relaxation and pelvic mobility. Some women also lean against the birth ball on hands and knees to ease back labor pain.
- **Birthing stool.** A birth stool is a seatless or partial-seat stool that allows a woman to deliver in a natural squatting position while providing support.
- **Massage devices.** Massage from a partner or doula during labor can be a great relaxation technique. There are dozens of devices available on the market, but a small rolling pin or a sock containing tennis balls can sometimes fit the bill quite nicely.
- **A cooler.** A small cooler can come in handy for cold compresses, light snacks, and drinks.

QUESTION?

What's the story with food and drink during labor? If I want it, can I have it?

Some hospitals may try to limit you to ice chips and other fluid nourishments. While a meatball sandwich is probably not the best choice during active labor, there's nothing wrong with something light to keep your strength and energy up if you are having a normal, low-risk birth. For more on food and drink during labor, see Chapter 13.

Check with your facility for information on access to any equipment you might need. Your midwife and/or doula may also have some of this equipment on hand to provide as part of her services. If it isn't available and you want it, buy or rent it early so you can bring it with you on the big day.

Head Shots

Like every modern parent, you probably are planning to capture some portion of the big event for posterity. Including your photographic expectations in your birth plan helps you ensure that they pass muster with your birth facility and gives you an easy checklist when it comes time to pack. It's quite possible you don't want your partner snapping pictures of every contraction instead of attending to your needs. Written requests stating that photos should only be taken during certain stages of labor and birth, or only when you ask for them, can prevent your overzealous shutterbug from getting carried away.

While birthing centers are usually amenable to any requests you have regarding photographing and recording the birth, getting the pictures you want may be a bit trickier if you're planning a hospital birth. There may be rules against filming of the actual birth itself or regulations forbidding the use of any special equipment, such as a tripod, that might get in the way. With today's tiny digital recorders, some of these fears of bulky equipment getting in the way and wires to trip over may be unwarranted. Talk to your hospital and provider about these issues so you can know what to expect.

Planning with Your Provider

Reviewing your birth plan with your provider well in advance of your due date is essential. If there are any aspects of the plan your provider disagrees with or will potentially refuse to comply with, you want to know early rather than being faced with an unpleasant surprise while in labor.

Many physicians and midwives will schedule a separate office visit for the primary purpose of going over your birth plan. If your provider doesn't suggest one, take it upon yourself to ask for a dedicated appointment to review your needs and wishes.

ALERT!

Ask your provider and hospital or birth center about their fetal monitoring policy. Walking in labor can ease discomfort and speed progress for many women, but being tethered to a monitor can prevent you from moving through contractions. With a low-risk birth, intermittent (that is, occasional) monitoring should not be a problem in most facilities.

Consider the version of the birth plan you take in to your provider to be a first draft, open to revision. Some practitioners may get defensive about the idea of a birth plan, believing that it conveys a lack of trust in their clinical abilities. Others may be concerned that if complications arise and the birth goes off-course from the plan, they may have a disappointed patient on their hands. And some physicians are simply grounded in the notion that their job is to "deliver" the baby rather than let the patient give birth and own the birth experience.

An open and honest approach can help dissuade any negative feelings about the birth plan. Being receptive to suggestions and communicative, rather than defensive, can do a lot toward lowering your provider's guard and getting him or her to work effectively on your plan.

Getting Everyone on the Same Page

So how do you make sure that your birth plan both reflects your needs and will be accepted (and more importantly, followed appropriately) by your provider? First, while you may have firmly grounded expectations of your birth, be willing to listen to the proposals and issues your provider may have and to work together toward a resolution.

Here are some other tips for getting the most out of your plan:

- **Make requests, not demands.** Keep the language cooperative and communicative so your provider doesn't feel intimidated by the tone.
- **Get to the point.** Think brevity and bullet points. The medical staff that attends your birth needs to be able to see your wishes clearly and quickly, especially if time is of the essence.

- **Short and sweet.** Don't present your provider with the *Encyclopedia Britannica.* You don't need to choreograph every contraction.
- **Convey trust.** Let your midwife or physician know that you trust her to follow the spirit of your birth plan.
- **Offer alternatives.** Be sure to outline your wishes regarding interventions in case complications arise.

Being Prepared: Interventions

Even the best-laid birth plans can go awry. One of the most important elements of a birth plan is a section on provisions for the unexpected. Some women may feel that they "failed" at birth when things don't end up exactly as planned. By building alternative scenarios into your birth plan, you can lessen any later disappointments.

Look at possible worst-case scenarios. Outline your preferences should interventions have to happen, and state your wishes regarding steps to be taken to prevent interventions. For example, you may want to ask for a trial of perineal massage and compresses if your perineum isn't stretching adequately to allow for baby's exit before allowing an episiotomy to occur.

Your pain-management preferences will be a big part of your birth plan. If you take prepared childbirth classes, you'll learn about some options there, and your provider can also outline options for you. If you're interested in natural birth, a midwife or doula may be a better source of information than a physician, as her experience in nonmedicated births tends to be broader.

It's also a good idea to include a section about your preferences regarding cesarean birth, even if yours is a normal low-risk pregnancy and you plan on delivering vaginally. Cover such issues as type of anesthesia, presence of your coach, being able to view the birth, and who will hold and be with the baby first. You will probably never need such provisions, but if you do, it will be one less thing to worry about when the time comes.

Try not to be so restrictive in your language that your provider feels like her hands are tied in your care. And remember that as labor progresses, it's possible that you may want to make some adjustments to the birth plan as well. You may plan on an epidural and then decide during labor that you don't need it. Or you may decide on having a natural childbirth and in the end decide that some pharmaceutical pain relief is the right thing for you. As long as you have an active and self-determined part in any alterations to the plan, last-minute changes are normal and acceptable.

QUESTION?

I'm having a C-section. Should I even bother with a birth plan?
Yes! Even with a cesarean birth, you still have choices to make. Do you want to spend time with the baby immediately following the procedure? Will your support person be present? What kind of postpartum arrangements will you have in place? A birth plan can benefit (and empower) every woman, no matter what type of birth she is having.

If you're having a planned cesarean section for whatever reason, it's likely that the hospital will have specific rules and regulations regarding operative procedure. However, there are certain things you can and should have a say in that a birth plan can help pin down.

Talk to your doctor about what may be flexible (such as seeing the birth in a well-placed mirror or having your significant other cut the cord) and what is nonnegotiable (things like anesthesia or surgical prep). The birth-plan checklist in Appendix A contains a list of potential considerations for women having a C-section birth. For more on cesarean birth, see Chapter 16.

The Perfect Debut

Is there any moment more powerful than your first face-to-face with your newborn? By the time this moment comes, you will have spent nearly ten months dreaming about it, possibly years more if pregnancy was difficult to achieve. Of course you want it to be just right, so take the time to think about and include your preferences in your birth plan.

Barring any complications, birthing centers typically let you and your family spend as much time cuddling and bonding with the new baby as you'd like before doing any routine fingerprinting or testing. As your first official parental duty, you and your partner help and hold baby during the weigh-in, measurement, and after-birth cleanup. There is no separation involved.

A hospital, on the other hand, may have certain protocols in place for newborn care, including immediate blood tests, eyedrops, heat lamps, and vitamin K injections. If you're planning a hospital birth, talk to your care provider and a hospital representative now to find out what the exact protocols are. A few questions to ask include these: Will you be allowed to hold your newborn skin-to-skin while the placenta is delivered and she is evaluated, or will you just get a peek and a promise of a swift return? Do you or your partner have the option to cut the cord, and must it be done immediately? If the baby requires medical attention at birth, will your partner be allowed to stay with her? Chapter 19 discusses newborn tests and procedures in more detail. It's a good idea to educate yourself on the issues surrounding them now so you can inquire about policy and state your wishes in your birth plan. Even if the protocol is very strict, at the very least you will know what to expect.

FACT

Vitamin K assists in blood clotting and is usually formed in the intestinal tract, but newborns aren't able to produce it at birth. In the early 1990s, several studies found an association between vitamin K at birth and childhood cancers; however, subsequent studies have found no link between the two. While vitamin K is usually given by injection shortly after birth, studies have also found that several oral doses of vitamin K are just as effective and possibly less traumatic for both you and your child.

Postpartum Preplanning

Your birth plan doesn't end with baby's entrance into the world. Adding a postpartum section to the birth plan can be a big help in getting you organized and keeping you and baby on a reasonable schedule once your new family is back at home.

Here are some things you might want to include:

- **Maternity and paternity leave.** If you and/or your partner are taking it, outline how much and when (for example, six weeks from the due date, twelve weeks after birth). Be sure to investigate your leave and insurance options.
- **Home support system.** Will you have some live-in help for a few weeks, or are you flying solo?
- **Backup.** Line up friends and neighbors who will make the occasional grocery store run, drop off a meal, or do other errands for you during those early days.
- **First meetings.** Are close relatives or friends planning a visit after the birth, or are you keeping baby to yourself for a while?
- **Doctor's visits.** Both you and baby will be visiting your respective doctors in the weeks following the birth. Put this on your birth plan now so you won't forget to schedule appointments when the time comes.

Remember, your birth plan can be a great tool in achieving the birth experience you and your partner want. Start early so you can make fully informed decisions and work with your provider to make the plan workable to everyone involved. The birth plan checklist in Appendix A can help guide you through the process.

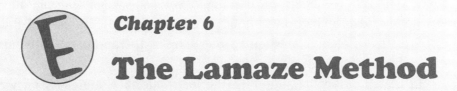

Chapter 6

The Lamaze Method

Perhaps the best-known birth philosophy, Lamaze has been an American household term since the late 1950s. Most people identify Lamaze with panting and blowing, and while breathing exercises are an important part of this method, there is much more to it than that. Lamaze is about managing pain through knowledge, exercise, and relaxation skills—a technique known as psychoprophylaxis.

Physician and Founder Fernand Lamaze

According to Fernand Lamaze's granddaughter and biographer, Caroline Gutmann, Lamaze was inducted into the world of obstetrics by Louis Dubrisay, the physician who delivered his only daughter (a birth Lamaze did not attend). Early in his career, Lamaze was an advocate of offering birthing women anesthetic pain relief—at a time when the view was largely unpopular in France. He did not develop his now-famous psychoprophylactic method of childbirth until relatively late in life, when he was in his sixties and had a thriving upper-class obstetrical practice.

In 1950, Lamaze had attended the International Congress of Gynecology in Paris, where he heard Professor A. Nicolaïev speak about a nonpharmaceutical method of decreasing pain in childbirth that was being successfully practiced in Nicolaïev's home base of Leningrad. Prior to moving into the field of obstetrics, Lamaze was a student of neurology, which may have explained his heightened interest in this radical new idea and the science it was based on—the behavioral conditioning theories of Russian researcher Ivan Pavlov.

FACT

Pavlov, as you may know from high-school psychology, is the behavioral psychologist who discovered that dogs could be conditioned to associate the sound of a bell (an unconditioned stimulus) with their dinner (a conditioned stimulus), so that they would eventually salivate at the sound of the ringing bell whether food was present or not (known as a conditioned reflex). Similarly, if the unconditioned stimulus was repeatedly introduced without the conditioned stimulus (that is, the bell without the food), this conditioned reflex could be eliminated, a process called extinction.

The following year, Lamaze traveled to the Soviet Union as part of a delegation of French physicians. Here he visited the Marx Maternity Hospital, where pregnant women were conditioned to have positive, instead of painful, responses to pain. Lamaze learned more about the psychoprophylactic method both here and at the Pavlov Institute. Toward the end of his trip, he was permitted to attend a labor and birth that demonstrated the effectiveness of the method. The experience had a profound impact on Lamaze. Upon his return to France, he dedicated himself to adapting the techniques toward a more universal audience, building on a more humanistic foundation than the one the Soviets used as a basis for their method.

Conditioning a Birth Response

The idea that fear and anxiety can amplify the pain response was nothing new. Dr. Grantly Dick-Read had been working on his own method of childbirth education and birth based on this exact theory since the 1930s. (For more on Dick-Read and the fear/pain response, see Chapter 8.) But while Dick-Read based his work on the idea that simply eliminating the fear of the unknown would eliminate the pain response, Lamaze taught that education was only part of the equation, and a woman must be reconditioned to experience the pain of childbirth as a positive life force, concentrating not on the discomfort but on her own ability to work past it and give birth to her baby. For many years, the medical establishment had been reinforcing the conditioned belief that birth was a painful physical malady requiring medical management, and Lamaze set out to break that association.

"Thank You, Dr. Lamaze"

By the time Lamaze published his landmark book *Painless Childbirth* in 1956, pregnant women throughout France were banging down the door of Bluets (the maternity hospital Lamaze directed). In the United States, however, Lamaze was still largely unknown. The 1959 publication of an insightful and witty book by Marjorie Karmel, entitled *Thank You, Dr. Lamaze: A Mother's Experience in Painless Childbirth,* changed everything. An American under Lamaze's care, Karmel had her baby in Paris—unmedicated and with her husband in attendance (two ideas deemed radical in the States at the time). The book, which detailed two births using psychoprophylaxis (one in France and one in the United States), became an overnight sensation and generated widespread interest among pregnant women and obstetricians.

Back in her home base of New York, Karmel joined forces with physical therapist and pioneering childbirth educator Elisabeth Bing to form the American Society for Psychoprophylaxis in Obstetrics (ASPO) in 1960.

Today, ASPO has become Lamaze International, with more than 11,000 educators certified in the Lamaze birth philosophy and training seminars held worldwide.

The designation "LCCE" stands for "Lamaze certified childbirth educator." If your childbirth educator has this credential, it means that she has participated in an accredited training program, has met specific educational standards, and has passed a rigorous certification examination.

The Philosophy of Today's Lamaze Method

Today's Lamaze method is quite different than the one Fernand Lamaze introduced to the world over fifty years ago. Lamaze has changed focus as the body of childbirth knowledge and literature has evolved. Instructors now teach women to follow their instincts and trust "their inner wisdom" throughout the pregnancy and birth process. Fathers are no longer trained as coaches; rather, each father is taught ways to provide comfort and support for his mate at her direction.

The Lamaze International Birth Philosophy Statement, a guiding principal that all Lamaze educators are expected to follow in their teachings, is as follows:

- Birth is normal, natural, and healthy.
- The experience of birth profoundly affects women and their families.
- Women's inner wisdom guides them through birth.
- Women's confidence and ability to give birth is either enhanced or diminished by the care provider and place of birth.
- Women have a right to give birth free from routine medical intervention.
- Birth can safely take place in birth centers and at home.
- Childbirth education empowers women to make informed choices in health care, to assume responsibility for their health, and to trust their inner wisdom.

While Lamaze promotes natural birth, it stops short of saying that labor and birth should be drug- and device-free. Instead, Lamaze educators advocate the responsible use of interventions for medically indicated purposes and not as routine procedures.

Woman's Inner Wisdom

The original Lamaze method encouraged women to focus away from their bodies in order to get past the pain of contractions and relied quite heavily on external cues from a "coach" pacing breathing or issuing orders. Today, Lamaze instructors teach women to look inside themselves for ways to cope with labor. While breathing exercises and relaxation for pain management are still an integral part of the method, it's now more about attuning yourself to respond appropriately to your body's signals rather than completely removing your mind from labor's physical discomfort.

Empowerment and Informed Free Choice

Today's Lamaze also promotes a woman's right to choose—this includes her birth place and surrounding environment, her support team, and her provider. Providing a complete education on birth options and potential interventions and complications is part of that process.

QUESTION?

Is Lamaze the same thing as prepared childbirth classes?
While the terms "Lamaze method" and "prepared childbirth" are often used interchangeably, Lamaze is a separate birth philosophy all its own. Some classes that are billed as prepared childbirth may be Bradley oriented, or they may include a little bit of Lamaze in addition to other birth theories. If you're looking for a Lamaze class, the best way to ensure that the curriculum includes Lamaze theory is to check the course description and to find out if the instructor is an LCCE.

Lamaze classes educate women on "working within the system" to get the birth experience they want, with an emphasis on how to minimize the impact of interventions and undesirable birth settings or attendants should that situation arise. Lamaze is criticized in some circles for this approach, as some childbirth advocates believe it can leave women with the assumption that interventions may be inevitable or that birth should be hospital-managed rather than woman-directed.

The Purpose of Pain

Labor pain is caused by the powerful contractions of the muscles of your uterus. It can also be manifested as lower back pain if your child is in a posterior, or downward facing, position. In addition to signaling that the time is right for birth, pain has other positive roles in labor and delivery. Pain signals trigger biochemical changes in the body that help labor progress and improve your ability to cope with the pain.

Lamaze International calls the pain of labor "protective," in that it acts as a signal to move through contractions, movement that encourages the descent of the baby and facilitates the ripening of the cervix. That ripening triggers further release of oxytocin, which strengthens contractions. In Lamaze-focused birth, pain is not a roadblock but an active sign that progress is being made. At its core, it focuses on casting pain in a positive light and working with it, not against it.

Labor pain also triggers the release of endorphins, those neurotransmitters (or brain chemicals) that attach to nerve receptors and depress or decrease the sensation of pain, making it more tolerable. In large amounts, endorphins are also associated with feelings of euphoria, like the rush you get once your baby is delivered and in your arms.

When narcotics or anesthetics are administered in labor, pain signals shut down and so does the production of endorphins, short-circuiting this biochemical defense system. Once an epidural or analgesia "wears off," pain may be perceived as significantly more intense because of this drop-off of endorphins.

Lamaze and Reframing Pain

Although Lamaze was widely touted as a "painless" childbirth method, it's important to note that women trained in Lamaze still feel contractions—

some quite acutely. What one woman may consider mildly uncomfortable, another may think is barely tolerable. The difference is in how they perceive and react to the pain. Lamaze uses conditioning techniques like breathing and relaxation as mental analgesics, meant to lessen pain or make it more manageable rather than eliminate the sensation completely.

FACT

A 2001 Italian study published in *Biology of the Neonate* found that women who had vaginal births and unmedicated labors had a much higher concentration of beta-endorphin levels in their colostrum than did women who underwent cesarean section. Beta-endorphins in colostrum and breast milk are thought to help newborns recover from the stress of labor and birth and may have a positive association with motor development in infancy.

Breathing Patterns

Good oxygen flow helps power your muscles, keeping fatigue at bay. Lamaze-patterned breathing also gives women a task to concentrate on and a distraction from pain. Some breathing patterns also help aid the mechanics of the birth process. There are several specific breathing patterns taught by Lamaze instructors. These include the following:

- **Cleansing breaths.** A cleansing breath is a deep breath taken at the beginning of a contraction and as a contraction ends. The purpose of this type of breathing is to relax you for the contraction and refocus you once it has ended.
- **Slow-paced breathing.** As the name suggests, to perform slow-paced breathing you deliberately slow your breathing rate to about half the norm in order to relax and relieve anxiety, inhaling through the nose and exhaling through the mouth. Abdominal massage and visual focus techniques usually accompany this type of breathing.
- **Modified-paced breathing.** Breathing at twice your normal rate of respiration can help you stay mentally alert. This type of breathing is used when contractions are close together and the second stage of labor is imminent.

- **Patterned-paced breathing.** This is rapid, "panting" type breathing that can help to refocus you on the task at hand. The thought processes involved to keep breathing in a particular pattern will keep you centered on your breathing and not the contraction pain. A pattern of light breaths followed by a pattern of blowing can help suppress the urge to push, as well.
- **Pushing breathing.** Breathing for the pushing stage of labor consists of several cleansing breaths that are held for six to ten seconds while you push during contractions. Holding the breath is a way of using the diaphragm to assist in the pushing process.

Although most laypeople will equate the word Lamaze with panting and puffing, patterned breathing is but one tool taught to pregnant women to help manage their pain. Women are taught to pick a focal point to rest their eyes on during contractions, a practice that helps them to concentrate completely on the rhythm and pattern of their breathing. Effleurage, or light massage, of the abdomen is also encouraged in tandem with breathing during contractions. The massage soothes pain and releases tension and provides another tool for working past the pain. Like patting your head and rubbing your stomach at the same time, choreographing your breathing patterns, massage, and sight line will require considerable mental efforts that will focus you on the task and distract you from labor pain.

Many women feel the urge to push prematurely during transition as the pressure on their rectum increases. To quell the urge, Lamaze instruction suggests rapid panting, breathing in and forcibly blowing out air (also called puff or blow breathing). Have a paper bag on hand in case of hyperventilation.

Body Awareness and Relaxation

Also key to Lamaze is the ability to recognize tension and to systematically release it from your body. Muscles that are relaxed will function more effectively and be less painful in labor. Lamaze classes use different exercises to teach awareness of tension and release by systematically contracting and then relaxing different muscle groups. Deep cleansing breaths are used to prepare body and mind for relaxation.

Exercises that keep the body limber and in good alignment can help women in both birth and in late pregnancy, when the shape and heft of their burgeoning bellies work against gravity, often resulting in back pain and fatigue. Lamaze exercises are usually a series of gentle stretches, with instruction on proper sitting and standing posture and on pelvic-strengthening kegel exercises. Pushing positions like the supported squat may also be practiced.

Learning Lamaze

Lamaze instructors usually encourage enrollment in their classes toward the end of pregnancy, in the seventh or eighth month. The rationale is that women who take classes earlier than this may forget some of the essentials by the birth or become bored with the exercises and home practice. On the other hand, classes taken any later may not give the mother-to-be sufficient time to practice and women who give birth earlier than their estimated due date may miss valuable instruction.

Many Lamaze courses are hospital-based, and as such may focus on the procedures and policies of the host hospital. On the plus side, if you're giving birth at the hospital in question, you'll learn more about what to expect and will get a first-hand look at the facility. Your class will be a good place to get all your more practical questions answered.

However, a course that is funded by the hospital may also have certain biases built into the curriculum. The instructor may not be as free with certain information considered outside the institutionalized obstetric mainstream. For example, if the lithotomy position is the overwhelming favorite of physicians at a given facility, an instructor employed by the hospital may teach that flat-on-your-back birth is the standard of care. Or she may avoid the topic of alternative birthing positions, not wanting to disappoint her students should they not be able to birth the way they want.

Of course, all instructors will filter their teachings through their own personal lens of belief systems and life experiences. However, some women believe that finding a class and instructor unaffiliated with the medical establishment will provide them with an education that is less about rules and regulations and more about a safe and effective birth experience. See Appendix B for information on contacting Lamaze International to find an instructor in your area.

Lamaze Instruction

Lamaze International, the official governing and certification body of the Lamaze method of childbirth and childbirth education, suggests that classes in the method contain a minimum of twelve hours of instruction. They should also include plenty of time to practice relaxation and exercise skills. Lamaze International also recommends that classes remain small to facilitate student participation and personal instruction, with a maximum enrollment of twelve couples. Most Lamaze courses are either taught as a once-weekly class over a period of five to six weeks or as a single weekend session.

Basic skills and issues taught in the Lamaze curriculum include the following:

- The physiology of normal labor and birth
- Relaxation skills and breathing techniques
- Communication between partners
- Communication and informed consent with medical providers
- Effective labor and birth positions
- Massage and other comfort measures
- Information on pain-relief options, including pros and cons
- Possible complications of labor and birth, and the risks and benefits of potential interventions to treat them
- Breastfeeding information
- Physical and emotional postpartum expectations
- Support methods for the father or another labor-support partner

Relearning Lamaze

If you choose the Lamaze method of childbirth and it works well for you, many Lamaze instructors offer "refresher courses" for second-time parents if you plan on another pregnancy. These short workshops can help you refresh your relaxation skills without having to go through all the basics on the physiology of birth that you've already experienced firsthand. They will also bring you up to speed on any new developments in Lamaze and childbirth research since your last pregnancy.

Partners and Practice

Your labor and birth partner—be it spouse, friend, partner, family member, or doula—is also an important part of a Lamaze birth. Lamaze was among the first to move fathers into the delivery room and the role of active participants in the birth experience. Originally, Lamaze promoted the role of father as a birth coach who monitored his partner's breathing and relaxation and corrected her form, directing the birth.

Today, Lamaze instructors teach birth partners to provide continuous and calm support, directed by the birthing woman's needs. There is an emphasis on facilitating communication and teaching your partner to recognize your unique physical cues and respond appropriately to them.

FACT

Lamaze International advocates continuity of support during birth, and recommends that "one-on-one continuous nursing support" be provided to laboring women. Most Lamaze classes will include discussion of doulas and their role in the birth process, encouraging their use for women and/or couples who don't anticipate being adequately supported during their birth.

Part of honing your partner's ability to manage this role is practice. While you'll get some opportunity to do this in your class, it's important to go over breathing and relaxation techniques together on a regular basis at home so you're in synch for the birth. You'll both be more likely to retain the information you picked up in class if you spend time practicing, and you'll also feel more prepared for the birth and thus less anxious. Doing your "homework" together can be fun as well. Practice massage so he knows what feels good and what doesn't. Switch places so you can model a comfortable technique.

Lamaze and After Birth

When Lamaze first appeared on the childbirth scene, the focus was on maternal pain management only, with little effort made to discover ways that neonatal care might improve. The after-birth experience of mother-and-child bonding has a greater emphasis in today's Lamaze.

Lamaze educators encourage women to have immediate skin-to-skin contact with their newborns whenever possible, in order to regulate baby's body temperature, promote early breastfeeding, and facilitate mother-child bonding. Rooming-in, or keeping and caring for the baby in mom's room, is also encouraged in hospital birth situations. Lamaze International cites easier and often more frequent breastfeeding, early attachment, and infant health benefits such as better sleep quality and weight gain as reasons for choosing rooming-in instead of nursery care.

The relaxation exercises learned in Lamaze can also serve you well during the postpartum period as you try to adjust to the lack of sleep and added stresses that being a new mom can bring. Use them to release tension that may be inhibiting your breastfeeding efforts or exacerbating your fatigue.

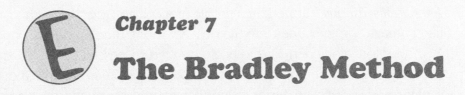

Chapter 7

The Bradley Method

D r. Robert A. Bradley, creator of the Bradley method of natural childbirth (also known as husband-coached childbirth), is largely credited with getting dads into the delivery room. Whether you choose dad or someone else to be your birth partner, you both need to be prepared to put in some time beforehand—Bradley childbirth involves a good deal of education, with a strong emphasis on natural (in other words, unmedicated) labor and delivery and on making sure parents are extensively instructed about birth practices so they are able to make responsible birth choices.

Physician and Founder
Robert A. Bradley, M.D.

Obstetrician Robert A. Bradley started his research into unmedicated, instinctual childbirth in the late 1940s while he was a resident at the Mayo Foundation and as he continued his work at the University of Minnesota. After the *Minneapolis Tribune* featured high-profile press coverage of his method, which (like Lamaze) brought dads into the delivery room, Bradley gained popularity. He moved to Colorado in 1952 to begin his own successful obstetrics practice. A decade later, he published a study recapping his experiences with thousands of natural, dad-coached births using the method described in the medical journal *Psychosomatics* (in an article entitled "Fathers' Presence in Delivery Rooms," 1962 Nov–Dec; 3(3): 474–9).

Bradley wrote his signature text, *Husband-Coached Childbirth,* in 1965. This revolutionary book gave natural-childbirth proponents one of the first handbooks devoted to unmedicated, intervention-free birth. But widespread instruction in the method wasn't available outside of the doctor's home base of Denver until 1970, when Bradley and two of his satisfied birth customers, Marjie and Jay Hathaway, cofounded the American Academy of Husband-Coached Childbirth (AAHCC). The Hathaways had flown from California to Denver in 1965 to give birth to their fourth child, James, under Dr. Bradley's care. They were so satisfied with the experience that they started developing a curriculum for Bradley instruction that eventually ied to the AAHCC. Today, the AAHCC proclaims to have trained more than 200,000 couples for Bradley birth, with an unmedicated birthrate of 86 percent.

The Bradley Method Philosophy

Unmedicated, natural vaginal birth is the primary goal of Bradley instruction. Classes are intensive, and parents are taught to be proactive, not passive, in making birth decisions. The father, or other designated partner, plays an important role in Bradley birth and undergoes significant training in coaching the mother through the various stages of labor and birth.

The twelve Bradley Method ideals endorsed by the AAHCC, as stated in their Declaration of Principles, are as follows:

1. Natural childbirth
2. Active participation of the husband as coach
3. Excellent nutrition, the foundation of a healthy pregnancy
4. Avoidance of drugs during pregnancy, birth, and breastfeeding unless absolutely necessary
5. Training: "Early-birth" classes followed by weekly classes starting in the fifth month, continuing until birth
6. Relaxation and NATURAL breathing
7. "Tuning-in" to your own body
8. Immediate and continuous contact with your new baby
9. Breastfeeding, beginning at birth
10. Positive communications and consumerism
11. Parents taking responsibility for the safety of the birth place, procedures, birth attendants, and emergency backup facilities
12. Parents educated about unexpected situations, such as emergency childbirth and cesarean section

Like Lamaze, Bradley teaches relaxation as its primary method of pain management. However, the Bradley camp is highly critical of Lamaze for what it considers to be unnatural methods of removing a woman from her birth experience instead of allowing her to participate fully in and master it. Although the two methods do have many similarities, Dr. Bradley and the AAHCC have been quite vocal about what they perceive as major flaws in the Lamaze method—unnatural breathing, lack of depth of educational instruction, and an acceptance of interventions and pain relief.

Relaxation

The progressive relaxation techniques taught in Bradley classes help women to become more aware of their bodies. Students are trained to recognize tension and stress by tightening and relaxing muscle groups and becoming familiar with the sensations of relaxation. Becoming attuned to the subtle tensions that can creep in unnoticed is key. Chronic stress can breed chronic tension and inhibit complete relaxation. A tight neck or a clenched jaw can be an insidious form of muscle strain that takes practice to identify and purge from the body.

In the Bradley- and AAHCC-endorsed text, *Natural Childbirth the Bradley Way*, author Susan McCutcheon urges women to think their way through contractions, physically relaxing but always remaining mentally alert and assessing the body for any tension. Bradley instructors teach that the only muscle that should be working during a contraction is the uterus.

While both Bradley and Lamaze focus on relaxation skills, the Bradley Method differs from Lamaze in the role that breathing plays in the process. Lamaze breathing is patterned and designed to provide a distraction or external focus away from labor pain. Bradley breathing, also called abdominal breathing, is steady, slow, unforced, natural breathing that causes the abdomen to rise and fall. Tuning in to the rhythm of the breathing is encouraged to enhance relaxation.

Mental Imagery

Another technique taught in Bradley classes is mental imagery. Bradley mental imagery is directed inward; rather than using guided-imagery techniques of picturing successful outcomes (such as a happy, healthy baby or a metaphor that symbolizes birth), mental imagery involves actually picturing the uterus contracting and working to open up the cervix and help push the baby into the world. The rationale is to provide a positive association with the sensation of contractions and to again frame birth as a natural, physiological process. Students are taught to use mental imagery in conjunction with total body relaxation and abdominal breathing during each contraction.

Informed Parental Responsibility

The Bradley Method stresses the role of both parents as informed consumers in the marketplace of health and childbirth services. Parents are taught about the physiology of birth, the risks of interventions and pain medications, and their rights as patients in order to choose the safest birth experience possible (which from a Bradley viewpoint is a nonmedicated birth). Women and their partners are charged with the responsibility of education and birth choices. Parents are encouraged to seek out care providers and a birth setting that also promotes natural childbirth.

While the focus on parental responsibility can certainly make Bradley instruction an empowering experience for many women and couples, it requires a significant commitment of time and effort. Bradley classes and the at-home practices associated with the method arc lengthy, and Bradley advocates that women and their partners proactively seek out a birth place and birth attendant that will provide the best chance for an all-natural birth, even if that means traveling long distances and investing significant resources to do so.

QUESTION?

The Bradley course offered in my town is $500! Isn't that a little steep?

Bradley Method courses do tend to be more expensive than other Lamaze and prepared-childbirth classes, primarily because there are more sessions involved. Typically running between $250 and $500 for the twelve-class series, Bradley course fees also include the price of the student workbook. In addition, instructors often make themselves available for follow-up phone calls from students. Check with your insurance company about coverage, and if money continues to be a problem, talk to the class administrator about the possibility of a sliding fee scale.

Bradley and Natural Childbirth

Natural childbirth is a term that is often misunderstood, misappropriated, and maligned. Childbirth is, of course, a natural physiological process by definition. It's only in the past half-century that technology and medical obstetric management have become so ingrained in the U.S. health-care arena that the perception of birth as a pathological or disease process requiring close medical oversight and interventions has come to dominate popular culture. Medical measures like forceps delivery and routine episiotomy have become part of the mainstream.

For Dr. Robert Bradley, who was born and raised on a Kansas farm where livestock gave birth and flourished without forceps, episiotomy, or epidurals, natural birth meant just that—birth as instinct, led unaided by medications or technologies. He did make allowances for a few noninstinctual components to his method, most notably the husband-coach.

Training and Instruction

Bradley classes are the lengthiest and most intensive of the popular childbirth education methods. A typical class will meet for a total of twelve sessions over a period of three months, starting in the fifth or sixth month. Because Bradley focuses on a healthy pregnancy for a healthy birth, an "early bird" class is often offered in the first trimester.

Instruction is usually augmented by substantial reading material (certified Bradley classes include a 130-plus-page workbook with instructional material, home assignments, labor exercises, and more). Classes typically have no more than eight couples to ensure that instructors can build a rapport with students and provide personal attention to all.

Certified Bradley instructors have received training from the American Academy of Husband-Coached Childbirth. You'll know if your instructor is certified if she carries one of these designations after her name—AAHCC; affiliated Bradley instructor; or Bradley-certified childbirth educator. Instructors with one of these credentials have completed required academic work and a period of student teaching, and they have also passed a series of competency tests at an AAHCC Bradley training workshop.

Bradley Instruction

Instructors who teach the Bradley Method advocate a completely drug- and intervention-free birth experience. As such, much of the curriculum is focused on steering clear of interventions. For example, you may learn ways to stretch the perineum without episiotomy or receive advice on spending the bulk of your labor at home to avoid an unnecessary cesarean. However, courses do cover what to expect should a cesarean or another intervention become unavoidable.

Bradley is based on the idea that adequate preparation and training are the best ways to promote a natural birth. Women taking Bradley classes are taught lifestyle strategies like proper nutrition and exercise to promote a healthy pregnancy and to help avoid potential delivery complications.

If natural (without medication) birth is high on your priority list, when choosing a Bradley-certified instructor you should ask about their "success rate"—in other words, what percentage of their students go on to have an unmedicated vaginal birth. The AAHCC stresses in its statement of policy that a teacher's first responsibility is to the students, "regardless of who is paying for the classes." The organization encourages instructors to operate independently of hospitals and physician practices to ensure that political pressures and vested interests of those institutions don't bias their curriculum. The organization also states that most Bradley instructors pursue certification after achieving a Bradley Method birth themselves, so if you're inspired by those who practice what they preach and speak not just from textbooks but experience, Bradley instruction may be the way to go.

FACT

To gain entrance into the Bradley teacher-training program, the AAHCC requires that potential instructors have personal experience with the Bradley Method. Specifically, they must have taken Bradley classes themselves during pregnancy, have breastfed their babies and attended La Leche League meetings, and have read the two teaching texts of the AAHCC—*Husband-Coached Childbirth* and *Natural Childbirth the Bradley Way*. Potential instructors who do not meet all of these criteria must obtain a special AAHCC exemption, and, if approved, they must do additional practical coursework to compensate for the deficit.

Bradley classes also include extensive instruction on what natural birth really is as opposed to the medical model of birth. Women and their partners are taught the lingo of birth "problems" that under some circumstances may actually be variations on the norm—failure to progress, prolonged labor, cephalopelvic disproportion, dystocia—so that they understand what is actually a danger to mother and baby and what may simply be a situation of the labor or birth not meeting their physician's expectations.

For example, a long labor or dilation that is proceeding at less than a centimeter an hour is not an indication for medical help unless the mother or baby is in distress, yet a number of interventions may be offered at this point with the assumption that they will speed the delivery of the child. Bradley instructors teach students what questions to ask—for example, "Is the baby's heart rate okay?"—in order to assess whether interventions are actually medically indicated or just indicated by the hospital's or doctor's schedule. Because the Bradley method assigns this advocacy role to the coach to allow his partner to focus on the birth, this instruction is often geared to him.

Coaching the Coach

Dads—or other labor support partners—are a big part of the Bradley way of birth. Since Bradley first brought fathers into the delivery room in the fifties, and the American Association of Husband-Coached Childbirth was formed in 1970, the Bradley method has been identified with dad-directed natural birth. Bradley dads are taught to play an active role in both the pregnancy and the birth, supporting their partners and participating in the same depth of education as the mother-to-be in the childbirth classroom.

Some critics of the Bradley method oppose the notion of "husband-coached childbirth," saying that a) not all husbands are cut out to be coaches, and b) the term "coach" implies that the partner is directing the action, which takes control of the birth away from the mother. Bradley promoters counter that their method teaches the coach to play the important role of advocate for the mother and also to provide support that is physical (through massage and other techniques) as well as emotional (by encouraging their partner through periods of self-doubt).

Husbands are also asked to coach the pregnant woman in making healthy lifestyle choices throughout her pregnancy. This assumes a certain level of tact and emotional sensitivity on the coach's part; it's easy to see how the "coaching" father could quickly become the nagging pain in the neck if he isn't skilled in either of these areas.

Yet in theory and purpose, the Bradley husband-coach isn't much different than the Lamaze support person, and Bradley instruction doesn't actually require a husband coach—just an interested and committed partner (of any gender and relationship). In fact, a good deal of the argument against the husband coach is purely semantics. If the AAHCC were to let go of the label "husband-coached childbirth" in favor of a more woman-centered, inclusive title such as "partner-supported childbirth," these criticisms might lessen considerably.

Attention all coaches: Don't let your title go to your head. Effective coaching in childbirth requires support and appropriate responsiveness, not calling out plays and barking orders. Your partner and child are leading this team. So think of yourself as a cheerleader, encouraging your partner when she needs it, and a referee (or perhaps a good agent), your partner's advocate with birth-facility staff.

Practice and Preparation

Bradley instructors often liken childbirth to an athletic challenge—something that requires months of training and hard work to prepare your body for. As you prepare your body physically, you will become emotionally ready for the birth experience as well. Women who have spent months working on exercises, relaxation techniques, and educating themselves about birth choices won't have the fear and anxiety of the unknown that many first-time mothers face when labor begins.

To get ready for the triathlon (labor-transition-birth) of childbirth, Bradley training is long and homework-intensive. Home practice focuses on these elements:

- **Building stamina.** Regular, heart-pumping exercise like walking, hiking, or swimming to prepare the body for the duration of the big event is encouraged. (Always check with your doctor before starting a new exercise program in pregnancy.)

- **Promoting flexibility.** Squats, kegel exercises, and tailor sits are just a few of the exercises introduced in a Bradley curriculum to stretch and tone the muscles used in childbirth and minimize perineal tearing.
- **Teamwork.** Because Bradley teaches husband-coached (or partner-coached) childbirth, practicing relaxation techniques, different pushing positions, and comfort measures at home is encouraged to improve communication between partners.
- **Relaxation.** Relaxation is a skill that takes practice to perfect. Home-relaxation exercises are used to help you tune in to your body and to help you learn how to tune out stress.

The Birth Environment

Because Bradley instructors spend a lot of time talking about ways to avoid hospital-based interventions in labor, they also usually recommend waiting until labor has progressed significantly and contractions are close together (about a minute long and three minutes apart) to proceed to the hospital. When they can be attended by supportive and competent birth attendants, home or birthing center births are considered preferable environments.

ALERT!

Babies can be born en route to the hospital, especially when most of the hard labor is done at home. Since laboring at home is encouraged, one of the final classes in the Bradley curriculum teaches coaches just what to do if the baby is born before you reach your destination. The baby will follow the same path whether she's in a hospital room or pulled over on the side of a freeway, but after an unexpected birth coaches do need to remember not to cut or pull on the umbilical cord before the placenta is delivered.

Bradley-trained couples who choose to have their baby in a hospital rather than at home or at a birth center are taught to have their guard up from the moment they enter the hospital until the minute they are discharged. This can have positive results in that a woman will be prepared to manage her own labor and birth instead of allowing the hospital to "actively manage" it for her. However, being conditioned to feel like the hospital is enemy territory can also work to breed anxiety, which will greatly impede your ability to master the relaxation techniques Bradley promotes. Instead of viewing the hospital as a necessary evil, focus on effective communication with the staff and perhaps even teaching them a thing or two with your birth experience. Of course, taking the time early in pregnancy to choose providers you trust and who respect your decisions will go a long way in making your birth environment—wherever it may be—a comfortable place.

Bradley and After Birth

Toward the end of your Bradley education, you'll receive instruction on the benefits of breastfeeding and on newborn care, postpartum recovery, and common issues that new parents face. Immediate and continuous mother-to-baby contact is encouraged, as is immediate breastfeeding to help hasten the third stage of labor (expulsion of the placenta) and to promote bonding.

FACT

La Leche League (now La Leche League International) was founded in 1958 to support and educate women on the benefits of breastfeeding their infants. The name "La Leche," Spanish for "the milk," was originally chosen because it was considered inappropriate to use the words "breast" or "breastfeeding" in public at the time. To date, the program has accredited more than 41,000 La Leche League leaders worldwide.

Many Bradley instructors are also La Leche League leaders; in fact, prior attendance at a La Leche League group is a requirement of being admitted into a Bradley teacher-training program. If you're planning on breastfeeding, you may find this an added educational bonus and source of support.

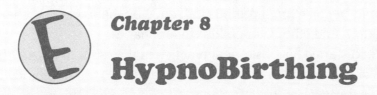

Chapter 8

HypnoBirthing

HypnoBirthing is a relatively new kid on the childbirth education block, but the principles it is founded on—the fear-tension-pain cycle—derive from the works and research of the original natural birth pioneer Dr. Grantly Dick-Read. Dick-Read was the first to realize that stress and anxiety are detrimental to women in childbirth. HypnoBirthing builds on his work by training women to release tensions and enter a state of deep relaxation that soothes labor discomfort while giving them greater control over their bodies and their birth.

Natural-Childbirth Pioneer Grantly Dick-Read, M.D.

Grantly Dick-Read is considered the father of natural childbirth, coining the term itself with his first book, *Natural Childbirth* (1933). His landmark text, *Childbirth Without Fear: The Principles and Practices of Natural Childbirth* (1944), would become an enormous influence on the work of Michel Odent, Robert Bradley, and other later childbirth luminaries.

Dick-Read started his obstetrical practice in the 1930s in an environment where twilight sleep and chloroform were standard operating procedure. In the previous thirty years, obstetricians had gone from shunning all anesthetics in childbirth to rendering every laboring woman they encountered unconscious. Yet the underlying attitude of a physician-driven birth, that of little regard for the mother's needs, had held steadfast. (See Chapter 1 for more on the history of anesthetics in childbirth.)

Dick-Read Observes Fearless Birth

According to anesthesiology scholar Donald Caton, Dick-Read first encountered a natural and fearless birth while serving as a World War I medical officer, when he witnessed women from Belgium and Greece give birth with ease and quickly resume their work in the fields.

After becoming a U.K. obstetrician in the 1930s, Dick-Read attended many home births. He carried chloroform with him as an anesthetic but found that some women neither needed nor wanted the anesthetic. These mothers were attended by women who were family, friends, or neighbors and their traditional, rural births all shared a common feature—laboring mothers who accepted their birth as a natural occurrence and who felt comfortable and well-supported.

All of these observations led Dick-Read to believe that a pain-free birth was achievable if a woman could relieve herself of the fear that had become inextricable from pain. In what he called the "fear-tension-pain" cycle, fear of pain begets physical tension in labor, which begets labor and birth pain. Break the cycle, and break the pain. The key to stopping the fear, in Dick-Read's opinion, was to educate women about the birth process and let them participate fully in it. He was the first of his time to emphasize that birth was indeed a natural process and not an illness or infirmity (hence the name "natural childbirth").

Even though Grantly Dick-Read was the first to promote natural childbirth, his meaning of "natural" is different than the drug-free experience we equate with natural childbirth today. Dick-Read believed that drugs had their place in birth if there were complications or if other means of relaxation were not proving effective in removing tension from the laboring woman. Dick-Read was known among his colleagues as a difficult man who could often be contradictory, and his view on the subject changed several times throughout his obstetrical career.

Dick-Read was also a strong advocate of birth without interference from obstetricians. He believed that a father's presence at the birth was important and that infants should not be separated from their mothers after birth—two more radical ideas for the times.

Promoting Childbirth Without Fear

Among Read's contemporaries, his first book, *Natural Childbirth,* was considered more than a little unorthodox, and Dick-Read was ostracized by many of his London colleagues. He would later run up against professional and licensing issues both in London and in South Africa (after he relocated there in 1948), but it is unclear whether or not these were a result of his radical views on natural childbirth.

In 1943, he published *Revelation of Childbirth* in the United Kingdom, and the book was released in the United States the following year under the title *Childbirth Without Fear.* When it hit American shores, its reputation had preceded it; Dick-Read's U.S. colleagues were more accepting of his theories, however, and in 1947 he accepted an invitation from the Maternity Center Association to speak at the MCA's annual meeting and to tour the country. Shortly thereafter, the MCA launched a pilot prepared-childbirth education project incorporating Dick-Read's theories, and soon the media picked up the story. Popular magazines like *Life* and *Reader's Digest* related Dick-Read's theories to the masses, and women began to seek out more information on the "new" idea of natural childbirth.

HypnoBirthing History

Marie Mongan, M.Ed. M.Hy., a certified hypnotherapist and mother of four, created HypnoBirthing (also known as "the Mongan Method") using Dick-Read's techniques and her own childbirth experiences. In her book, *HypnoBirthing—A Celebration of Life*, Mongan describes how she was anesthetized against her wishes when she gave birth to her first two children in the late 1950s, but was "permitted" to give birth without any drugs (and with her husband in attendance) for the last two. For all four birth experiences, she felt no pain, but her doctor and the hospital medical staff were skeptical and dismissive of the Dick-Read theories that she readily shared with them.

Several decades later, Mongan began to study hypnotherapy as an adjunct to her counseling practice, and she came to the realization that her earlier birth experiences following the Dick-Read method were actually a form of self-hypnosis. She started to develop a formal program of childbirth preparation termed "HypnoBirthing." The first "hypnobaby" was her own grandson, born in 1990 to her relaxed and confident daughter.

Since that time, Mongan has established HypnoBirthing as an increasingly popular childbirth method, with approximately 1,800 certified instructors worldwide who have helped women bring an estimated seven to eight thousand babies into the world using self-hypnosis techniques for labor and birth.

According to HypnoBirthing International, there are certified HypnoBirthing instructors teaching the method in the United States, Australia, Brazil, Canada, Chile, Costa Rica, France, Germany, Holland, Ireland, Israel, New Zealand, and the United Kingdom.

Birthing as Instinct

The foundation of HypnoBirthing is that childbirth is a basic, natural function, which, when allowed to occur unimpeded in a mother who is free of fear and preconceptions about labor and birth, can proceed quickly, painlessly, and joyously. HypnoBirthing instructors teach that each woman has a natural instinct for birth and that she should trust herself and her body fully to relax and simply do what's right as labor progresses. This same message is repeated throughout the courses and home practice in the form of positive affirmations, imagery, and relaxation exercises.

Bonding Before Birth

HypnoBirthing teaches mothers that prenatal bonding with their children is important to achieving a positive birth and postpartum experience. Women are encouraged to develop a relationship with their child in the womb through conversation and affirmations and to send positive messages to the baby for a safe and natural birth.

Hypnosis and Pain Relief

Hypnosis is simply a state of deep relaxation—both psychological and physical. When muscles are relaxed in a laboring woman, two things happen. First, her uterus works more efficiently in contracting and releasing because there is no muscle tension in surrounding areas and no stress hormones to work against the process. Second, she is able to produce endorphins, or natural painkillers, that reduce the discomfort she does feel.

Anesthesia from Within

Endorphins are a class of neurotransmitters that help to ease pain by attaching to nerve receptors. Similar in structure and purpose to synthetic opiates like morphine, endorphins can cause feelings of euphoria. Endorphin production kicks into high gear as part of the pain response; however, certain physical conditions and response can either enhance its effects or lessen its efficacy.

Introduction of certain medical interventions also interrupts the body's natural pain-relief system. When labor anesthetics or analgesics stop pain signals, they shut down endorphin production as well. If the epidural or other medication loses effectiveness or it is discontinued before birth is complete, pain may be perceived as significantly more intense because of the reduced endorphin levels.

QUESTION?

I want to be completely aware during my birth. How can HypnoBirthing be such a natural experience if you're in a trance?
No one will make you cluck like a chicken or stare at the swinging pendulum in a HypnoBirthing class. Self-hypnosis is simply a state of deep relaxation in which you remain completely in control of your mind and body. Many HypnoBirthing advocates liken the mental sensation to the feeling of being on "cruise control" when driving or to being deeply involved in a book. To work, it only requires a willing participant and some dedicated practice.

Epinephrine (adrenaline) and norepinephrine (noradrenaline), also known as catecholamines, are the stress hormones responsible for the racing heart, blood-vessel constriction, and muscle tension of what is commonly known as the "fight or flight" response. Women who are frightened of or anxious about labor or birth have high circulating levels of these hormones, which can reduce blood flow to the uterus and have been shown to prolong labor in some clinical studies.

The deep relaxation methods of HypnoBirthing are designed to prevent the stress response and capitalize on the natural biochemical comfort of a laboring woman's endorphins. Other methods that may enhance endorphin production and lower stress, such as massage, are also taught.

The Power of Words

HypnoBirthing uses gentle, positive, woman-centered language to reframe the birth experience. Uterine contractions are called "surges and waves," the amniotic sac "releases" instead of "rupturing," and "pushing" is referred to as "breathing the baby down." The goal is to free women from their institutionalized conceptions of birth by replacing the traditional lexicon of birth with more positive language. Using these terms throughout pregnancy helps reinforce the concept of natural birth.

Affirmations, which are positive statements that are used to prepare mom mentally for a good birth experience, are listened to and verbalized frequently. The HypnoBirthing Institute has an audio recording of affirmation messages as part of their formal curriculum, along with a second recording entitled *Rainbow Relaxation*. This CD guides women through relaxation exercises by using the colors of the rainbow as a tension-releasing metaphor. Women are told to imagine each mist of color working to remove all the tension in a particular part of their bodies.

FACT

While HypnoBirthing, or the Mongan Method, is widely recognized as the first widespread and formalized curriculum for prepared childbirth with self-hypnosis, there are other hypnotic birth programs in the United States and abroad. In addition, many hypnotherapists in private practice offer pregnant clients instruction for developing self-hypnosis and relaxation skills, as well as hypnotic suggestions for making labor and birth easier.

The Power of Images

In addition to language that affirms the natural and safe process of birth, HypnoBirthing makes use of positive images that reinforce the same message. Common imagery includes the visualization of a flower opening to mimic the soft and steady opening of the cervix and blue satin ribbons that symbolize the long muscles of the uterus gently pulling together to open the cervix for baby's birth.

Imagery is used in combination with relaxation exercises. In HypnoBirthing classes, it's taught as guided imagery, as the instructor leads women through the different visuals and what each represents. Guided-imagery exercises taught in class are also reinforced on tape and with printed scripts.

Preparation and Instruction

HypnoBirthing classes are available in both private and hospital settings. The course curriculum consists of five two-and-a-half hour sessions taught by a certified educator. In addition to the standard elements that you'll find in most childbirth education classes, such as the physiology of labor, writing a birth plan, prenatal nutrition, signs of labor, and potential complications, the curriculum includes instruction on these HypnoBirthing basics:

- **The fear-tension-pain syndrome.** Educators explain the original Grantly Dick-Read concept of how fear makes labor and birth painful and how to break the cycle.
- **How hypnosis works.** HypnoBirthing instructors work to remove any pre-conceptions about hypnosis as mind control or an out-of-body experience.
- **Relaxation.** The essence of self-hypnosis is deep relaxation. A HypnoBirthing course teaches progressive relaxation and other methods for achieving this state.
- **Breathing.** Birth breathing, or "breathing baby down," is the HypnoBirthing equivalent to getting through the pushing stage.
- **Birth in other cultures.** Instructors provide a look at what natural birth is in societies that haven't overmedicalized the birth experience and how to learn from their experiences.

A HypnoBirthing course also includes films of actual births using the method. Instructors will show one of these films at almost every class to reinforce the idea that birth is a natural experience that shouldn't be feared and that the method can be used to achieve a safe and peaceful birth. Stretches are taught to prepare the body for birth, and instruction in massage and other comfort measures is provided.

The designation "HBCE" after a childbirth educator or care provider's name means that she is a HypnoBirthing Certified Educator and has completed comprehensive coursework in the method offered by the HypnoBirthing Institute. A certified HypnoBirthing professional labor companion (HBPLC) has undergone training for attending and supporting a HypnoBirthing birth.

Practicing the Techniques

Deep relaxation is a skill that must be practiced to perfect, so HypnoBirthing instruction offers home audiotapes for guided relaxation exercises and affirmations. Students are encouraged to play the tapes and do the home exercises as frequently as possible, as repetition is a key part of establishing the relaxation response and the subconscious acceptance of the affirmations within them.

Fathers (or other birth partners) are also an integral part of the experience. Dads are encouraged to participate, and they are provided with their own scripts to help support and guide their partners through birth. They are also taught comfort techniques that they can practice in conjunction with the scripts. While in HypnoBirthing classes, fathers participate in the same relaxation exercises as mothers do so they can fully understand the hypnotic state and how they can best support it during labor.

If your baby is in a breech position, your HypnoBirthing instructor can teach you exercises designed to turn her into a vertex, or head down, position. These consist of more deep relaxation exercises, combined with guided imagery of the baby turning in the womb. The concept is that your deeply relaxed uterus will give your baby the room she needs to reposition herself.

FACT

A 1994 study in the Archives of Family Medicine of 100 pregnant women with breech fetuses reported that among those women that underwent hypnosis design to promote relaxation, 81 percent had their babies turn into a head-down position, compared with 48 percent of those women who didn't receive the therapy. The study authors suggest that there may be a psychological link to breech presentation.

The Birth Environment

One of the big selling points of HypnoBirthing is that it can be used effectively in any setting because it relies solely on the relaxation skills of the woman giving birth. To be effective, therefore, it also requires hours of home study, during which you train your body to relax on demand—the ability you will call upon when labor begins.

A quiet atmosphere will be helpful in achieving relaxation, so if you're giving birth in a hospital setting, request that noise, chatter, and nonessential visits be kept to a minimum. You may also want to play some quiet background music or white noise tapes to filter out the outside world.

If you've had prior bad experiences with a hospital birth that you feel will inhibit your ability to relax completely, you may consider having your child in a birth center or home setting. If you do give birth in a hospital, little else is needed beyond a few comforts from home and a supportive partner.

Because HypnoBirthing involves little "extra work" or special demands on the part of a health-care provider, you shouldn't have any problems finding a practitioner who will work with you on achieving a successful HypnoBirth. Prior provider experience with the method isn't really a prerequisite as you and your partner will be doing the hard work, which you will be ready for after faithfully attending your classes and home practice sessions. However, it may be helpful to educate your provider about the method if he is unfamiliar with it so he knows you are striving for an unmedicated birth. As always, you should find a physician or midwife you feel comfortable around and can communicate openly with. You should also create a birth plan early so that you can review your needs and wishes with your provider well in advance of the birth.

If you're having a HypnoBirth outside your home, be sure to bring a tape or CD player along to the hospital or birth center along with your relaxation audio recordings. You may have your methods down pat, and verbal affirmations and cues from your partner will help you through, but it can't hurt to have your relaxation tapes as a backup in case they're needed.

After HypnoBirthing

Many women who have used HypnoBirthing report that the skills they learned in the process helped them to establish breastfeeding and to bond with their babies in the first days after the birth. If episiotomy stitches or a cesarean are required, the relaxation methods may also help reduce both postsurgical pain and the need for pain medication.

The sense of calmness from practiced deep relaxation may also help you adjust to the hectic and sleepless life of a new parent more easily. Some women report that even their infants seem calmer, more alert, and happier after a HypnoBirthing experience, although this could be evidence of a new mother's love affair with her new baby more than any clinical phenomenon. However, some clinical studies have linked prenatal stress and anxiety in mothers with childhood behavioral and emotional problems, so perhaps the positive impact of a stress-free birth is present in these children after all.

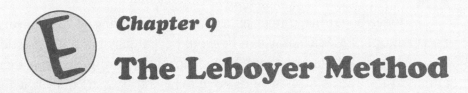

Chapter 9

The Leboyer Method

Birth the Leboyer way is based on the premise that birth is traumatic for the baby, so a newborn's transition into the world should be made as gentle, calm, and loving as possible. The birth atmosphere is dim, warm, and quiet—much like the womb that the baby has just left. Comfort measures of massage and warm water are used to greet the new baby and acclimate him to his new surroundings.

Founder and Physician Frederick Leboyer, M.D.

One of the most influential men in the history of "natural" childbirth, Frederick Leboyer realized that babies feel pain, anxiety, and fear—perhaps even more intensely than adults—and believed that traditional birth practices were ignoring this basic premise and harming infants on an emotional and physical level.

Leboyer began his career as a physician, studying at the University of Paris School of Medicine, where he would eventually build his practice and become head of staff of the affiliated hospital. During his time there, he attended the births of thousands of infants, yet it wasn't until leaving institutionalized medicine that he developed the theories he would become famous for. Leboyer traveled to India, where he observed childbirth practices and studied Karnatic music. He also underwent psychoanalysis during this period, an event that had a profound impact on him as he explored his feelings about his own birth experience. All these experiences contributed to his theories of birth that make him famous once he published his best-known work, *Birth Without Violence,* in 1975.

FACT

For Frederick Leboyer, birth is a spiritual experience as well as a physiological and emotional one. In his books *The Art of Breathing* and *Inner Beauty, Inner Light,* he writes extensively on the use of both yoga and Karnatic music—a form of rhythmic chanting music from India that promotes abdominal breathing—for a positive pregnancy and birth.

The Leboyer Philosophy

Leboyer believed that labor and birth were an inevitable trauma to a child, as his world closes in around him and he is forcibly pushed down the birth canal by the force of uterine contractions. What was considered a "modern birth" in the 1970s—bright lights, loud noises, bottom slaps, and mother/infant separation—further compounded the suffering and, according to Leboyer, left an indelible mark on the baby's psyche that would stay with him for life. Leboyer believed that these methods were inhumane and ignorant to the sensitivity of the newborn, and that replacing them with a comforting and nurturing environment was the only way to heal the trauma of birth itself.

A Soothing Environment

The overriding goal of Leboyer birth is to make the place the newborn will enter soothing and womb-like instead of frightening and anxious. In Leboyer's words, "If there is such a thing as a sanctified place, surely it is the room the child is about to enter." Therefore, Leboyer births take place in dim lighting, with hushed voices, and perhaps with gentle music playing. A tub of warm water is available for the baby's first bath shortly after birth. Movement of the child and contact with him is slow and tender. The birth is centered upon the newborn, and anything potentially frightening or painful is removed from the experience. It is "birth without violence."

Birth Without Violence

Published in 1974, Leboyer's *Birth Without Violence* was a landmark in modern childbirth history, a poetic and profound work that questioned standard birth practices of the day and proposed a natural birth model that focused on the needs and emotions of the newborn.

What still makes this relatively brief little volume so intriguing today is its prose, written in a free-form poetic style, that vividly depicts birth from the fetal and newborn viewpoint. Leboyer describes the experience of a "traditional" birth, with all its jarring noise and lights, rough handling, bottom slaps, and cold scales and painful eyedrops, and likens it to sadism and torture.

Birth Without Violence also featured dozens of black-and-white photographs of peaceful, alert babies—some smiling—minutes or hours after their birth. These images were contrasted against photos of screaming newborns birthed "traditionally." One particular scene that is the object of Leboyer's pity and scorn is a photo of a screaming baby suspended upside down by a smiling physician while mother and father look on in equal rapture. The juxtaposition of these transfixing photos, combined with Leboyer's unique writing style and groundbreaking ideas, propelled *Birth Without Violence* to international prominence.

Leboyer's vision of a birth that comforted a newborn and caused a positive emotional response from the infant, and particularly his description and photos of what is now known as the Leboyer bath—baby's first warm-water dip shortly after birth—resonated with mothers and childbirth educators alike. The revised edition of the book remains in print today and is still a provocative and popular read among women worldwide.

QUESTION?

I heard Leboyer babies don't usually cry at birth. Don't babies need to cry to start breathing?
Crying is a manifestation of emotional or physical discomfort, not a physiological response that triggers breathing. Leboyer was the first to recognize that crying at birth is neither necessary nor inevitable. The babies he delivered using his method were alert, quiet, and even smiled in the minutes after the birth—something most child development experts had thought was impossible for infants so young.

The Importance of "Where" and "Who"

Finding a place and a practitioner conducive to a Leboyer birth is the biggest challenge of planning your birth. It may be easier to achieve a Leboyer birth at home, where the environment is completely under your control. However, if home birth is not an option or makes you anxious, Leboyer birth is achievable at a center or even a hospital if you have a willing care provider and plan in advance.

While many childbirth educators have been influenced by Leboyer's work, and his once-radical theories of the newborn as a sentient and sensitive being are now considered an integral part of the "natural" childbirth movement, there is no formal curriculum of childbirth preparation classes for a Leboyer birth. In fact, Leboyer himself doesn't hold much stock in childbirth education. In a 1995 interview with Nicholas Albery, author and founder of the Institute for Social Inventions, he said, "Some women believe you can take six quick lessons before birth, like before taking a car for a drive. But there are things which cannot be taught."

Provider Issues

While the principals of Leboyer birth are common sense, low-risk, and really don't require extensive investments in time or equipment, some providers may still be opposed to the idea of this "radical new practice" that has been in existence for well over twenty-five years. Some of this resistance may be a perceived loss of control. Asking a physician to speak in whispers and work in low light means that you're dictating the birth circumstances, which may—right or wrong—be threatening.

If you feel your provider may be hesitant to attend a Leboyer birth, here are some ways to get the two of you on the same page:

- **Lose the label.** Outline your requests in terms of the specifics you want (that is, low light, minimal noise) and don't label it a "Leboyer birth." If your practitioner is wary of anything outside of mainstream medicine, simply eliminating the terminology may do the trick.
- **Educate her.** Find out what your provider's knowledge of Leboyer is. If she hasn't read *Birth Without Violence*, bring her a copy. Tell her you'd be interested in discussing any clinical knowledge she has about the method. Arouse her interest in this birth as a learning experience or a new type of challenge.
- **Plan it well.** Get your birth plan together and map out exactly how you will achieve your goals. For example, if your birth hospital LDR rooms are sunny with no room-darkening blinds or curtains, you can hang a dark blanket. Once your provider has seen evidence that you have thought things through carefully and there's nothing dangerous or unreasonable about your requests, he may rethink his initial opposition.
- **Get someone you're more in synch with.** If all else fails, tell your provider thanks but no thanks and find someone who will honor your birth requests. Chapter 3 has more on finding a provider that fits your needs.

The Birth Place

Dim lights in the antiseptic, shiny white hospital labor and delivery room? Warmth and quiet in the hustle and bustle of a busy maternity unit? It's easy to feel that Leboyer hospital birth is somewhat of an oxymoron.

The good news is that with your provider's cooperation, a flexible and accommodating nursing staff, and a little planning and imagination, you can transform even the coldest, most Spartan hospital room into a Leboyer birth place.

The biggest obstacle you may run into with a hospital birth are facility regulations regarding postpartum neonatal evaluation—both those that require things you may not want, such as treating your infant's eyes immediately at birth, or separation for weighing and examination, and those that don't allow for things you do want, like delayed cord clamping and cutting and the all-important first Leboyer bath. Some of these regulations may be determined on a provider level, while others are governed by the hospital or birth center. Speak with your provider about any institutional protocols at your birth place. You may be able to opt out of some procedures, or at least delay what the hospital or center deem "essential" until you've completed the Leboyer bath and had an adequate amount of one-on-one time with your newborn.

QUESTION?

I'm having a cesarean. Can I still have a Leboyer birth?
Because a cesarean is a surgical procedure that takes place in an operating room, the chances of having a low-light atmosphere for birth aren't very good (for both practical and safety reasons). The baby also won't be able to lie on your abdomen right after emerging—for obvious reasons. However, you can still request that talking and unnecessary noise be kept to a minimum as the birth occurs, and you can also ask that your partner be allowed to give the baby a Leboyer bath.

Women choosing a home birth are fortunate in that they are able to control things like lighting, noise, and first infant-mother contact. These variables should be outlined in your birth plan. You will also want to get an appropriate-sized tub for baby's after-birth bath. A sink is too small, and a bathtub can be too big and sometimes too awkward. Some women find that a large ice-chest filled with warm water is the perfect size. Make sure whatever you use has been cleaned and sterilized beforehand.

The Mother's Role

Leboyer has been criticized by some for making the birth more about the child and less about the woman who gives birth. Some contend that his birth philosophy, particularly his picture of labor from within as a hellish, horrifying experience for the baby, burdens women with unnecessary guilt—particularly if there are problems with the birth and interventions are required.

There are some portions of Leboyer's work that contribute to this image that he advocates a non–woman-centered birth experience. In *Birth Without Violence*, Leboyer recognizes that the newborn should be reunited with his mother instantly by being placed on her belly to hear the same heartbeat he heard inside her for so long. Yet his depiction of a new mother is one who is a bundle of postpartum nerves: "Her hands are not yet steady and sure . . . the intensity of what she's just lived through can still be affecting her so strongly that it overwhelms the child. In these crucial moments, the child needs peace, quiet and calm." Ultimately, Leboyer blames this maternal deficiency on socially ingrained inhibitions, and he trusts the baby's first bath to "a loving midwife" or another participant in the birth.

Yet in the same work, Leboyer still seems to believe that women are redeemable in this sense, for he closes with a challenge, telling his female readers to gather their courage so that no one will "take away from you what is your most precious birthright, your greatest treasure: a fully conscious, enlightened delivery."

Certainly, the birth environment Leboyer promotes, with its muted sounds, soft lights, and soothing music, is beneficial for reducing stress and anxiety in the mother as well as the child. Leboyer also makes other statements about the importance of relaxation for the mother, such as his belief that a pregnant woman who is about to give birth must "step out of time," as he puts it, to become completely relaxed and anxiety-free for the birth.

The Birth

Dim, quiet, warm, and gentle—those are the four prerequisites of a successful Leboyer birth room. The number of "nonessential" personnel should be limited and the door closed to outsiders. The room should also be warm and free of drafts so the baby isn't greeted with a rush of cold air. There should be just enough light for the provider to visualize the perineum and baby adequately. Overhead lighting is almost always too bright. If a lamp is available, draping it in a scarf or towel to diffuse the light can provide the right atmosphere.

FACT

Despite the fact that your baby has been in the dark since conception, infants can see about nine to twelve inches away at birth. However, their vision is not fully developed and things will look blurry to them. Providing your newborn with high-contrast patterns and bright colors to look at can help to stimulate visual development. Newborns also prefer looking at faces—especially familiar ones like mom and dad—to other objects.

As labor crescendoes and birth is imminent, everyone is instructed to speak only when necessary and to do so in a whisper. Some women may choose to have soft, relaxing music playing in the background at a low volume. Others may sing or chant quietly, especially if they have engaged in the practice throughout their pregnancy and the sounds are familiar to the emerging baby.

After the baby's head is delivered, he will soon have the impulse to breathe, although his chest is still squeezed in the birth canal. The rest of his body is freed as quickly and gently as possible to allow him to begin breathing. At this point, what Leboyer considers the painful journey of birth is over, and the newborn can be welcomed in a sensitive, loving, and compassionate manner.

On the Outside

When a newborn emerges from the birth canal, he is suddenly exposed to air and what must seem like vast space—two elements that are completely new and startling. Leboyer teaches that the infant should be gathered up and placed on his mother's stomach with his limbs tucked under his body. This reunites him with mom—on the outside this time—and also returns a sense of security. As the newborn adjusts to this new waterless environment, he will venture out into it, untucking his arms and legs and stretching them out into the world. The baby may move toward the breast to nurse, which is also encouraged.

A Gentle Transition

As the newborn lies on his mother's stomach, belly-to-belly and skin-to-skin, the mother gently massages her child's back, just as the uterus was massaging him in the womb. The umbilical cord is not cut until it has stopped pulsating with blood flow. Leboyer suggests that the added oxygen from the cord blood helps the baby better adjust to the breathing mechanism of his lungs and allows him to take smaller breaths rather than gasp for air.

The typical battery of postbirth evaluations and treatments are withheld or postponed in a Leboyer birth. Antibiotic eyedrops or ointments are strongly discouraged because of the discomfort and temporary loss of vision for the child. Things like weighing, footprints, heelsticks, vitamin K shots, and other routine procedures are thought to either pose too much of a sensory overload or be too painful, and are avoided—if not completely, for as long as possible. For more on neonatal testing, see Chapter 19.

ALERT!

In many places, state law mandates the administration of neonatal tests and treatments like vitamin K injections and eye prophylaxis. However, the timing of these tests isn't always written into the laws that govern them. Talk to your state health department about regulations concerning neonatal testing and whether or not you can legally request to hold off on some procedures until well after the birth.

After-Birth Bath

The Leboyer bath is probably the best-known component of Leboyer's birth philosophy. The bath is often performed by the father or birth partner, or by the mother (although she will need assistance). It requires a tub that is small enough to provide boundaries for the baby to feel when he outstretches his limbs, yet big enough to allow the newborn to float with support. Some facilities may have tubs specifically for this purpose. The bath water should be at body temperature.

To begin the bath, your baby should be held securely and very slowly immersed feet-first into the water, his head supported by the bather's arm or hand. Babies often become very alert and playful while in the bath, even though just hours, or minutes, old. Leboyer theorizes that the bath relieves infant stress by re-creating the recent memory of the womb and makes the first separation from mom a positive event.

How long the bath should last depends upon the water temperature and the baby's cues. If the water starts to cool off significantly, it's important to get baby out and wrapped in a warm towel or blanket so he doesn't lose too much body heat. Bath time is also over if the baby starts to appear startled or frightened. Again, he should be wrapped in a warm blanket before returning to your arms.

FACT

When your baby was inside the uterus, he floated around at a toasty 100.4°F. The temperature outside your body is considerably lower, and a normal body temperature for a newborn is between 97.7 and 99.5°F. To prevent hypothermia (excessive heat loss), the World Health Organization (WHO) recommends that the birth room be kept at a minimum of 89.6°F for a wet newborn and from 77 to 82.4°F for a dry infant who is placed skin-to-skin with her mother and covered with a blanket.

Once the first bath is given and the infant is returned to his mother's arms, Leboyer advocates a simple retreat for providers and others to allow the baby, mother, and father to continue their new relationship privately.

A Mother's (and Father's) Touch

The act of touching and being touched is a baby's first form of communication, according to Leboyer. He developed an interest in therapeutic touch after witnessing Indian mothers massaging their infants, a common part of regular baby care in India. Leboyer's book *Loving Hands: The Traditional Art of Baby Massage* discusses the benefits of massage in helping the newborn face its "monsters" (new sensations and experiences) in the first weeks and months of life. It also provides basic instruction—in words and pictures—for effective massage techniques.

Beyond Leboyer's perceived emotional benefits of infant massage, clinical research bears out its positive impact on the physical health of newborns. Numerous studies have indicated that therapeutic massage of premature babies promotes weight gain and alertness and reduces stress. Massage may even help improve your baby's sleep patterns. A 2002 study out of Tel Aviv University found that infants who were massaged daily by their mothers at a set time for two weeks had a better-established nighttime sleep cycle than those who didn't receive the rubdown.

Leboyer's Legacy

Leboyer had an enormous influence not only on how newborns were treated at birth but in ultimately changing the standards of medical care for infants at large. His assertion that infants feel and experience everything acutely—and, furthermore, that they remember it—caused parents to question once-standard procedures like circumcision (a procedure Leboyer asserted was neither medically necessary nor beneficial for the child), which had been practiced for years without anesthesia or analgesia. Parents also began to protest the practice of unanaesthetized neonatal surgery, and by the 1980s they were stepping forward to bring their concerns to the media, which quickly sparked additional interest in research that examined infant pain perception.

In 1987, the *Lancet* published a study that found that infants undergoing surgery who were treated with an anesthetic agent (fentanyl) had better outcomes than those who didn't receive the pain medication. Shortly thereafter, Harvard anesthesiology researchers published a landmark review in the *New England Journal of Medicine* that found that infants did indeed feel pain, perhaps even while still in the womb. Without Leboyer's pioneering work in raising the consciousness of parents and practitioners to the existence of infant sentience, medicine might still be denying the complete personhood of the newborn.

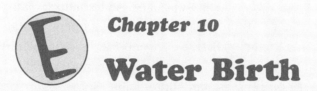

Chapter 10

Water Birth

Water has been used therapeutically for healing and comfort for thousands of years. Birth in water has a shorter, but no less significant, history—today, birth tubs or pools can be found in birthing centers and hospitals and can also be rented for home use. This method allows your infant to enter the outside world to be surrounded by warm, soothing water, providing him with a gentle transition from the warm fluid environment of your womb into his new world.

What Is Water Birth?

A water birth is, quite simply, a birth that takes place under the surface of the water. The baby emerges from the birth canal into the water of a birth pool, tub, or any other body of water—indoors or out—that the mother chooses to birth in. After her entry into the world, the baby is brought quickly and gently to the surface to meet her mom face to face and to test out her lungs. Many women and couples choose water birth because they believe it offers a gentler, more natural introduction into the world than a conventional land-based birth.

Women have always made good use of water for labor comfort—in the form of showers, wet compresses, and immersion. Some water births are unplanned; the mother chooses to spend part of her labor in water and is so comfortable and/or focused while in a tub or pool of warm water that she remains there as the baby begins to emerge. Other women plan specifically for a birth underwater, scouting out a birth facility that offers water birth, renting their own spas or pools for home use, and finding a provider who will attend the aquatic event.

Water Birth's Recent History

The first use of birthing pools in a hospital setting was in the early 1970s in France. Dr. Michel Odent, an instinctual childbirth researcher, breastfeeding advocate, and author of two important texts in the field (*Birth Reborn* and *The Nature of Birth and Breastfeeding*), brought an inflatable wading pool into the maternity unit at French State Hospital in Pithiviers, France. As Odent recounts in the journal *Midwifery Today,* the unit's drug bills started to decrease significantly as women were drawn to the comfort and privacy of the birth pool during labor. Although Odent, the director of the unit, originally brought the pool in to provide an analgesic measure for women, most of whom would leave the pool just prior to giving birth, he soon discovered that birth under water was not only possible but also, for many women, preferable.

After Odent published a summary of his water birth experiences in the medical journal *The Lancet* in 1983, news of his work reached American childbirth educators and midwives. The 1980s would prove to be a seminal decade for water birth in the United States. Interest in this intriguing new birth method was heightened further by the American publication of Odent's

Birth Reborn in 1984. A year later, the first U.S. birthing center offering water birth to its clients was opened by obstetrician Michael Rosenthal in Southern California. As media coverage and interest in the practice grew and the 1980s drew to a close, nurse and water-birth advocate Barbara Harper, author of *Gentle Birth Choices,* founded Waterbirth International. The organization, which is an arm of the nonprofit Global Maternal/Child Health Association (GMCHA), promotes water-birth education and advocacy. Its stated mission is "to ensure that water birth is an 'available option' for all women in all birth settings by 2015."

Russian researcher Igor Charcovsky was another childbirth pioneer whose experimentations into water and buoyancy and its beneficial impact on newborns and laboring women were instrumental in propelling the water birth movement. Charcovsky's work, documented in the book *Water Babies*, includes accompanying couples on a pilgrimage to a "birth camp" in the Black Sea where they give birth in tidal pools among the dolphins.

Today, over two-thirds of American birth centers offer water birth, and close to 300 U.S. hospitals have water birth programs (out of nearly 4,000 hospital-based maternity programs). Waterbirth International conservatively estimates that more than 30,000 water births have taken place in the United States in the past decade.

Benefits of Water Birth

Water birth offers both mother and child a number of potential benefits, including these:

- **Perineal pliability.** Soaking the perineum in warm water allows it to stretch more easily and may prevent tears and the need for episiotomy.
- **Less stress.** Water is soothing, and women who are at ease and relaxed will secrete fewer stress hormones (such as noraderanline and catecholamines).

- **Weightlessness.** Women submerged in water are able to assume more natural labor and birthing positions, such as squatting, that gravity may make difficult to sustain on dry land.
- **Self-comfort.** Besides the natural buoyancy that water provides the laboring mother, the relaxing effects of warm-water immersion can promote the production of endorphins as it reduces stress hormone production.
- **Control.** Many women who birth in water feel a greater sense of control over the experience. They can easily reach down and feel the baby's head and body as it emerges and even "catch" their newborn themselves.

Where to Have a Water Birth

Once you've chosen to have a water birth, you should start planning early. Finding a provider and a birth facility that will accommodate your needs may take some research, depending on where you live.

FACT

The first U.S. hospital to launch a water birth program for women was Monadnock Community Hospital. The Peterborough, New Hampshire, facility consulted with Dr. Michael Rosenthal, the only other practitioner in the country who was offering water birth on a regular basis, to develop water-birth protocols after a woman expressed interest in a water birth in 1989. It wasn't until 1992 that the hospital actually hosted its first water birth, but as of early 2004, it has been the birth place of hundreds of water babies.

If you don't have any facilities in your area that do water births, aren't happy with the ones that do have the service, or don't qualify for a water birth due to facility restrictions, home water birth may be an option. If that's the route you choose to go, you'll have even more homework on your hands as you select a pool that will provide comfort and safety for your birth.

Home Versus Center

All the benefits of traditional home birth—privacy, ownership of your space, control—also apply to a water birth at home. But there are some perks to water birth at a well-equipped center or hospital. First and foremost, if the facility is designed for water birth, you don't have to deal with the expense and logistics of renting, transporting, constructing, and cleaning a portable pool or spa. Birth centers that have a high rate of water births also offer the added benefit of practical experience and proven safety protocols.

On the flip side, if you choose to try water birth outside of your home, you are subject to any rules and restrictions your birth facility has in place, which may or may not meet your needs. To learn about potential contraindications to water birth and how to discuss them with your provider, see the section entitled "Lifeguard on Duty: Safety Issues," later in this chapter.

Consider the Equipment Involved

Renting a pool involves a lot of advance planning. Start investigating your options early so you'll have the logistics down well in advance of the birth. Thanks to a growing interest in water birth, there are many businesses renting birth tubs or pools throughout the United States. Your midwife may be able to refer you to a local rental source. If none is available nearby, there are also tub providers that will ship units cross-country.

You will also have to plan ahead for the amount of work involved in keeping the pool clean and find a place to set it up. It's important to clean the pool thoroughly before use, according to the manufacturer's or rental company's directions. Be sure you or your partner are prepared for the work involved. Most portable pools use a disposable plastic liner for infection-control purposes, but the hoses, pumps, jets, and drains still need to be appropriately sanitized to kill bacteria. Bacteria and water pH test kits may be offered as accessories to test the pool water for safety.

Before setting up a home pool, you will need to make sure the floor is well protected—a waterproof tarp will do the trick—and the place where you will be situating it is supported well enough to hold the weight of the pool once it's filled. Again, the manufacturer's directions for use should list the weight of the pool when it's filled with water. For more on choosing a pool, read on.

Do I need to worry about infection from a birthing pool or tub?
Although there is a theoretical risk, as long as tub-cleaning and water-quality protocols are followed and no one in the pool has an open wound or known communicable infection, there is little to worry about. A Cochrane Review of three trials of 988 births found that there was no difference in neonatal infection rates between water-birthed babies and those delivered on dry land.

The Perfect Pool

There are many different types of birth pools and tubs available, from the low-rent simple child's inflatable pool to large, installed Jacuzzi whirlpools. The pools and tubs you'll find in birthing centers and hospitals, when they're available, are usually more than adequate for the job. But when you're picking your own rental unit, there are a few issues to consider.

Questions to ask yourself when choosing a pool include the following:

- **Will it keep the water warm?** Some pools offer a heating device, while some are insulated to retain the warmth of the water, and others just rely on refills to stay at optimal temperature.
- **Will it fit?** Make sure the tub isn't too large for the space you have in mind, and isn't too heavy for where you'll be placing it.
- **How is cleaning and sanitization handled?** The pool may have a filter system, or it may require a chemical regimen to kill bacteria. Some pools come with disposable liners. In many simple pools, emptying and refilling is the only way to keep water clean and bacteria-free.
- **Is it big enough?** A deeper pool may provide more buoyancy and possibly more pain relief. A pool should also be wide enough so that you can easily change positions and work with your contractions in the water. And if you expect company in the water, make sure there's room for that, too.
- **Is it bright enough?** A tub liner that is dark in color may make it harder for your provider to observe the birth itself. Some tubs come with lights, but a waterproof flashlight will also work. So will a light-colored tub in a well-lit room, if the brightness doesn't bother you.

- **Is it comfortable enough?** Some tubs offer built in seats, inflatable or padded edges, whirlpool jets, and other perks that can make laboring more comfortable.
- **Can it be set up easily?** This may be low on your priority list since it will only be set up once, but a tub with an instruction manual the size of the Manhattan phone book may not be what you want to face with labor approaching. Ease of set-up and durability should play some part in your pool selection.

Warm or Cool?

Every birth pool or tub should have a thermometer, either as part of the unit or as an accessory, to monitor the water temperature. It is essential that the water not go over 100°F to prevent dehydration in mom and a rapid heart rate in baby. The ideal temperature for a water birth is thought to be right around normal body temperature.

How cool the water can get and still be beneficial for mother and safe for baby is a matter open to some debate. Newborns don't have the insulation and fine-tuned internal thermostat that adults do, making hypothermia a risk for babies exposed to cold water for long periods of time; skin-to-skin contact with mother can help a newborn maintain his body temperature.

Some researchers theorize that cool water can trigger the breathing reflex in a newborn before she has surfaced and therefore should be avoided. However, it's also well known that many women have given birth in the tide pools of the Mediterranean, the Black Sea, and other cooler waters with no ill effects. Further research is needed on the issue to clarify whether cool water poses a danger of aspiration to the infant. Most providers who attend water births will adjust the temperature to whatever the mother feels most comfortable with given the surrounding climate and the stage of labor she's in.

Keeping It Clean

To reduce the risk of infection and to stay comfortable during the birth, you should pay close attention to the cleaning instructions for your birth tub or pool. If your tub comes with disposable liners, the process will be easier. Still, any pool accessories that touch the water will require special care and sanitization.

The best way to ensure a clean pool is to wait to fill it with fresh water until it is needed. If you do give it a test run before labor, make sure you empty and dry it thoroughly after you're through to prevent bacteria growth. Your pool may come with a germicide, bactericide, or other sanitizing solution to treat it with between uses. Follow the spa or pool manufacturer's directions for cleaning.

The hose you use to fill the pool should be one that is designed and labeled for use with potable (safe for drinking) water. When you're purchasing your hose, make sure the length is sufficient to reach from your water source to the pool or tub location. You don't want to be stuck with a 12-foot hose and a 20-foot hallway on birth day. In cases in which you plan on filling the pool more than once, you'll also need a second hose for draining to avoid contamination.

Many birthing pools also come with a net. If your pool kit does not provide one, a small fish net can be used to skim debris from the pool. It's normal to pass some stool when pushing in labor. As long as the stool is solid and removed quickly from the water, it poses little risk of infection to mother or child.

For women giving birth in a hospital or center, there are typically stringent infection control guidelines in place for sanitizing the tub and birth area. Water quality is also tested to ensure it meets hospital standards. Your birth facility can provide more information on its cleaning procedures if you have any questions or concerns.

Taking the Plunge

So now that you've got your pool, what do you do with it? When to get into—and out of—the water is a concern for many women. Some women want to jump right in at the first contraction. Others will wait until labor is well established before easing into the water. While many providers will allow you to follow your own instincts, there are some good reasons for not getting in the pool prematurely.

The Five-Centimeter Rule

A 1997 Swedish study found that women who entered a birth pool before five centimeters dilation ended up with longer labors and a higher incidence of epidural and oxytocin use than those who entered the water at five centimeters or greater. For this reason, your provider may recommend staying out of the water until you're dilated at least five centimeters, as the buoyancy may slow contractions and make labor less effective.

That doesn't mean you can't have the benefits of water in the meantime. A shower may work well as a temporary alternative for pain relief, and the upright position it requires should speed things along. If you just can't wait to get into the water and you haven't reached five centimeters yet, most providers won't stop you from getting in early. If contractions wane, however, they may suggest that you try leaving the pool for some walking or time in the shower to re-establish contractions and increase dilation.

FACT

There's no reason to leave the water when baby's heart rate needs to be checked. Your provider can use a waterproof Doppler device to assess your baby's heart rate as you labor in the tub or pool. If fetal monitoring is indicated, there are also waterproof transducers and leads available that can make monitoring in a tub or shower possible.

Weightlessness and Labor

The depth of your birth pool or tub will depend on the type of unit you have set up. You should be in at least eighteen inches of water—enough to cover your belly—to achieve the beneficial effects of buoyancy in the water. A standard bathtub usually can't accommodate this goal, but many Jacuzzi and whirlpool-style tubs are deep enough. Some larger birth pools or tanks may offer 2 to 2½ feet of water to labor in.

If you're curious about how your pregnant body might benefit from this fluid environment, make a date to visit a swimming pool. Not only is swimming (or even walking) in a pool good exercise, but you'll also feel just how relaxing being immersed in water is. If you've been feeling back strain or other aches and pains from the extra load you've been carrying, you may get a sneak preview of just how comforting the gravity-free zone of the pool can be.

Maximizing Comfort

Hands-on comfort techniques like massage and counterpressure will feel just as good in the water as on land. If you feel comfortable having your partner in the water with you, make sure he (or she) brings swim attire along. Women giving birth in a tub or Jacuzzi may have less space available for company in the water. Find out the dimensions of the tub when planning your birth so you won't be disappointed later.

A study published in the *British Journal of Medicine* (2004) found that among subjects with slow-to-progress labor (dystocia), those that labored while immersed in water required fewer obstetrical interventions and epidurals than those who were given standard labor augmentation procedures, such as amniotomy and oxytocin.

Some tubs offer built-in seats for resting. If yours doesn't, a plastic stool will serve just as well. Make sure the feet are covered so that the liner of the pool won't be damaged. A washcloth and a rubber band for each foot will do the job nicely. You may also want to find an inflatable pillow or neck rest, especially if your tub or pool doesn't feature padding around the edge. Finally, make sure the tub floor and the area outside of the tub offers a skid-free surface. A few well-placed towels, or the skid-free decals available for home tub use, will work.

A Natural Welcoming

After months upon months in a warm, fluid environment, abruptly entering the bright lights and cool air of the outside world is understandably a shock to the newborn. One of the major benefits of water birth is a gradual introduction of the newborn to his new world, where he floats through warm water into his mother's arms and takes his first breath snuggled wet-skin-to-wet-skin.

Familiar Surroundings

Even the quietest and dimmest birth environment is an enormous sensory change for the newborn. It is theorized that infants may benefit from the sound-insulating properties of water, as well as from being at ease with the familiarity of surrounding fluid. Barbara Harper notes that a baby born into water may find his sudden freedom of movement less startling within the natural resistance of water rather than the strange new touch of air.

The water in a birth pool is ideally kept around body temperature, so in theory the newborn will experience little perceptual difference between the liquid surroundings of amniotic fluid and the warm birth tub.

The First Breath

When babies leave the birth canal and enter the birthing tub, they continue to receive oxygen as they have since conception—via the blood flowing from mother to child through the umbilical cord. The physiology of a newborn baby prevents him from experiencing aspiration of water into his lungs. Although the process isn't completely understood and has been studied most extensively in animals and not humans, a diving reflex or instinct prevents inhalation of water by triggering a swallowing reflex when any liquids enter the larynx. In a normal, healthy baby that is not under stress or hypoxic, breathing cannot and will not begin until the baby surfaces just after birth and emerges into air. Some infants born underwater may take up to a minute to begin regular spontaneous breathing after exposure to air. For this reason, some providers may give a water-born baby an additional thirty seconds to one minute before taking the first APGAR score. (See Chapter 19 for more information on baby's first checkup.)

There have been some reported cases of infants experiencing water aspiration (water in the lungs) during a water birth. The circumstances and length of time the baby was submerged after birth in these cases was not well documented, so definitive conclusions about the causes behind them cannot be made. Animal studies of fetal lambs have shown that the reflexes that prevent inhalation until air contact is made at birth can be inhibited by a lack of oxygen to the fetus, also known as hypoxia. Therefore, researchers have theorized that babies who are extremely hypoxic may aspirate water into their lungs when they gasp for air at birth while still underwater. However, infants in this condition would have irregularities in their heart rate that would be evident to a competent midwife or physician before the birth, and the mother would be advised not to deliver underwater.

ALERT!

A baby born into a tub or pool should not be kept underwater for longer than necessary. The water-birthed infant who is submerged is getting oxygen through the umbilical cord and placenta. If the placenta separates from the uterus while the baby is still underwater, he could asphyxiate. About ten seconds is all it usually takes to slowly and gently bring the baby to the surface.

Lifeguard on Duty: Safety Issues

There are a few safety issues that require special attention in a water birth. As previously mentioned, the wet surfaces the mother will be standing and walking on should be skid-free and not slick. Water must be kept clean and at an appropriate temperature, which should be monitored regularly with a floating thermometer or comparable device. The ambient temperature in the surrounding environment should also be warm so that the mother won't become chilled if she needs to leave the tub for any reason. The warm water and the hard work of labor can make dehydration a risk, so women should be encouraged to drink plenty of fluids to stay hydrated and keep their energy up.

Cord Care

One potential problem in water birth is a torn or damaged umbilical cord from pulling the baby up to the surface too rapidly following delivery. A slow and careful ascent can prevent cord issues. The depth in the majority of birthing pools and tubs is shallow enough that a change of the mother's position would be enough for the baby to be raised gently to the surface, even if the umbilical cord is particularly short. If you plan on giving birth in a deeper pool, your provider may also suggest adjusting the water depth prior to the birth so that bringing the baby to the surface is easier.

Hospital Restrictions

Some hospitals may not allow water birth due to "liability issues" with their insurers or a lack of knowledge or experience in water birth. Others may not have regulations against it but may require you to rent, transport, and set up your own birthing pool.

Most hospitals and some birthing centers will have strict protocols as to who qualifies for water birth and what circumstances can make laboring or birthing in a pool contraindicated. These guidelines will vary by facility. As a general rule, they tend to be more rigid in hospitals than in birthing centers.

There are some labor and birth circumstances that can raise a red flag for many facilities. Here are some possible contraindications to water birth:

- Abnormal fetal heart rate
- Active skin or blood infection
- Active genital herpes
- Meconium-stained amniotic fluid
- Excessive vaginal bleeding
- A multiples pregnancy
- Premature labor
- Ruptured membranes
- A mother who is HIV-positive or has hepatitis
- A baby in breech position
- Preeclampsia, uncontrolled gestational diabetes, or other pregnancy complications

It's important to note that not all of these potential contraindications are supported with clinical evidence, and what is forbidden in one facility may be okay in another. For example, at least one study has found that women who have already had their amniotic sac rupture are at no greater risk of infection in a water birth than those with intact membranes. And some practitioners would argue that a breech baby is actually easier to deliver in a weightless environment than on land. Where sufficient evidence is not available, some hospitals prefer to err on the side of caution, restricting water births in the name of safety. These are concerns you should discuss with your provider well before the birth.

Women who are having a water birth at a hospital or center will probably be required to sign an informed-consent form that addresses the facility rules and regulations regarding birth and obligates you to follow those protocols. Ask for a copy of the document well in advance of the birth, preferably when you're writing your birth plan, to avoid any unpleasant surprises in the eleventh hour.

After a Water Birth

Once the baby has arrived and is safe in your arms, you still have to deliver the placenta. Some women are comfortable right where they are, and they prefer to complete the entire process in the pool. Others may be ready to head to dry land. Whatever you are most comfortable with is fine.

When the placenta is delivered in the water, the cord is usually kept intact until delivery is complete. Most women will breastfeed immediately to encourage stronger contractions to help finish the job. After the placenta is delivered, it is examined to ensure that it is intact and no fragments remain in the uterus, and then held or floated in a plastic tub or bowl while the provider, mom, or dad cuts and clamps the cord.

If the placenta is delivered out of the pool, the cord is cut and clamped first. Some providers prefer that the placenta be delivered on land so blood loss can be assessed more accurately. An experienced water-birth practitioner should be able to detect excessive blood loss in the tub by the color of the water.

Dealing with Providers and Insurance

Financial limitations and provider reluctance are two common stumbling blocks for women seeking a water birth. Health insurers sometimes view a birth pool as an unnecessary "recreational" expense and deny coverage. And because water birth has really only had widespread availability in the United States for less than a quarter-century, many providers have limited experience with it and may be hesitant to attend the unfamiliar. In both of these cases, being a well-informed consumer and gathering clinical citations and other solid data that backs your view of the benefits of water birth can help you influence and inform the decision-makers at insurance companies and hospitals, as well as your provider.

Paying for the Pool

If you're giving birth at a facility with pools or tubs available, the costs are inclusive in the basic fees for the birth itself. However, women who are having a home water birth or who are going the B.Y.O.T. (bring your own tub) route may have to shell out several hundred dollars for pool rental. The costs will depend on the type of pool rented, any shipping fees, and other required accessories like hoses and cleansers.

QUESTION?

I'm having a home birth. Can't I just give birth in my tub rather than renting an expensive pool?

If your bathtub is big enough and deep enough to be up to the challenge, there's no reason not to. However, some benefits of a pool designed for birth that you may not have considered include ample room for a partner, portability, easy access for your provider, and of course plenty of space for changing positions and getting comfortable.

Insurance Issues

Unfortunately, your insurance company may not reimburse for rental of a tub if it doesn't consider it a necessary expense—even if the water birth ends up saving them money in epidural costs (including both the pharmaceuticals and anesthesiologist billing). Waterbirth International suggests asking your provider to write a prescription for the pool as a pain-management tool and requesting that the company you rent it from invoice it as a durable medical device used for pain management.

Remember that you can usually appeal any claims your insurer denies. Sometimes clinical studies and documentation of the health and financial advantages of water birth are enough to influence an insurance company's take on covering water–birth-related expenses.

Physician/Midwife Issues

While most providers recognize the benefits of water immersion for labor comfort, the idea of actually giving birth under water is still considered a bit too "New Age" for many practitioners. Depending on where you live, finding a provider who will attend a water birth may be a challenge. Because of their focus and philosophy of nonintervention and woman-controlled birth, midwives are more likely to recognize the benefits of water birth. That isn't to say that there aren't physicians who support and attend water births. However, obstetricians are often governed by hospital policies and personal liability considerations that guide their practice away from less-traditional birth options.

If you're happy with your provider, decide on a water birth, and then discover that he or she isn't too keen on the idea, find out why. Your provider could be uncomfortable due to personal inexperience, misinformation on current practices, or a simple lack of education on the concept. You might present it as a new challenge for your provider to experience or suggest that a midwife with water-birth experience might provide a consult about the process. If it's the second or third reason, doing some research and bringing the information to your provider's attention may be enough to ease any resistance. Waterbirth International offers support and advice for women seeking a water birth, including a bibliography of clinical studies examining the practice. They also have a referral database of facilities and practitioners offering water birth in the Unites States. See Appendix B for more information.

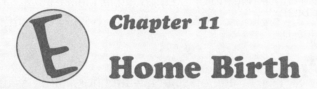

Chapter 11

Home Birth

irth in the home is a wonderful and empowering option for many women. A home birth offers comfort, control, and a natural labor and birth experience. Women who birth at home find that they can let go and follow their instincts more readily than those who may be forced into an "actively managed birth" with restrictions regarding how they labor and a preordained clinical timeline for the birth itself. Still, home birth isn't for everyone, and it requires a good deal of commitment and self-education to be successful.

Why Home Birth?

Giving birth in the place where you feel most comfortable and in control is important, which is why many women choose to have their babies in the cradle of their family—the home. While the vast majority of American babies are born in hospitals, the number of home births is increasing as women search for a natural birth alternative outside of the medical model.

Some reasons women choose home birth over a hospital or birth center include the following:

- **Provider preference.** Depending on state law and hospital rules and regulations, exclusive midwife care for your birth may only be available in a home setting.
- **Fear of unnecessary interventions.** Some women feel that a hospital environment promotes interventions by pigeonholing all women into one model of birth without taking into account inherent physical and emotional differences that could impact length of labor and other aspects of delivery.
- **A need for greater freedom in birth choices.** If the only area hospital mandates continuous fetal monitoring or doesn't allow water birth, you might find that a home birth offers you the options you need.
- **A bigger role for you and/or your partner.** You or your spouse can catch the baby if you want to, something that isn't really done in hospital settings. You manage the environment of your labor and birth instead of having it managed for you.
- **A desire for a smooth transition from birth to family.** Birth at home means that your baby is delivered right into the arms of his family, with no need for separation for newborn testing and no hospital stay.

Home birth provides you with complete control over your surroundings—everything from who attends the birth to how the room is lit—which makes it a very attractive birth option for some women. However, there are some potential downsides to assisted home birth, such as these:

- **Family or societal pressure.** Not everyone is keen on the benefits of home birth, and you may face the displeasure of others who don't share your viewpoint. Remember, this is your decision.

- **A big responsibility.** Home birth requires that you dedicate yourself to fairly intensive self-education about labor and birth. This can, of course, be a positive aspect for many, but some women may not be able or willing to take on this responsibility.
- **The unexpected.** If complications do occur that are beyond your birth assistant's clinical skills, there could be serious repercussions. An emergency transport plan (see below) can help minimize this risk.

Finally, any woman who has a complicated or high-risk pregnancy should seriously consider a hospital birth. Just what is considered "high-risk" can vary by practitioner (and can be influenced by things such as insurance and liability concerns), so do get a second opinion if you don't feel the first has assessed your situation fairly. Just be sure to consider all medical advice carefully.

Is Home Birth Safe?

Home birth may be the most comfortable option available, but is it safe? It seems to depend on who you ask—proponents of either side of the argument can point to clinical studies that back their viewpoints. A 2002 University of Washington study that examined data from eight years of planned home births versus hospital births concluded that there was a greater risk of neonatal death and postpartum bleeding in the home birth population. This study is frequently cited by those who believe home birth to be an unsafe birth option.

However, critics maintain that both the design and the analysis of the study were flawed because it classified infant deaths as home-birth deaths even if the mother was ultimately transported to a hospital and the birth and death occurred there. The study did not exclude infant deaths that were unrelated to the birth setting, nor did it fully analyze the case histories of the infants and mothers involved. Instead, it examined birth-certificate data only, which the authors admitted was limited and sometimes questionable.

Home-birth proponents can point to several large-scale studies in Canada, the Netherlands, and the United States that support the safety of birth in the home for low-risk women with a trained birth attendant. One report, known as the Farm study, is an analysis of home births versus hospital births in rural Tennessee. The Farm study found that low-risk home births that were attended by lay midwives were accomplished as safely as, and with fewer interventions than, physician-attended hospital births.

FACT

While the majority of U.S. births in 2001 took place in a hospital setting, 65 percent of those that occurred outside of a hospital happened at home.

Unfortunately, there are no clear-cut answers to the safety of home birth—or hospital birth, for that matter. Each poses risks inherent to the setting, and each woman must weigh those risks and potential benefits for herself.

Vaginal Birth After Cesarean at Home

The American College of Obstetricians and Gynecologists (ACOG) advises that vaginal birth after cesarean (VBAC) always be performed "in institutions equipped to respond to emergencies with physicians immediately available to provide emergency care." In other words, ACOG believes that VBAC needs to be done in the hospital with a doctor either attending or nearby. They cite the risk of uterine rupture as the reason behind this recommendation.

National midwifery organizations take a more moderate approach. Although state law, practice location, and liability concerns may affect whether your midwife will or will not attend a home VBAC, it's fair to say that if you want to have a vaginal birth after cesarean at home, an experienced midwife is your best chance.

Be sure to ask her what your provider's VBAC success rate is and what her strategies for labor support are for women having a VBAC. You should know that her VBAC success rates will depend in part on her patients' medical histories, including the reason for the prior cesarean. For example, a woman who had her labor stall at ten centimeters and ended up with a cesarean may be a less likely candidate for successful VBAC than someone who had a previous C-section because the baby was breech. But overall, a particularly low VBAC success rate could raise a red flag, while a high VBAC success rate is generally a positive sign.

Full, informed consent about the potential dangers of VBAC, no matter what the setting, is an essential step in the process. Your provider should explain the potential risks and benefits of VBAC, and if you're not planning to give birth at a hospital, you need to sit down together and review a written plan for transport to the nearest hospital should an emergency arise.

Although clinical studies haven't yet thoroughly investigated the success rates of home VBAC versus hospital VBAC, many women believe that a supportive home setting is more conducive to a successful VBAC birth because it keeps the normalcy of labor and delivery in focus. VBAC in a hospital entails mandatory intravenous lines, precautionary internal fetal monitoring, and even terminology such as "trial of labor" that can make a woman feel as though she's an accident waiting to happen—destined for another cesarean.

That's not to say that home VBAC is for everyone. Some women will feel more comfortable having immediate access to a surgeon and to neonatal pediatric care should it be required. You need to examine your own personal preferences and comfort level and make the choice that's right for you.

And of course, the same contraindications for VBAC—such as a classical (vertical) incision and any past history of uterine rupture—still apply no matter what the location, so if you fit these criteria a cesarean in a hospital is your safest alternative. (See Chapter 16 for more on VBAC.)

Assisted or Unassisted

A home birth is either assisted—attended by a midwife or other health-care professional—or unassisted, with no health-care provider in attendance. Yes, some women do give birth by themselves or with just their partner or a close friend or family member or two by their side.

The unassisted childbirth movement is rooted in the idea that birth is as intimate an experience as sex itself and should be just as private. Advocates of unassisted birth believe that the natural and instinctive act of childbirth doesn't require the presence of anyone but the woman giving birth and whomever she chooses to have with her, since birth itself predates all modern medical technologies and organized medicine as we know it.

ALERT!

If you do make the decision for an unassisted home birth, an infant CPR class is essential. Your local hospital, Red Cross chapter, or YMCA are good places to find low-cost programs in your area.

Along with unassisted home birth comes the responsibility to be able to deal with complications should they arise, particularly if the nearest hospital or medical facility is some distance away. If the baby is breech, or if complications such as shoulder dystocia or a prolapsed umbilical cord occur, will you be able to handle it? Unless you have a medical or midwifery degree yourself, or you have been trained in emergency care, you and your partner will need some kind of guidance in appropriately managing potential complications. And if this is your first birth, the need for education is even more acute. Some women find that self-instruction, such as through books and support groups, provides them with enough information to feel comfortable with handling crises.

If you're contemplating unassisted home birth, keep in mind that some women find they can get the best of both worlds with a carefully selected midwife. When you interview midwives, look for one who will maintain a hands-off approach and let you control the birth but who will be there to provide competent care and advice should things not go as expected.

House Calls and Home Birth

Home birth is a primarily midwife-dominated profession. Still, there are some physicians who will still attend home births, and a few practices even focus exclusively on home birth. Depending on where you live, legal issues and financial constraints may limit your birth choices. Some states do not legally allow midwives to attend home births. And in some places, the cost of liability insurance and other practice issues have pushed midwives out of the business of home birth completely.

FACT

Women who have difficulty finding a provider who will attend their home birth can contact one of the national midwifery organizations or the home-birth information clearinghouses for contacts in their area. Appendix B offers resources for both.

Legalities

Home birth is not explicitly outlawed in any U.S. state; however, the prohibition many states have against midwives attending home births effectively eliminates the option of a legal, assisted, home birth for many women who want it.

According to the Midwives Association of North America, as of December, 2003, sixteen states did not allow direct-entry midwives (those certified as CM, CPM, LM, or LDM) to practice, either by explicit statute or by lack of formal licensure procedures or regulations. In addition to these states that don't allow direct-entry midwives to practice at all, others limit the types of birth that direct-entry midwives can attend, based on factors such as circumstances or location of the birth. Certified nurse-midwives (CNM) are licensed to practice in all fifty states, but again, some states limit the types of birth they can attend. Your state department of health can provide more information on the laws in your area.

Insurance Issues

Since there are no facility charges with a home birth, your expenses are limited to provider care and necessary supplies. If your insurance does not cover midwife services, then you could run into some major expenses with home birth. Keep in mind that some states, like Pennsylvania, mandate that health insurers must reimburse midwife care, so be sure to check the regulations in your state.

In addition to the actual delivery, many midwifery practices include both prenatal care and postpartum checkup in their home-birth fees, which run on average from $1,250 to $3,500, depending on where you live. These fees often include part or all of birth supplies and childbirth education.

All in all, home birth is less expensive than birth in a hospital or even a birthing center. Since the bottom line dictates policy for many health insurers, that is one thing that works in your favor when seeking coverage for home birth.

Getting Ready

Since you don't have to worry about getting to a hospital by a specific point in labor or planning for an extended stay away from home, getting ready for your home birth simply means getting the necessary supplies in-house, planning ahead to be laid up for a while, and making a few phone calls once labor begins.

Keep a list of important phone numbers right next to your phone so they're handy. At the very least, this list should include the numbers for your midwife and/or doula and an emergency transport facility.

Lay in extra nonperishable groceries and protein snacks that can sustain you during labor and postpartum. If you have the time or the energy, freezing some meals and casseroles may be a good idea to get you through that first week after the birth.

Supplies

Your midwife will typically either provide most of the necessary items for a home birth or provide you with a list of supplies you should purchase. A few standard items include plastic sheeting to protect bedding or floors, absorbent Chux underpads, umbilical cord clamps, sterile gloves, bulb syringe, peri-bottle (for cleansing the perineum postpartum), super-absorbent sanitary pads, sterile gauze pads, alcohol for sterilization, and a cap for your newborn. Medical or surgical supply companies often offer these items in a home birth kit.

Other things, like bed linens, towels, and clothing and diapers for your newborn will be your responsibility to supply. Your midwife may suggest that you take extra steps when cleaning your bed linens, such as washing them in special detergent or running them through the dryer on high and bagging them until use.

Pain Relief

Home births are natural births, which means that no narcotics or anesthetics are used (unless you're one of the rare few who have a physician attending your home birth, and even then pharmaceutical pain relief options will be limited). But comfort measures such as warm soaks, showers, and massage are at your disposal, and since it's your space, you can do whatever feels good. See Chapter 14 for more information on pain relief in labor and birth.

The Home Team

Another perk of a home birth is that you dictate exactly who is there and what roles your attendants play. You make the visiting hours and age restrictions yourself—kids are welcome (if you want it that way), and since you are chief cook and bottle washer, you don't have to worry about strangers from the food service or housekeeping staff popping in to tidy up just as the baby is crowning and you're feeling most exposed.

To keep intrusions at a minimum, put up a "Do Not Disturb—Birth in Progress" sign on your outside doors (even the most determined door-to-door solicitor wouldn't dare to go against that directive). And take the phone off the hook (or put your calls directly into voicemail). Let friends and family waiting for word outside the home know that you will contact them in due time, and ask them to respect your wishes about giving you the time and space to focus on the birth and immediate postpartum period.

In Case of Emergency

Although chances are your home birth will go just fine, there is the possibility that complications may arise that would require your transport to a hospital. No matter how remote that possibility is, you and your provider should have a written plan in place so you are ready should it occur.

In fact, some states have specific laws that require a transport plan to be created for home birth situations. This plan will outline details such as the facility you wish to be transferred to, what kind of emergency situations may require transport, and who will pay for transport other than your own vehicle, such as an ambulance, should it be required. The transport facility should be within thirty minutes of your home.

After you and your provider discuss the plan, she may ask you to sign off on it to indicate you understand and accept it and to give her the authority to release your medical records to another provider in an emergency.

FACT

Even if you are planning on a home birth, it's a good idea to preregister at your local hospital. If emergency transport is required, you'll have all the paperwork already in place and your partner won't have to spend time getting you checked in.

Ask your midwife about continuity of care should a transport be necessary. Will she accompany you to the hospital and continue to attend the birth? Does she have privileges at the hospital closest to you, or does she belong to a practice that does? Your midwife may be working in consultation with a physician who would meet you at the hospital. In the event that another provider has to take over due to hospital regulations or the nature of the complications, will your midwife still stay by your side as additional birth support should you want her to?

Making a Mess

Birth is not a tidy process. You, and most everyone in attendance, will experience plenty of contact with blood and other bodily fluids. The average vaginal birth involves about a pint of blood loss—factor in amniotic fluid, placenta, and other afterbirth, and you've got a bit of a mess to clean up afterward. Since you don't have the benefit of a hospital housekeeping staff, you should make a few provisions now to keep the mess manageable for yourself. Items like plastic sheeting and absorbent pads for your bed will probably be on the birth kit supply list you receive from your provider. Buy extras so you can stay mobile without worrying about what your body might leave on the rugs or furniture.

The Cleanup

Most midwives who do home births will also clean up the birth area for you—or have an assistant who will clean up—as part of their services. This may not sound like a big deal now, but when you've just given birth and are gazing into the eyes of your newborn, the last thing you and your partner want to deal with is changing sheets and scrubbing an errant blood spot out of the carpet. Some midwives may even do your laundry and fix you a light snack. Ask your midwife if she provides these home care services when you're discussing your home birth options.

A Big Splash

Another potential housekeeping hot spot is the bathroom. You may find that your bathroom facilities just don't meet your needs when you're trying to get comfortable to ride out your contractions. And a standard bathtub can really get constricting if you'd like an underwater birth, and (unless you have a Jacuzzi) doesn't leave much room for your partner or support person to join you. After you've squirmed into a comfortable position, you may have left half the tub water on the bathroom floor.

Fortunately, you have other options. Ask your midwife about a birthing pool rental. Resembling a portable hot tub, these portable pools can provide excellent pain relief and are the perfect place for a home water-birth should you chose to have one. (See Chapter 10 for more information on birthing pools.) If money is tight or you can't find a rental option in your area, consider an inflatable wading pool that is at least thigh-high. Although it won't be as deep as a standard birth pool, most provide enough water for buoyancy, and the sides are supportive, yet comfortable. A waterproof groundcover to go under the pool or tub is a must. Drop cloths or plastic shower curtain liners are inexpensive ways to protect your floors.

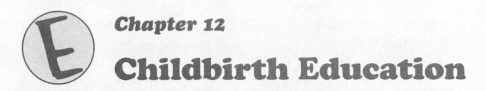

Chapter 12

Childbirth Education

If you're feeling fearful or anxious about the birth experience, childbirth education classes can help by defining some of the unknowns and separating fact from fiction. Even if you've been through birth before, childbirth education has a lot to offer. Knowing what to look for in a childbirth educator, how to select a class, and what to expect when you arrive in the classroom can help you get the most out of the experience.

"Prepared" Childbirth

Childbirth education is a little like your first sex ed course in school. You and your classmates probably giggled nervously, sharing a great sense of anticipation that some great truth would be revealed to you once the teacher started talking and the film projector got rolling. But in the end, aside from knowing a few more official names for things than you did before, you still didn't grasp exactly what it meant, or was like, to have sex. In the same way, childbirth education lays out the mechanics of the process, but you won't fully appreciate the experience until you're in labor.

That doesn't mean classes are a waste of time or inevitably a disappointment. Far from it—they have the important purpose of helping you develop the skills you need for a successful childbirth, in addition to providing practical information about the birth experience. The tool set you acquire here—breathing techniques, prenatal exercise, labor positions, relaxation methods, partner support—will go home with you, and what you choose to do with them can make a big difference when labor rolls around. As with any tools, the more you practice, the more skilled you become with them. With regular use, they'll feel natural by the time birth arrives.

FACT

Some teen mothers-to-be may feel uncomfortable about the prospect of attending class with women who are not their peers. Many hospitals and birth facilities offer birth preparation classes designed specifically for teenagers. These classes cover the same birth basics as a regular childbirth class but also address adolescent issues such as getting adequate support as a single mom, special nutritional needs, and instruction on parenting skills and child development.

Choosing a Class

In the previous chapters, you have learned the basics of several popular childbirth methods. The following chart will help you review the basics of each method before you choose which type of class is right for you.

Comparing Childbirth Philosophies

Method	Philosophy	Pain Control	Course of Study
Active Birth	Birth as instinctual	Upright positions and prenatal yoga	5 prenatal classes
Birthing from Within	Birth in awareness	Focuses on embracing pain to cope; drugs if necessary	6 prenatal classes/ 2 postpartum classes
Bradley Method	Parental responsibility and husband-coached childbirth	No drugs; relaxation and natural breathing	12 weekly prenatal classes
HypnoBirthing	Breaking fear-tension-pain cycle	Self-hypnosis through relaxation and guided imagery	5 prenatal classes
Lamaze	Natural birth guided by a woman's "inner wisdom" and childbirth education	Breathing, relaxation, massage; drugs if necessary	12 hours of prenatal instruction
Leboyer	Infant focused; birth without violence	Relaxation benefits baby and mother	N/A*
Water Birth	Water speeds labor, increases comfort	Buoyancy and warmth of water ease pain	N/A**

*Formal instruction in Leboyer is not currently available, but some educators may incorporate his ideas into their teachings.

**Some facilities that offer water births may have formal preparatory classes available, but there is no certifying organization or set curriculum for water-birth instructors.

Most mainstream childbirth education classes taught at hospitals try to offer a bit of everything—breathing from Lamaze, coaching à la Bradley—under the umbrella of "prepared childbirth." Others offer additional classes that are more specific to the particular genres.

Birthing centers may provide wider options and more method-specific classes. If your local hospital doesn't offer what you're looking for, and you're not sure where else to find it, a midwife or doula can be a good source of alternatives. Some things to consider when choosing a class include the following:

- **Curriculum.** Does the course outline address your specific needs in terms of philosophy and goals? If it's unclear from the literature, call and ask the instructor.
- **Class size.** In general, smaller is better. A small class size ensures that the instructor can answer all questions posed and circulate among participants during exercises to check form and offer tips. Smaller classes also offer a more intimate setting to become acquainted with other couples in the group.
- **Convenience.** Schedules vary, but most classes are either offered over a period of weeks, or as a "power weekend" workshop. The latter may fit your schedule better, but it can be exhausting for some women. Location may also play a factor in your class choice.
- **Cost**. The cost of most childbirth classes is nominal, and most health insurers generally cover the fee as part of your prenatal care. But some private instruction or method-specific classes may carry a heftier price tag.
- **Class leader.** A course is only as good as its teacher. Choose your instructor carefully. (For more on choosing an instructor, read on.)

Most health insurers will cover prenatal classes as part of basic prenatal care. A call to your insurance provider can confirm your eligibility. Hospital-based classes usually only involve a nominal fee, while independent instruction on specific methods (for example, Bradley Method or HypnoBirthing) can be a bit pricey. However, if you are uninsured, or your insurer doesn't provide class coverage, check with the class administrator—a sliding-scale fee or installment payment plan may be available.

Choosing an Instructor

The personality and teaching style of the instructor can make or break a childbirth class. Is the instructor comfortable with the curriculum and candid when answering questions from the class? Does she encourage discussion and address each concern about the birth experience with honesty and appropriate suggestions for coping? Are her lessons presented in a format that the layman (or woman) can understand, without oversimplification? A good instructor should have all these qualities. She should also operate with the underlying attitude that the women before her have the power to make the necessary choices and call the shots during their birth experience.

When looking into a potential class, ask if there are referrals (couples who have taken the class and are willing to talk about their experiences) available for the instructor. You may also request to sit in on fifteen minutes or so of the instructor's class to determine if her teaching style is right for you.

Certification and Experience

There are several organizations in the United States that certify childbirth educators. Instructors who are certified through the International Childbirth Education Association (ICEA) have met extensive educational requirements and have passed a certification examination. ICEA-certified childbirth educators have the designation "ICCE" (for international certified childbirth educator) after their name. The ICEA is also a good source of referrals for childbirth educators should the options available at your hospital or birthing center not fit your needs. Contact them by phone at ✆ 952-854-8660 or online at ✑ www.icea.org.

The Association of Labor Assistants and Childbirth Educators (ALACE) also provides certification for childbirth educators, although the membership of this organization is smaller than ICEA. Instructors who have completed certification requirements with ALACE have a CCE (certified childbirth educator) designation after their name. ALACE can provide referrals to their member educators via its Web site at ✑ www.alace.org.

If you are interested in instructors who are certified in a specific method of childbirth education, the best way to verify their credentials is to go to the official certification organization for the method (Lamaze International, for example). Appendix B contains a list of these organizations, along with contact information for each.

Philosophy

Your potential instructor may also have teaching credentials in a specific childbirth method or philosophy. The American Academy of Husband-Coached Childbirth (AAHCC) offers childbirth educators specific instruction in Bradley Method coaching, while Lamaze International offers certification in the Lamaze method. Instructors who have earned Lamaze certification have the designation "LCCE" (Lamaze-certified childbirth educator) after their names.

The course description should make clear what type of birth philosophy the instructor aligns herself with, if any, so that you can make appropriate choices about your participation.

FACT

Childbirth education isn't the only type of prenatal class available. There are also prenatal exercise classes, breastfeeding classes, instruction in pregnancy massage, courses on baby care basics, pregnancy nutrition-and-wellness workshops, and classes tailored specifically for dads, grandparents, and siblings. Pregnancy is a perfect time to take advantage of expanding your education, especially if your insurer is willing to foot the bill.

What to Expect from Class

You've found the perfect class, gotten good reports on the instructor, paid your fee, and are ready to roll. Although your mileage will vary based on the type of class you enroll in, here's a basic idea of common elements you can expect:

- **Reading material.** You'll get plenty of reading material to bring home with you. Some classes may also offer a "goodie bag" of baby-care product samples to take home as well.
- **Audiovisual aids.** Most instructors have at least one movie in their educational arsenal to give you a close-up view of a real birth. The use of slide shows and overhead projectors for other visual aids is also common.
- **Hands-on practice.** You'll get down on the floor and try out relaxation techniques, breathing methods, exercise moves, and more.
- **Lecture.** Your teacher will talk you through lessons and should allow plenty of opportunities for questions and interaction as part of her lectures.

- **Facility tour.** An added bonus of taking a course at the facility where you'll be giving birth is that it usually includes a guided tour of the labor and birth area.

Depending on the curriculum and the time frame of your class, your instructor may request that you bring along some items from home. Pillows (for labor and breathing exercises), paper and pen for notes, and money for lunch are common supplies. Also feel free to bring along any items that will make the experience more comfortable for you, such as a bottle of water, light snack, and layered clothing should the room temperature be too warm or too cool.

Education, Not Dictation

Basic childbirth preparation classes should present all potential options and outcomes—from completely natural to cesarean delivery along with everything in between—in an objective and clinically accurate manner. They should also steer clear of simply parroting hospital or birth-facility policy, although making students aware of policy in the context of other available choices is encouraged so that women can reach their own conclusions about birth at the facility. Unless the class is billed as concentrating on a particular birth philosophy, the instructor should not try and impose her personal views on matters such as drugs in labor or other potentially hot-button issues on her students. A balance of risks and benefits and pros and cons is important so that you have the information you need to make informed choices.

Your childbirth educator will probably cover the basics of birth plans with you. This is a good opportunity to ask any questions you might have about creating yours. If you already have one put together, or are in the process of doing so, bring it to class with you, and you may be able to get some feedback.

Even if a class is focused on a particular birth method that is typically intervention-free, it should still offer information on medical technologies that could conceivably come into play during the birth process, such as forceps use and cesarean section. There should also be at least basic information provided on analgesic and anesthetic pain relief, offered in a factual and nonjudgmental manner.

Commiseration

One of the best parts of the childbirth education experience is getting to know other couples who are going through the same pregnancy trials and tribulations that you are and who are experiencing the same fears and anxieties as well. You may know intellectually that you're not alone in this endeavor, but getting into the trenches with other women who can relate (and how!) will drive that point home. And of course being a part of the group panting-and-grunting exercises, the graphic audiovisual aids, and getting into more awkward positions than you can shake a stick at will provide a unique bonding experience for you all.

If you live in a small community, the women you meet in class may end up being the start of a new mothers' group or playgroup in a few months. Some childbirth classes also offer a postpartum get-together so you can show off the fruits of your labor and talk about some of the issues new parents face.

Homework

Your instructor will probably suggest that you take your new skills home with you and practice for your next class session. It may feel a little awkward at first, but take fifteen minutes to a half-hour out of each day to do it. Repetition is the best way to get comfortable with breathing, relaxation exercises, birthing positions, and other techniques you learn for labor and birth.

Don't let your partner wiggle out of the homework routine. He needs to practice his supporting role as well. And some things you learn in class—like massage techniques—can be an enjoyable exercise for both of you. Take turns giving rubdowns so your partner can get a feel for the type of touch that you enjoy.

Homeschooling

If you're having a home birth, you may wonder about the need for formal instruction. A hospital class—with all the information on interventions and tours of the maternity ward—may not feel right to you. But childbirth education is just as important for women who are giving birth at home, if not more so. Most women desiring home birth rely on natural pain-control methods, so taking a Lamaze or Bradley course to prepare for effective pain management is a smart idea. Many midwifery practices also offer childbirth education classes geared specifically toward women who desire a home birth.

ALERT!

Again, even if you are expecting an intervention-free birth at home, it is important to educate yourself about potential interventions and circumstances under which you may require transport to a hospital. A home-birth class should offer this information.

Refresher Courses

Couples who have been through childbirth once before may wonder about the necessity of spending time in class once again. If your birth experience was not what you wanted the first time around, a fresh look at your alternatives may be welcome. And if it's been a few years since you've been through the process, changes in standards of care, birth techniques, and pain relief options may make revisiting the classroom well worth your while.

Some facilities offer a "refresher course" specifically geared to parents who have done this before. These classes will cover the basics and allow you to dust off your labor management skills, in addition to providing information on issues important to second-time moms, like helping your child adjust to the new baby in the family. But for others, your options may be limited to general prepared childbirth classes. Still, even if your birth was a stunning success the first time out, there's always something new to learn.

Share the Wealth

As a mother who has been through it before, you have something special to offer your classmates. They can only imagine what a contraction feels like, while you have felt the real thing. Sharing your experiences within the context of the instructor's lesson plan can be a positive learning experience for all involved. Keep in mind that your perceived expertise on the subject may cause your fellow students to put a special weight on your classroom comments. If you're the only second- (or third-) time mom in the group, you may find yourself with a semicelebrity status among these novices.

Remember, with fame comes responsibility. If your previous birth experience was not a pleasant one, try not to project any negativity about the birth itself—stick to discussing the particular circumstances around it. Point out things that could have been done that may have resulted in a better outcome. In other words, make it a learning experience rather than a horror story. You probably still remember the fears and self-doubts of your first time around, so keep them in mind during classroom sharing and bathroom-break chats.

VBAC Classes

For women who are interested in trying a vaginal birth after a previous cesarean, or VBAC, a course geared just for this situation can be quite helpful. Many facilities offer VBAC instruction, which teaches many of the same relaxation and breathing techniques taught in a non-VBAC class. These classes also address the special concerns of women who have undergone a previous C-section birth.

A good VBAC class should lay out the risks and benefits of VBAC, explain things like what a "trial of labor" is, and what circumstances make a vaginal birth or a repeat cesarean more likely. These are all topics your health-care provider should discuss with you as well. However, many women feel more comfortable asking follow-up questions about VBAC in a classroom setting surrounded by women in the same situation and where the instructor has no potential vested interest in the choice between VBAC or repeat cesarean.

Class for Kids

Children who are expecting a brand-new sibling can also benefit from pre-natal education. Many hospitals have sibling classes that introduce kids to the idea of what to expect when mom leaves for the birth and comes home with the new baby.

When looking for a class for your child, be sure that class size is limited so that each child gets the opportunity to participate and interact with the instructor. Classes should be divided by age group so that information can be presented on an age-appropriate level. Follow the same guidelines for checking out the instructor that you did for your own childbirth education class. Find out what the instructor's credentials and experience are, and ask the course administrator if she can put you in contact with parents who have had children participate in the program so you can determine if the instructor and curriculum are what you're looking for.

ALERT!

Even if your child is excited about attending your birth, don't consider bringing him into the experience with no knowledge to prepare him. He needs adequate and age-appropriate education to understand that the things he will see—like mom's apparent pain and blood—are normal parts of the natural process known as childbirth.

When Your Child Will Attend Your Birth

Some birth facilities offer classes for children who will be in attendance during the birth. Usually these are geared toward older children, but you may find some class options or private instruction for younger siblings.

If nothing is available in your area specifically geared toward preparing a young child to be present at your birth, then get some appropriate books and videos on the subject and do your own home-based instruction.

Practicing breathing techniques and vocalization in front of your children can give them a sneak preview of labor so they won't be surprised or frightened at the sights and sounds of labor. It's also important to reassure them that there will be an adult there to take care of all of their needs while you are otherwise preoccupied. (For more information on having your child at your birth, see Chapter 5.)

Life As a Big Sister or Brother

Sibling classes for younger children explore the emotional aspects of having a new baby in the house, including how things are changing at home during the pregnancy, how the family will adjust once the new baby comes home, and how the child is feeling in light of all these big events.

FACT

In addition to exploring and expressing their feelings, most sibling classes offer children an opportunity to practice holding and caring for a baby (a doll, not the real thing). Kids also get a chance to tour the area where mom will be having the baby, see the nursery, and ask questions about what will happen when mom goes to the hospital.

For children who are having a hard time adjusting to the fact that there will be a new baby in the house, sibling classes can give them a sense of purpose and place in your new family. Even if your child is thrilled about the prospect of a new playmate, he is sure to have some uncertainties about the whole process. A sibling class can give him some important answers.

Beyond Bradley and Lamaze

The childbirth philosophies covered in detail in this book are those that are taught on a widespread basis in the United States. However, there other curriculums and methods that are gaining popularity as women explore the many options available to them for prepared childbirth education. These include Birthing from Within, a method developed by a certified nurse-midwife who was trained in the Frontier Nursing Service, and Active Birth, created by a former National Childbirth Trust educator in the United Kingdom.

Birthing from Within

Perhaps the most spiritually grounded childbirth education philosophy, Birthing from Within (BFW) emphasizes the emotional experience of giving birth. The method was created by nurse-midwife, childbirth educator, and therapist Pam England in 1989 after she gave birth by cesarean section. England believed her birth outcome might have been different if she had been emotionally and spiritually equipped instead of just being intellectually prepared for the birth.

Birthing from Within is more about developing coping techniques and achieving a goal of what England calls "birthing-in-awareness," which can only be developed through a process of self-discovery. Classes use nontraditional techniques to explore fears and feelings about childbirth, including journaling and birth art.

BFW does not oppose the use of obstetric interventions when necessary or of pain control methods of any kind. England believes parents should be supported in whatever birth and parenting choices they make, as long as such choices are made with full awareness. The curriculum also emphasizes that pain is a necessary part of childbirth, but suffering isn't, and that pain-control techniques should be integrated into daily life—not just practiced on birth day.

Instructors in Birthing from Within classes are known as mentors instead of teachers. That's because they are there to help women and their partners discover their own birthing needs rather than as an absolute source of knowledge. Certified mentors attend a training program and complete a BFW course of study. The designation "BFWM" indicates that they have successfully completed a BFW mentor certification program. The BFW program also certifies doulas.

Birthing from Within instructors are located throughout the United States and Canada as well as several other locations abroad. Pam England also teaches workshops and performs mentor training out of the BFW studio in Albuquerque, New Mexico. More information can be found online at *www. birthingfromwithin.com.*

Active Birth

Founded by author and childbirth educator Janet Balaskas in 1981, the Active Birth movement is based on the idea that birth is instinctual and that each woman should be an active participant in her own pregnancy and birth, rather than having birth managed by others around her. It was created in response to the rise of "active management of labor" in the United Kingdom, a practice under which labor is augmented with interventions such as artificial rupture of membranes and oxytocin if labor doesn't meet specific benchmarks of progress (dilation of one centimeter per hour, for example).

Active Birth also emphasizes movement in labor and delivery, particularly those upright positions that encourage both maternal comfort and labor progress. Recumbent or lithotomy positions in labor and birth are strongly discouraged by Active Birth instructors.

In her book *New Active Birth,* Balaskas asserts that "A strong intention, relaxed body and an open mind are the main ingredients for an Active Birth." Balaskas does recognize that there are situations in which complications will require the "safety net" of modern obstetrical care. However, the emphasis is on lessening the chances of complications through education and proper preparation, such as yoga-based exercise.

FACT

While Active Birth education is widely available in the United Kingdom, the United States has yet to adapt the program on any widespread, formalized basis. However, the North London-based Active Birth Centre offers training materials to women worldwide on their Web site at *www.activebirthcentre.com* in addition to their classes in London.

Mix-and-Match

Many women study a variety of childbirth philosophies, either through formal instruction or by researching books and other educational materials, and then select the components of each that resonate with them. Birthing positions from Active Birth, spiritual preparedness from Birthing from Within, relaxation techniques from Bradley—all can work together to create the birth experience you choose.

Childbirth education is a vibrant and ever-changing field, constantly incorporating new science and experienced-based knowledge, while adapting to the changing needs of women, their families, and society. Today's woman has significantly more choices in creating her birth experience than her mother did; chances are by the time her daughter grows to womanhood, there will be a variety of new options and educational philosophies available for her birth.

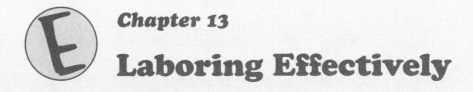

Chapter 13

Laboring Effectively

S uccessful labor is a state of mind as much as it is a physical process. If you're anxious, scared, and stressed, your body will react with pain and resistance. Educating yourself about what to expect can really help you to achieve a positive, prepared state of mind. Once labor begins, being comfortable and in control of the labor process and working with your body instead of against it will make your birth experience more productive and enjoyable.

The Stages of Labor

Your baby may start preparing for birth before labor even begins by settling lower into your pelvis. Called "engagement," "lightening," or simply "the baby dropping," this move downward places pressure on the cervix so it can begin the task of effacement (thinning) and dilation (opening).

FACT

Not all women experience engagement prior to labor. Some babies, particularly those born to second-time moms, may not move down into the pelvic cavity until labor officially begins.

Labor itself is divided into three stages:

- *First stage:* Lasts from early contractions until the cervix is ten centimeters dilated.
- *Second stage:* The pushing part; the actual delivery of your baby.
- *Third stage:* Delivery of the placenta.

First Stage

Typically the longest phase of the labor process, the first phase consists of three parts—early (latent) labor, active labor, and transition (descent) labor. Your cervix may already begin to ripen well before early labor starts. When the first stage of labor begins, your uterine muscles will squeeze, causing you to feel contractions, and the cervix will dilate further—four to five centimeters during early labor. Contractions will be coming every fifteen to twenty minutes and should be between sixty and ninety seconds in duration. Once you've established that contractions are regular and real, contact your provider and other support people on your birth team to let them know the show has begun. If you have any bleeding or loss of fluid, or if you notice decreased fetal movement, contact your provider immediately to let him know what is going on. (According to the American College of Obstetricians and Gynecologists, normal fetal movement is ten fetal movements in a two-hour period.)

How will you know a "real" contraction when it comes? As any woman who has labored can tell you, you'll definitely know. In case you're still wary of missing the signal, a labor contraction is one that 1) causes discomfort that does not improve significantly when you change positions; 2) comes at roughly regular intervals; 3) increases in intensity as time passes; and 4) leads to a change in the cervix.

Your provider will instruct you on when to head for the hospital or birthing center or when she will come to you, should you be planning a home birth. Because early labor can be long, this probably won't be until you're approaching the active phase of the first stage of labor, where contractions are at regular three- to five-minute intervals and last approximately forty-five seconds each. The strong contractions of active labor will dilate your cervix to approximately eight centimeters when the transition phase starts (as shown in **FIGURE 13.1A**).

FIGURE 13.1A

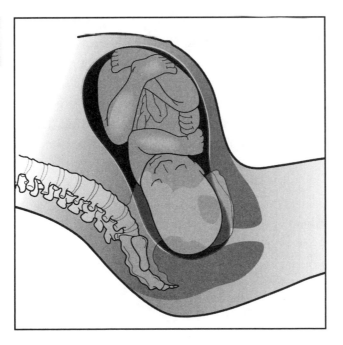

◀ The birth journey— transition phase

Transition is perhaps the most difficult part of labor because your contractions are coming fast and furious, and you're faced with the overwhelming urge to push—but can't yet. As your cervix dilates those final two centimeters to a full ten, you'll feel intense pressure on your rectum from the baby's head, and severe back pain. It's normal to feel nauseous and have the chills or sweats. Breathing exercises can help you quell the urge to push until full dilation is achieved and stage two begins.

Second Stage

As the second stage starts, the baby descends into the vagina, or birth canal (**FIGURE 13.1B**). Now you can finally push to help her along, and the elastic walls of your vagina will widen for her passage down the final five inches of the journey to the outside world. (See the section entitled "Pushing," on page 167, for tips on pushing effectively.) The gripping pain of contractions changes to a stinging or burning sensation as your perineum, the external tissue between the vaginal opening and anus, stretches to accommodate baby's emerging head and body. The burning sensation affects a circular area of the perineal tissues surrounding the vaginal opening. As the baby's head bulges out of your vaginal opening (known as crowning—see **FIGURE 13.1C**), your provider may ask you to stop pushing momentarily to prevent perineal tearing. This request may feel as futile as patching the Hoover Dam with a damp sponge, but panting can help you quash the urge to push until it's safe. Once you push the baby's head and shoulders out, the rest of her body will slide out easily by comparison.

FACT

If you aren't in the ideal pushing position to see your baby emerge, many hospitals and birthing centers offer mirrors to watch your baby as she enters the world. Ask when you tour the birth facility so you can know if you have the option. Even if mirrors aren't available, you may be able to make arrangements to bring in a small mirror for your use.

Second Stage . . .

FIGURE 13.1B

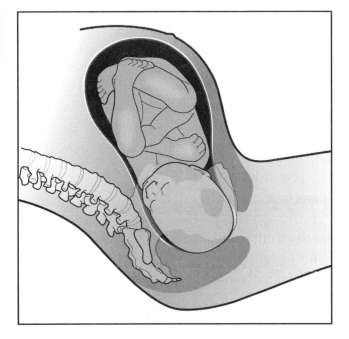

◀ The birth journey—
descent

FIGURE 13.1C

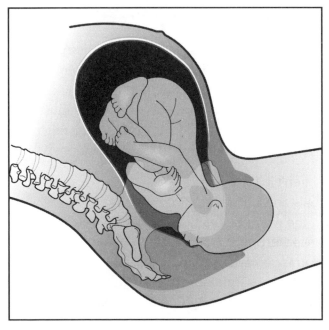

◀ The birth journey—
crowning

Third Stage

Once you've been through stages one and two, the third stage of labor is a cakewalk. Your placenta must be delivered and examined to ensure that you haven't retained any pieces in your uterus. Your provider may suggest an injection of Pitocin to strengthen your contractions enough to deliver the placenta efficiently. Other providers may wait until after the placenta has been delivered to suggest giving Pitocin, in which case the goal is to increase uterine contractions in an attempt to decrease uterine bleeding. See Chapter 19 for more on delivering the placenta.

Easing Baby's Passage

One of the most miraculous aspects of birth is that both your body and your baby seem to know exactly what to do—even if you're a first-time mom. Trusting yourself to listen to the signals your body is sending is half the battle in childbirth. There are also some conscious choices you can make along the way to help make the journey easier for your soon-to-be-born baby.

Gravitational Pull

Obviously if you walk, stand, squat, or assume any other upright position, your baby has the advantages of gravity working for him. Lying prone, whether by choice or by hospital policy, can make your discomfort greater and gives your baby no assistance at all. If you must stay in bed, make sure your head is well elevated so you're in a semisitting or full-sitting position.

Refer to the section titled "Birthing Positions," on page 168, for more information.

Oxygen and Blood Flow

This is where all those breathing exercises you learned in childbirth preparation class come in handy. The air you breathe is giving your baby sufficient oxygen via your bloodstream and is also helping your body and muscles work effectively through contractions. The very process of breathing keeps you centered and focused on the task at hand. Rhythmic breathing can help reduce stress and anxiety, which will make labor pain more manageable and relax your body more readily for birth. (For more on rhythmic breathing, see Chapter 14.)

Good Alignment

With that big pregnant belly before you, it's a natural reaction to want to arch your back to counterbalance the weight. But as your mother always told you, stand up straight. Keeping your body in good alignment even before labor begins eases back pain and helps to give your baby the room it needs to move into the proper position for birth. It also allows you to breathe more effectively once labor starts.

QUESTION?

I'm a natural-born sloucher. How can I improve my posture for birth?
Yoga is an excellent way to work on proper alignment of your body, and it promotes flexibility. Sitting on a birthing ball, either before or during labor, is also a good way to improve posture since it requires you to sit up straight for balance. If you do decide to try out a prenatal yoga class, get the green light from your provider first.

Walking Through Labor

While clinical studies have had differing results as to the effectiveness of walking for shortening labor, what is known conclusively is that for many women, walking can ease labor pains and improve their overall satisfaction with their birth experience. It can also give women a greater sense of control and self-empowerment, particularly in a hospital setting. For these reasons, walking is often encouraged. However, staying mobile can be a challenge if your situation requires continuous fetal monitoring, intravenous lines, or any other technology that anchors you to equipment. For more on walking in labor and maintaining mobility, see Chapter 14.

Back Labor

Sometimes baby descends with his face toward your abdomen rather than your spine, called the occiput posterior position (OP) or "sunny-side up." The pressure of the head on your coccyx, or tailbone, can cause severe lower back pain, known as back labor.

In addition to the discomfort of back labor, the posterior position can make labor a long and difficult road, because a posterior baby descends straight down with the top of his head, as opposed to an anterior (face down) baby, who tucks in his chin (called flexion) and descends with the smaller back of his head first (see **FIGURE 13.2**).

FIGURE 13.2

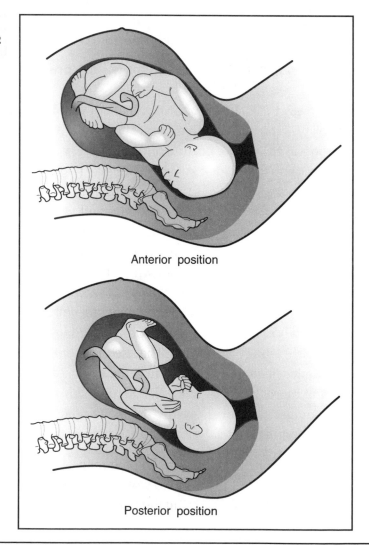

◀ Anterior versus posterior fetal position

Anterior position

Posterior position

Some women can deliver a baby that is posterior if their pelvis is wide enough to accommodate the broader load, but in most cases a provider will suggest that you encourage the baby to rotate through different labor positions and exercises. If you are dilated to ten centimeters but are having difficulty pushing out the baby because it is OP, sometimes your health-care provider can turn the baby with her hands or with the help of forceps.

ALERT!

A posterior baby has a much easier job of turning if she hasn't yet engaged significantly into the birth canal. A vaginal exam to check the baby's position in early labor can save much pain and potential interventions (including C-section) by giving you the opportunity to encourage rotation while it's still achievable. Many babies who are OP during labor will spontaneously turn prior to the second stage of labor.

Getting Through Back Labor

Assuming a hands-and-knees position will relieve the pain of back labor (by dropping your uterus away from your spine) and give your baby more room to rotate to an anterior position. Other effective pain-relief methods include massage and counterpressure and warm compresses or water jets (in a shower or whirlpool). Injections of sterile water papules, discussed in Chapter 14, have also been shown to be useful in relieving back labor pain.

To try to initiate fetal rotation, your provider may suggest pelvic tilts or rocking, which is simply lifting or rocking your pelvis back and forth while in the hands-and-knees position (**FIGURE 13.3**). The use of pillows or a birthing ball for support can help alleviate strain on your arms and wrists over a long period of time.

Epidurals and Back Labor

While an epidural can provide much-needed pain relief for women experiencing back labor, it also has the potential to worsen the situation by relaxing the uterine floor and potentially allowing the baby to engage further into the pelvis in the posterior position. Talk to your provider now about her strategies for dealing with back labor should it occur.

FIGURE 13.3

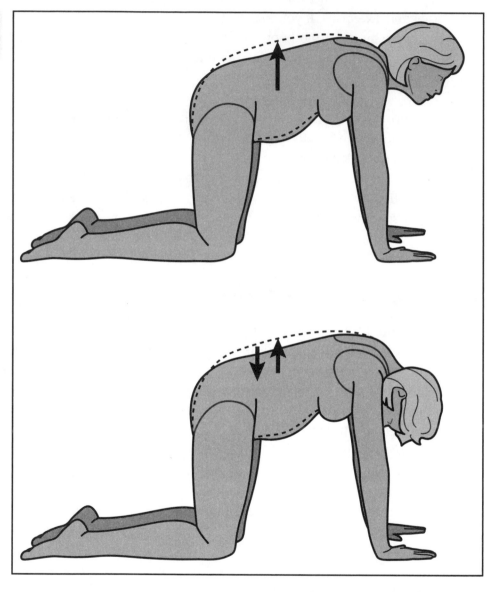

▲ Pelvic tilts can alleviate the pain of back labor and help encourage your baby to turn.

Time for Rest

Labor can be an exhausting affair, particularly if yours is a long one. If you are completely exhausted by the time you reach the second stage of labor, you may have a difficult time summoning enough strength to push effectively. It's not easy to sleep through contractions, particularly when they start coming close together, but you may be able to grab some small catnaps in between them early on. If you choose to have an epidural or other pharmaceutical pain relief, it can provide a much-needed respite for sleeping and regaining your strength.

Save Your Strength

One way to prevent complete exhaustion during the latter stages of labor is to save your strength early on. It's common for women, especially first-time moms, to want to walk a marathon and mow the lawn at the first twinges of contractions in an effort to speed things along. What often happens instead is that they end up exhausted and unable to marshal their strength when they really need it—during the second stage of labor. While some moderate physical activity is fine, don't overdo it and regret it later.

Once regular contractions begin, take a short nap if your comfort level will allow it. If labor begins in the middle of the night, but contractions are still far apart, try to go back to sleep. At the least, relax and take it easy for a bit, and store up your energy for the big task ahead.

Food and Drink in Labor

The same way rest can help recharge you for birth, taking nourishment can also help fuel your energy stores for the birth process. A light snack and plenty of fluids can keep you hydrated and powered up. If you do eat in labor, light, nonspicy, and easily digestible foods like broth, toast, crackers, and juice are your best bet.

Some hospitals and providers may restrict food and fluid intake because if an emergency situation arises and you require general anesthesia, there is a risk of aspiration of stomach contents, or vomit getting into the lungs. However, given that the vast majority of laboring women are not in a high-risk situation that would make cesarean and general anesthesia likely, a blanket policy banning food and drink in labor can do more harm than good.

Dehydration, discomfort, mental stress, and ketosis (ketones in the bloodstream) are all potential detrimental effects of banning any oral nourishment in labor. Intravenous fluids are given to help prevent dehydration in women who are not allowed to eat; however, IV fluids are more invasive and have their own set of risks (as described in Chapter 15).

Professional opinions on the food and drink issue differ. The American College of Obstetricians and Gynecologists advises that only small sips of water and ice chips be provided to laboring women and that women with long labors be given fluids intravenously, while the American College of Certified Nurse Midwives (ACNM) suggests that midwives allow their low-risk patients to listen to their bodies by "promot[ing] self-determination by healthy women experiencing normal labors as to appropriate intake."

FACT

"NPO" is the clinical acronym for *nil per os* (Latin for "nothing by mouth"). Hospitals have made NPO the norm for laboring women throughout the latter half of the twentieth century, despite the fact that general anesthesia is rarely used in childbirth today. At the very least, ice chips and water intake should be allowed as comfort measures for low-risk laboring women.

Reflecting these differing philosophies, you'll find that the policies on fluids and food by mouth are generally more liberal in nonhospital settings like the birthing center. Ask your provider and birth facility about their policies on food and drink in labor and the scientific rationale behind them so you can prepare and plan accordingly.

Pushing

Pushing is arguably the hardest task of labor (although some women may say transition is more difficult). Having enough energy to be up to the challenge is the key to effective pushing—another reason why rest in labor is so essential.

The best time for pushing is right at the peak of your contraction. You may be acutely aware of when that is, or you may need a little help from your provider and/or support person to get the timing down. If you've had an epidural or other anesthetic block, you will probably need some guidance to push at the right time.

The second stage of labor can last from minutes to hours. Women who have had a previous child usually have a shorter second stage than those who are first-time mothers. Because an epidural or other anesthetic block can make pushing less effective, women who have had an epidural are often allowed more time to push in the second stage of labor.

Vocalization can help you power up your pushing and reserve your strength. Use your voice to strengthen your efforts. Moaning, groaning, or grunting will also "remind" you to breathe, which is important since your baby is still depending on you for oxygen. Take a deep cleansing breath between pushes to keep your energy up. Some women will hold their breath briefly during the push, breathing deeply between contractions. Try not to hold your breath for too long—five seconds is probably a good rule of thumb. You can also try exhaling slowly during your pushes. This type of controlled pushing is less intense and can help prevent perineal tears.

Finally, focus only on the pushing and on seeing your baby. Do not worry about losing control. Women giving birth do urinate, defecate, and pass gas in the process. Your provider is quite used to encountering bodily fluids during the birth process, so don't let self-consciousness inhibit your pushing efforts. Before you know it, you will be well rewarded for all your hard work.

Birthing Positions

As previously mentioned, getting gravity on your side as you position yourself for birth is an excellent idea. Any upright or semiupright position—standing, leaning, walking, squatting, or sitting—can help move your baby in the right direction.

The rule of thumb in labor positions is if it feels good, do it. Experiment with different stances to see what works best for you. A doula or midwife can also be an invaluable source of suggestions for effective laboring positions. Here are some basic positions to try:

- **Squatting.** Assuming a squatting position, with the support of a person or birthing bar, can increase the diameter of the pelvic outlet and is a natural position for pushing.
- **Chair sitting.** Sitting on a birthing stool, chair, or toilet can help relax your perineum and pelvis.
- **Kneeling.** Getting on your knees and leaning against pillows, your support person, or a chair for support may ease back pain.
- **Standing or leaning.** Staying upright with a partner or support person to lean against can help. Some women find rocking or other rhythmic movement in this position a calming influence.

Squatting is one of the most effective positions you can use in labor and birth. It allows gravity to work in your favor during the pushing phase of labor and opens up your pelvic outlet another one to two centimeters. Just keep in mind that your provider needs to be able to both see and properly support the baby's emerging head to prevent tearing or birth trauma. The use of a birth stool is sometimes helpful in maintaining a squatting position, as the stool allows your midwife or doctor to see your vaginal opening adequately.

If a birthing stool or a squatting bar is not available for you to use as support as you assume a squatting position, a well-placed partner or chair for support can serve the same purpose. If you do choose this position for birth, be aware that because it usually shortens the pushing phase and speeds your baby's descent, there is a risk of perineal tearing. An experienced midwife or birth attendant can often prevent this with proper support, however.

The lithotomy, or flat-on-your-back, position is actually quite ineffective for labor and birth. Your heavy uterus is pressing down on the vena cava, a major blood vessel, and potentially lowering your blood pressure and your baby's oxygen supply. You also have no help from gravity. Placing your legs in metal stirrups can make matters worse by putting pressure on your tailbone and narrowing your pelvic outlet. Still, some providers prefer this position because it allows them to see the baby's emerging head better. A modified lithotomy, called McRobert's position, may also be useful in cases of shoulder dystocia by increasing the diameter of your pelvic outlet.

Chapter 14

Managing Pain: The Options

Labor and birth pain is in the eye of the beholder, and every woman will have a different perception of just how comfortable her birth experience is. Anxiety and fear over childbirth and anticipated "unbearable" pain can actually make your birth more painful. In addition, factors beyond your control, such as the presentation or positioning of your soon-to-be-born babe, can also impact your comfort level. Fortunately, there are many natural and pharmaceutical options available for soothing labor discomforts.

Choosing Your Weapons

Many first-time moms are under the impression that childbirth is either natural and painful or medicated and tolerable. The fact is that there are a number of pain-relief options available to today's laboring woman—both drug-free and pharmaceutical—ranging from meditation and massage to nitrous oxide and narcotics.

Prepared childbirth education classes are an excellent source of information on pain management options and will help you reach an informed decision about which methods you want to try in labor. Talk to other women who have been through birth about what pain-relief methods they found effective. Keep in mind, however, that what was right for them may not necessarily be what you're looking for out of your birth experience.

Use your partner or support person as your buffer against the outside world, in order to allow yourself to concentrate completely on the task at hand. Having positive, supportive people at your birth will reduce your anxiety level and therefore improve your overall sense of comfort and well-being during labor and delivery.

Movement and Positioning

The easiest drug-free way to increase your comfort level is to get moving. Walk down the hall or around the room, and experiment with different positions that may ease the pain, such as on all fours, squatting with support from a partner, or kneeling while leaning over a bed or chair. A rocking chair may provide some comfort and help you relax. If it feels good—do it. Many women also find it is helpful to have body pillows and birthing balls available for sitting on, leaning over, or supporting themselves.

If you want to walk in labor and are delivering in a birth center or hospital, talk to your provider about the fetal-monitoring policy of the facility. If it's standard protocol to have you hooked up to a monitor for the duration of your labor, it could put a roadblock in your walking plans. Some facilities may have wireless monitoring units that use telemetry to transmit baby's signals to a base unit. If those aren't available, request intermittent fetal monitoring, which involves periodic checks rather than continuous observation.

There's really no reason a woman with a low-risk birth can't have intermittent fetal monitoring and be allowed to walk as she wants. In fact, the American College of Obstetricians and Gynecologists says that intermittent fetal monitoring is just as safe and effective as continuous monitoring. An IV line could also cramp your style, but at least you can push an IV around on a rolling pole, which may actually be good support for you as you do your laps.

QUESTION?

Will walking the hospital hallways help to shorten my labor?
Clinical studies are inconclusive as to whether walking can help shorten your labor time, but it is known that many women find walking both physically and emotionally more soothing than being stuck in a bed. In addition, the forces of gravity will be working with you if you choose to walk in labor, helping your baby out with her descent.

Relaxation and Visualization

The idea of relaxing while your uterus is clenching like a fist may sound like a hopeless cause. But, used properly, relaxation techniques between contractions can help reduce any mental anxiety and make pain more manageable, particularly in early labor.

The best way to get the most out of relaxation exercises during labor is to use them often during pregnancy so they become second nature. Progressive relaxation, which is a series of muscle tightening and release exercises, should be practiced in a comfortable and quiet room where you can lie down. Recline with your head and back elevated, either on a bed with pillows behind you or in a reclining chair. Starting from your head and working down to your toes, tense and then release each muscle group. Inhale with the tension, and exhale with the release. As you breathe in and out, try to clear your mind of all thoughts but the sensation of tension and release.

There are many relaxation tapes available on the market, and Appendix B offers resources for relaxation exercises.

Guided imagery, or visualization, can help to control labor pain by giving you a sense of control or mastery over the pain itself. The exercise is a two-part process that builds on relaxation techniques. The first component involves achieving a state of deep relaxation through the breathing and muscle relaxation techniques already described.

After you are relaxed, the second part of the process—the actual imagery exercise—comes into play. Use your imagination to turn your pain into something less frightening and more easily controlled. For example, you may think of your contraction pain as brightly burning lamp. Through guided imagery, you can imagine yourself controlling the switch that slowly dims the lamp, extinguishing your pain perception.

Mental rehearsal is another visualization technique to use during pregnancy. Mental rehearsal can help you handle anxiety about the upcoming labor. This technique involves repeatedly visualizing yourself during labor and birth, successfully delivering your child without anxiety, pain, or stress.

Vocalization is a good tool for riding through your contractions and reducing stress. Low groaning, humming, or chanting through the peak of a contraction helps many women cope with and feel some control over the pain; screaming or high-pitched vocalizations can have the opposite effect and promote tension. Don't be self-conscious about vocalizing. Even the most self-reserved women find that any tendency toward shyness pretty much flies out the window with that first big contraction.

Breathing Techniques

Boiling water and funny breathing have to be the two biggest clichés of childbirth. Every woman (and man) who has ever turned on a television knows that a panting pregnant woman is a sure sign of imminent childbirth, and that the first thing to do when labor strikes is to boil plenty of water. But unlike the boiling water, which is only helpful if you're craving a cup of tea, breathing can play a very important role in guiding your concentration and making your pain manageable in labor.

Lamaze is a big proponent of patterned breathing. There are several types of breathing taught in Lamaze, each with a different purpose. (See Chapter 6 for an overview.) Breathing techniques are often used in combination with imagery to achieve deeper relaxation. Having a focal point to look at during breathing exercises—either a pleasing photo or simply a chosen place somewhere in the birth room—can help with concentration.

Lamaze isn't the only childbirth philosophy that teaches controlled respiration; the Bradley Method advocates abdominal breathing for relaxation. Most childbirth preparation classes involve some sort of breathing exercises. Practice at home so it becomes second nature by the time your birth arrives. While breathing won't magically eliminate pain, it will give you a greater sense of control, keep you focused and relaxed, and make the pain more manageable.

ALERT!

Rapid, shallow breathing in labor is a sign of hyperventilation, which can reduce the oxygen supply to your baby. Using specific breathing techniques during labor and delivery can help to minimize the risk of hyperventilation occurring. If it does happen, breathing into a paper bag can help stop hyperventilation quickly; have your labor support partner pack one just in case.

Warmth and Water

Many women find that hydrotherapy—the use of water to reduce labor pain—can be a potent tool. The massaging action of showers, the buoyancy of a birthing pool, and the combined action of both in a whirlpool tub can relax your body and mind. Hot and cold packs can also work wonders on localized pain in lower back, perineum, and abdomen.

The soothing relief of warmth and water can be particularly helpful in cases of back labor, when the back of your baby's head places pressure on your spine. (See Chapter 13 for more information on back labor.) If you're having back labor, a series of injections of sterile water papules under the skin in the base of your spine (the sacrum) can also provide pain relief.

This technique, sometimes called a water block, works by effectively "shorting out" the nerve pathways carrying the pain signals in the spine with the sting of the injections themselves. Because medication is not involved, an anesthesiologist is not required to perform the procedure—your healthcare provider should be able to administer it for you.

Water Therapy Options

A shower with a directional showerhead can provide warm, pulsating massage relief to your back, abdomen, and any other painful areas of your body during labor. The shower should have a support bar to ensure steady balance. Some women prefer to sit on a stool or supported birthing ball in the shower.

The "weightless" environment of a birthing pool can help ease contractions, and many women find that having warm water all around them, not unlike the environment of their fetus, is a calming and comfortable environment for labor. (See Chapter 10 for more on birthing pools.) Whirlpools offer the massaging action of showers along with the added buoyancy of a pool or tub. Water should be no warmer than body temperature to avoid putting stress on the fetus.

FACT

TENS therapy, also known as transcutaneous electrical nerve stimulation, is used by some women for pain relief in birth. Electrode patches are applied to your spine and connected via wires to a small TENS unit. The unit transmits electrical impulses through the skin, which feel like a slight tingling or buzzing. TENS works by boosting your body's production of endorphins and blocking pain signals. However, it can take some time to build effectiveness, and some women may find the technique limiting because the electrodes cannot get wet.

Using Compresses

Alternating hot-and-cold compresses on the back or abdomen can also provide good pain relief. Cold packs can numb a particularly painful area;

hot-water bottles or heating pads can soothe sore muscles. And warm, moist compresses on the perineum serve the dual purpose of easing discomfort and helping to promote elasticity of the perineal area for birth. Make sure compresses are comfortably warm, not hot; hot compresses can cause swelling and increase the risk of perineal tears and should be avoided.

Massage

A good backrub can be a godsend during labor. If your partner or labor support person isn't talented in the art of massage, simple tools like a tennis ball in a sock or a small rolling pin can help improve his technique. You can also purchase massage tools, either manual or electronic, from many retailers. Sometimes a simple foot rub can help reduce your stress level and therefore improve your comfort. Certain massage oils can add the extra benefit of heat to the rub; make sure the smell agrees with you beforehand, though.

A technique known as counterpressure can be particularly helpful in cases of back labor. Counterpressure is simply pressing down firmly on areas that are causing pain. Make sure you give your support person feedback on what feels good and what doesn't, and try a few practice sessions before the big event.

Systemic Analgesics

Analgesics work by depressing the nervous system and therefore lessening the sensation of pain. They do not render you unconscious, although they may render you silly. The narcotics meperidine (Demerol), nalbuphine (Nubain), butorphanol (Stadol), and fentanyl (Sublimaze) are all analgesic drugs that are commonly used to relieve labor pain.

QUESTION?

What's the difference between an analgesic and an anesthetic?
An analgesic reduces pain, but doesn't eliminate it completely, while an anesthetic removes sensation, and therefore pain, completely. Both can be effective tools in management of labor pain.

Analgesics are administered as an injection. When used at the right point in labor and in the correct dosage, analgesics will not cause your baby any serious side effects. However, because analgesics do cross the placenta, the administration of narcotics too late in labor can cause sluggishness in baby that can result in low blood oxygen levels and difficulty latching on and sucking during after-birth breastfeeding attempts. They can also decrease normal variability patterns in the fetal heart rate.

Blocks and Epidurals

Regional anesthesia is a drug that numbs or deadens the sensation in a specific portion of the body. Unlike narcotics, which can make you feel sleepy or stoned, a regional anesthetic like a spinal block or epidural leaves you mentally alert. According to the Mayo Clinic, an estimated 2.4 million women who give birth in the Unites States each year receive an epidural for pain management.

Because epidurals and blocks can slow labor, some providers may strongly suggest that you reach a certain dilation benchmark (usually four to five centimeters) before receiving one. However, ACOG has issued a statement saying that the standard of practice should be that an epidural is never denied to any woman in labor who requests one for pain control, no matter how far she is dilated. Women who have their labor induced may have more severe contractions before significant dilation even occurs, and often find a need for epidural relief well before the four-centimeter mark. It's a good idea to discuss any concerns about epidural timing with your health-care provider before the birth.

Lumbar Epidural

The most common type of regional anesthetic used in labor is a lumbar epidural, which temporarily deadens the nerves from your navel to your knees. If you decide to have an epidural, an anesthesiologist will be called in to administer it. The procedure takes just a few minutes to complete. You will be asked to roll over on your side or sit at the edge of the bed to expose your lower back, which will be swabbed with an antiseptic solution to prevent infection. The anesthesiologist will then insert a thin plastic catheter into the area between your fourth and fifth vertebrae, which is called the epidural space. Once in place, the catheter is taped down and the anesthetic is injected into it. You can then assume a more comfortable position.

FACT

There are a variety of regional anesthetics that can be used in epidurals for labor and birth; two of the most common drugs are bupivacaine (Sensorcaine) and ropivacaine (Naropin). The anesthetics work by blocking the nerve impulses that regulate sensation and pain. They are sometimes administered in combination with epinephrine, which speeds the onset and prolongs the efficacy of the anesthetic, or with a narcotic analgesic such as fentanyl (Sublimaze).

If you weren't hooked up to an intravenous line and saline drip already, one will be started prior to the epidural. The epidural can cause hypotension (low blood pressure), so having the IV in place can not only keep your fluid volume up but also provides easy access for an injection of drugs to treat you should your blood pressure drop dangerously low. You will also be encouraged to keep your head elevated, as lying flat on your back could make hypotension worse. If you were not having continuous fetal monitoring before the epidural, you will start now.

A lumbar epidural takes about twenty minutes to fully take effect. Once it does, the numbness lasts several hours. While the epidural deadens the nerves, it has no effect on the involuntary muscles that control your contractions, which will continue even though you may now be blissfully unaware of them.

Walking Epidurals

For those who want the pain relief of an epidural, but aren't interested in being confined to their hospital beds, there is an option. A low-dose combined spinal epidural, more commonly known as a walking epidural, numbs the same area as a standard lumbar epidural but allows you to retain enough sensation to move around and walk. This type of epidural is administered with a fine needle that is guided through the epidural catheter and into the spinal fluid (not the epidural space), where anesthetic medication is injected.

Let your anesthesiologist know if you have had any bad experiences with anesthesia in the past. You should also feel free to ask any questions (or designate your partner to ask questions) about a block or epidural procedure before it begins. If you're having a scheduled cesarean, your anesthesiologist should stop by for a brief visit as part of your prep to answer any questions you might have.

Spinal Block

A spinal block is used in cesarean delivery to numb the area from your waist down. A dose of anesthetic is injected into your lower back into the fluid-filled space that cushions your spinal column, known as the intrathecal space (a spinal block is sometimes called an intrathecal for this reason). Much faster than an epidural, a spinal block takes effect almost immediately. Spinal block may also be used in cases of an assisted birth to relieve any pain associated with forceps use.

Possible Pitfalls

So are there downsides to an epidural? Some clinical studies have found that the first and second stages of labor are often prolonged with an epidural, especially in women who are giving birth for the first time. However, other studies have not noted a statistically significant difference in labor times for women having an epidural, so further research is needed to investigate any adverse effects of epidurals on length of labor.

Epidural use has also been associated with an increased use of oxytocin in labor and with a greater incidence of forceps use, particularly when epidural anesthesia is administered after eight centimeters of cervical dilation. Epidurals can also cause elevated body temperatures in both mother and child. And, as with any procedure that punctures the skin, there is a risk of infection with an epidural or a spinal block.

There is conflicting evidence as to whether or not epidural use increases your chance of cesarean; some retrospective studies have found an association, while other studies have not.

Another potential drawback is the possibility of a postdural puncture headache (often called a PDPH). This severe headache occurs when the dura that sheaths the cerebral spinal fluid (CSF) around the spinal column is unintentionally punctured and fluid starts to leak into the epidural space. The resulting drop in spinal fluid pressure is what triggers the headache, which usually gets worse upon standing.

FACT

In the United Kingdom and Europe, nitrous oxide (Entonox, or "laughing gas") is commonly used to provide pain relief and reduce anxiety in labor. Because it has a short half-life, can be controlled by the laboring woman, and doesn't impact the fetus, it is often a desirable alternative to other forms of pharmaceutical pain relief. However, nitrous has a delayed effect, so it must be breathed in about a minute prior to a contraction in order to be effective, making its use somewhat more difficult.

Postdural puncture headache is more common in spinal blocks because it is easier for the dura to be unintentionally punctured in that procedure. However, the size and type of needle used and the technique with which the needle insertion is done have an influence on whether or not you develop CSF leakage. If you do get a PDPH, rest and rehydration can usually resolve the problem. In some cases an injection of blood into the epidural space, called a blood patch, may be required to seal the puncture site and stop the leakage.

Other Regional Blocks

Other less common regional blocks sometimes used to relieve labor pain include a paracervical block, which involves an injection into your cervix, and a caudal block, which is injected into the tailbone and numbs your abdominal and pelvic muscles.

In situations when your baby needs a little help coming out, you may be a candidate for another type of regional anesthetic block used at delivery. A pudendal block, which deadens the nerves in the pelvic floor and vagina, or a saddle block, which numbs your perineum, bottom, and inner thighs, may be given to provide pain relief if an episiotomy or a forceps or vacuum extraction is required.

Give Yourself Choices

As you can see, every method of pain relief has its pros and cons. You must weigh the risks and benefits in light of your particular birth needs and come to your own conclusions about what's right for you. Although you may have made some general decisions about how you'd like to handle labor pain on the birth day, give yourself permission to change your mind—without guilt—at any time. For first-time moms, making a cast-in-stone commitment to one pain-management method now is like buying a car without a test drive. And even if you've been through labor and delivery before, this time around may be completely different.

Don't let the emotions and attitudes of others influence your decisions, either. You are the one having this baby. If your sister thinks you're nuts for not wanting an epidural or if your neighbor looks down her nose at you because you aren't interested in natural birth, remind yourself (and them too, if you're so inclined) that this is your show and you'll do what's best for you and your child. And by all means, keep that kind of negative energy away during birth. Backseat drivers in the labor and delivery room will do nothing but breed stress and anxiety.

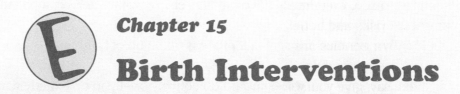

Chapter 15

Birth Interventions

Along with the pain relief options discussed in the previous chapter, a twenty-first century woman has a dizzying array of technology at her disposal to employ in the birth process. Yet labor and birth remain, in essence, completely natural processes that women have been experiencing forever without the aid of monitors, synthetic induction, or extraction tools. Knowing what is available, and more importantly, when interventions are necessary versus when they are simply prophylactic, is essential to making informed decisions at your birth.

Informed Consent

In simplest terms, informed consent is making sure you as a patient fully understand a given medical intervention and any risks associated with it well enough to make an informed decision on whether or not to agree to the procedure. Unless you are mentally or physically incapacitated for some unforeseen reason, you ultimately have the final say on what interventions are used or not used in your birth.

Ideally, informed consent is a process made up of three major steps.

1. **Education.** Your provider should objectively brief you on exactly what the intervention entails, and explain the risks and benefits to the procedure in laymen's terms.
2. **Alternatives.** Your provider should inform you of any possible alternatives to the intervention, along with the pros and cons of each.
3. **Assessment.** Your provider should ensure that you've understood everything that was just explained and ask if you have any questions before you make your decision.

In practice, the process of obtaining informed consent may be colored by a provider's own beliefs or personal agenda, either consciously or subconsciously. Fears of malpractice or liability issues, provider care preferences, and even scheduling issues can influence the process. This is why it is so important for a woman to learn all she can about the pros and cons of interventional procedures before birth. Informed consent is much easier to give, or deny, if your first lesson about a given procedure happens well before birth rather than in a potentially stressful environment or emergency situation.

When you are preparing your birth plan, keep in mind that unexpected emergencies may come up. Along with educating yourself about emergency procedures, don't be afraid to ask your provider about potential situations and come up with possible game plans. A frank discussion about birth plans should always include mention of the fact that no one can predict what will happen, and that last-minute changes of plan are not uncommon.

Preparatory Procedures

Intervention choices may begin in early in labor when you first enter a birth facility. Prepping procedures will vary depending on facility policy and your provider's preferences. The following sections discuss some prep procedures that you may potentially encounter.

To Shave or Not to Shave

Although the practice is much less common than it once was, a few hospitals still perform a shave of the perineal and/or pubic area. The rationale is that it improves visibility and minimizes infection. If your hospital advocates the shaving routine and you'd rather avoid being shaved, you can either do it at home yourself, if you prefer, or discuss the possibility of not having this largely unnecessary procedure.

Formal Attire

If giving birth at a hospital, you'll be handed that old favorite, the backdraft hospital gown, to put on after admission. While the back opening can allow an anesthesiologist easy access for an epidural or other anesthetic block, it can be uncomfortable and embarrassing for many women. Ask about wearing your own nightgown from home, or bring a robe along for extra coverage.

Enema Anyone?

An enema before birth can help clean out your bowels and theoretically will make the trip down the birth canal easier for your little one, which is why some hospitals still use them as part of their prepping procedure. However, enemas can also be uncomfortable and unnecessary. The fact is that contractions will naturally loosen your bowels, and many women have spent a great deal of time on the toilet already during early labor, emptying them the standard way. If you feel you don't really need an enema and the hospital offers one, explain that you're already covered in that department.

FACT

Having a bowel movement, or two, during the pushing phase of labor is a common occurrence. Don't be mortified if it happens to you—any health-care provider who has attended a birth has been exposed to all sorts of bodily fluids during the birth process. If you're really embarrassed by the possibility of this scenario, you can always choose to have an enema in early labor.

Locks and Lines

Some hospitals may insert what is known as a heparin or saline lock into your arm as standard procedure. The lock is simply a needle encased in a plastic hub that is inserted into a vein and attached to your arm with surgical tape. A small amount of saline or heparin, a blood thinner, is then flushed through the lock to prevent clotting. If intravenous medication is suddenly needed in labor, the lock provides easy access. An intravenous line, or IV, can be attached to the lock at any point. If you have the lock on for more than eight hours without any attached tubing, it may be flushed periodically to prevent clotting.

Other facilities may start you on an IV at admission to keep you hydrated. Medication can also be added to the IV if necessary. If yours isn't considered a high-risk birth and you don't want an IV, there's really no reason you can't hydrate yourself the old-fashioned way—by drinking fluids. For more on the issue of food and drink in labor, see Chapter 13.

Intravenous lines are not without risk. As with any procedure that penetrates the skin, they have the potential to introduce bacteria and cause infection, although proper sterile procedure can greatly minimize the chances of this occurring. In addition, if a glucose drip is given to a laboring mother, there is an increased risk of hypoglycemia (low blood sugar) for the baby at birth. It can also cause electrolyte imbalances such as hyponatremia (sodium depletion), in mother and child. Any type of intravenous fluid drip also introduces a risk of fluid overload in a laboring woman if not managed properly.

Finally, if you're having a cesarean section or having an epidural or another type of anesthetic block that will give you no muscle control over your urine flow, you'll require a urinary catheter. You can ask for insertion of the catheter, an uncomfortable business, after the anesthetic has been administered.

A full bladder in labor can keep your baby from descending properly, as well as being just plain uncomfortable. If you can and wish to make it to the bathroom on your own, include that in your birth plan. Otherwise you may be using a bedpan or, in cases where you have an anesthetic block, require catheterization.

Fetal Monitoring

During labor, an electronic fetal monitor is used to monitor your baby's heart rate (fetal heart rate, or FHR) and your contractions (uterine activity, or UA) to ensure that labor is progressing normally. The monitor will also alert your provider to excessive fetal stress from oxygen deprivation or umbilical cord problems. Some fetal monitoring units measure your blood pressure and heart rate as well as fetal blood oxygen levels.

On the down side, continuous electronic fetal monitoring has been associated with an increased incidence of C-section and operative delivery such as forceps or episiotomy birth, and all the associated risks of those procedures.

If you're having a home or birthing center birth, you may have the option of having your baby's heart rate monitored with a fetoscope, a stethoscope, or a handheld Doppler device like the one your provider may have used during prenatal checkups. (These devices are also used in hospitals, although not as frequently.) Using these devices, the FHR is taken after a contraction, and your provider will monitor it for a full minute, counting the beats in each five-second interval until he has twelve sets of five-second FHR samples to ensure that the variability of the heart rate is "reassuring." This technique, called intermittent auscultation, may be preferred by women who don't like the restrictions of traditional electronic fetal monitoring.

Internal and External

With external fetal monitoring, two belts are positioned on your abdomen—one low and one higher—to measure the FHR and UA. A small sensor called a transducer is on the skin-side of each of the belts. The transducers pick up the heartbeat and contractions and transfer the information back to the base unit.

The base unit provides a visual representation of the FHR and your contractions on a computer screen. The base unit may also print out a paper strip of tracings that provides a hard copy of the progress of your labor, a good practice if health-care providers are attending to other labors and are in and out of your birth room.

If you are given oxytocin (Pitocin) to induce labor or strengthen contractions, it's quite possible the provider and/or facility will require continuous fetal monitoring, which will keep you in bed. Again, talk to your provider well in advance of your due date so if oxytocin is offered during your birth, you'll know the potential perks and pitfalls.

If yours is a high-risk pregnancy and your amniotic sac has broken, an internal monitor may be recommended. An internal monitor uses the same base unit, but instead of belt transducers, a tiny spring-like coil of wire is inserted vaginally. The coil is inserted just under the skin on the baby's scalp and provides an electrocardiographic (ECG) analysis of the FHR. Internal monitoring is almost exclusively used in a hospital setting, and women who are internally monitored are generally restricted to their beds. If you have concerns about the possibility of internal monitoring, talk with your provider about the circumstances under which it might be required and what your options are.

Maintaining Mobility

The downside of continuous monitoring is that it keeps you confined to a hospital bed and restricts your movement. In most normal labor situations, continuous fetal monitoring is not necessary. A quick monitor check every fifteen to thirty minutes (depending on your stage of labor), called intermittent fetal monitoring, should be sufficient if you wish to remain mobile in labor.

Another option is going wireless. Many birth facilities offer fetal monitors that employ telemetry, a technology that allows you to move about without having to be physically connected to the main base unit. There are even some waterproof telemetry units on the market with transducers that can withstand a dunk in the tub, shower, or birthing pool.

Induction of Labor

If you are one week or more past your due date, your provider may suggest induction. Other indications that your labor process may need jump-starting include premature rupture of membranes (PROM, or breaking of your "bag of waters" or amniotic sac), abruptio placentae (placental separation from the uterine wall), fetal distress, and preeclampsia/eclampsia.

FACT

It's important to note that only an estimated 5 percent of births actually occur on the due date, and many women cannot determine their date of conception with absolute certainty, so due dates are far from concrete. A more accurate determination of whether or not your baby has outstayed his welcome in the womb is his size and level of amniotic fluid present (determined by ultrasound).

A full-term gestation is considered to be thirty-seven to forty-two weeks, or three weeks before and two weeks after your due date. If you go one week past your due date, your provider might recommend some fetal monitoring, including a nonstress test to look at the baby's heart rate and an ultrasound to examine the level of amniotic fluid around the baby. This combination of monitoring and ultrasound is referred to as a biophysical profile. If your nonstress test or amniotic fluid is abnormal, you may be offered an induction of labor.

Inducing labor involves not only stimulating uterine contractions but also ripening the cervix for baby's passage. If the cervix isn't adequately effaced (thinned) and dilated (opened), the chance of interventions increases. There are several methods at your provider's disposal to get the labor ball rolling.

Natural Inducement

Your midwife or doctor may suggest stripping your membranes. Membrane stripping, or sweeping, is the manual separation of the amniotic membrane from your cervix. Your provider will insert her finger into the cervix and sweep it gently from side to side, separating the membrane from the uterine wall. Sweeping the membranes releases natural prostaglandins, which help to ripen your cervix for labor.

Current FDA standards do not require herbal preparations to meet the same stringent quality and potency standards that prescription and over-the-counter drugs must meet. If your midwife suggests the use of herbs for induction, make sure the preparations she uses are manufactured under USP (United States Pharmacopeial) quality guidelines. Supplements or herbs with a USP designation have met specific purity, strength, and manufacturing requirements as defined in the USP National Formulary (or USP-NF).

Another method that may speed the onset of labor is breaking your amniotic membrane (or "bag of waters"). If you choose this method, your provider will use an amniohook, a long instrument with a blunt hook on the end, not unlike a crochet hook, to break the amniotic sac. If you do decide to let your provider perform amniotomy, you should keep in mind that if labor does not start naturally within twenty-four hours, a scheduled induction with Pitocin may be required because of the risk of infection. In some cases, a Pitocin intravenous drip may be started at the time the membranes are artificially ruptured.

Some midwives also use herbal preparations to stimulate uterine contractions. Blue and black cohosh, red raspberry leaves, and pennyroyal are sometimes used by midwives as induction agents, and evening primrose oil may be recommended as a topical agent for cervical ripening. Be aware that some herbs can cause potent contractions that may not be safe in your particular pregnancy. Never take herbal supplements without first consulting your health-care provider.

Nipple stimulation triggers the release of the hormones prostaglandin and oxytocin and may help get the contractions going in women with a favorable cervix. It shouldn't be done for more than a few minutes at a time, however, as too much stimulation has the potential to cause oxygen deprivation to the fetus.

Other natural induction methods that are used but have sparse to no clinical evidence to back their efficacy include the following:

- Castor oil by mouth
- A brisk and/or lengthy walk
- Spicy foods
- Sexual intercourse (semen contains prostaglandin and orgasm contracts the uterus)
- Masturbation

In most cases, natural induction methods won't have any effect unless your cervix is already ripened and baby is ready to arrive. Keep that in mind before mixing your castor-oil cocktail, and always talk to your doctor or midwife before trying any of these methods.

Mechanical Inducement

If your cervix is not ripening and induction is scheduled, your provider may suggest using a mechanical device to slowly dilate the cervical opening. There are several types of dilation devices used. A hygroscopic dilator is a thin tube of synthetic or natural material placed in the cervical opening. As it absorbs moisture, it expands, naturally opening up the cervix. This type of dilator is inserted much like a tampon, and because it works gradually it causes minimal discomfort compared to some other methods of mechanical dilation.

FACT

Most providers will allow the external portion of the balloon catheter to hang loose or, if they want to keep it out of the way, will tape it to the patient's leg with slack in the line. However, some feel that putting the catheter on traction (taping the catheter to the thigh so the line is taut) will increase its effect.

A Foley catheter is a catheter with a balloon attached to the end. The catheter is inserted through the cervical opening and the balloon is inflated to allow the catheter to remain in place. The balloon sits inside the uterus and acts as an irritant to increase the secretion of prostaglandins. This has an effect similar to continuously stripping the membranes.

Pharmaceutical Inducement

Prior to a scheduled induction, your provider may have you come in for one or more applications of prostaglandin gel on your cervix. The gel is applied to your cervix in either a vaginal insert or with a swab that is inserted into your vagina. Prostaglandin gel helps to ripen your cervix and may actually induce labor in some cases. For this reason, your baby's heart rate will be assessed during the gel application and for a period of time afterward.

A scheduled induction using Pitocin—a synthetic version of the hormone oxytocin—will take place in a hospital setting. Pitocin is administered via an intravenous drip. It stimulates intense contractions, so you will probably be hooked up to a fetal monitor to keep an eye on your baby's heart rate as the contractions start.

Mifepristone may be better known as RU-486, approved by the FDA in 2000 to chemically terminate early pregnancy as part of a treatment regimen that also includes the administration of misoprostol (Cytotec) to stimulate uterine contractions. This drug combination is widely used as an induction and cervical ripening treatment, although it is not FDA-approved for this "off-label" use.

Other pharmaceutical agents sometimes used to ripen the cervix and induce labor include the antiprogesterone mifepristone (Mifeprex, used to stimulate contractions) and the synthetic prostaglandin misoprostol (Cytotec, used for cervical ripening). It is important to note, however, that neither of these agents is FDA-approved for use as an induction agent (although some providers do use them as such), and their long-term effects have not yet been sufficiently studied. Misoprostol, in particular, has been found to cause hyperstimulation of the uterus when given in too large a dose. The ACOG does, however, endorse the use of both drugs in circumstances of uncomplicated regular vaginal birth. If you're being induced, it's important to speak with your provider about his "agent of choice" and discuss the risks and benefits. Women with a prior cesarean section are not candidates for certain induction agents due to the increased risk of uterine rupture.

Breech Babies

If your baby is in a breech presentation (not head down) at birth, your provider may suggest one of several options: trying to manually turn the baby (external cephalic version), performing a cesarean, or delivering the baby vaginally in the breech position.

Turning the Baby

External cephalic version, which involves manually attempting to turn the fetus in the uterus, may be performed at thirty-seven weeks or later if your baby is in the breech position and you have an adequate amount of amniotic fluid present. The procedure usually takes place in a hospital setting, and you may be given medication to relax your uterine muscles. Your provider will manipulate your abdomen with her hands, under ultrasound guidance, in an attempt to move the fetus into a head-down position (**FIGURE 15.1**).

Version should not be attempted before thirty-seven weeks because of the risk of preterm labor and the possibility of the baby returning to its breech position if version is performed too far from the due date. There are some risks to version, including the possibility of placental abruption and preterm labor, but they are relatively rare.

FIGURE 15.1

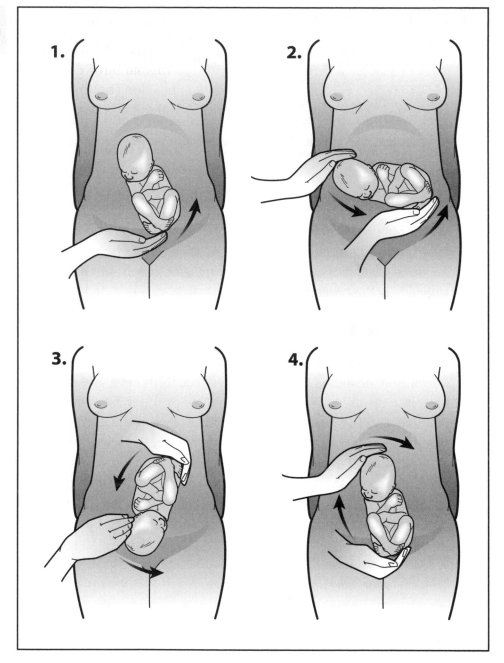

▲ Manual manipulation of the abdomen may successfully turn a breech baby. Images 1-3 show the steps in a manual forward roll, image 4 shows a manual backward roll.

Giving Birth Breech

If your baby is breech at the time labor begins, it does not automatically mean you must have a cesarean section. Vaginal birth may be an option for you if your baby is in the frank breech position (bottom down with feet up near the head) or a complete breech without a presenting foot (**FIGURE 15.2**). Some providers will only agree to a vaginal delivery of a breech if you have already successfully delivered a prior baby vaginally. It's possible that your provider may agree to a trial of labor, which may help your baby turn head down.

FIGURE 15.2

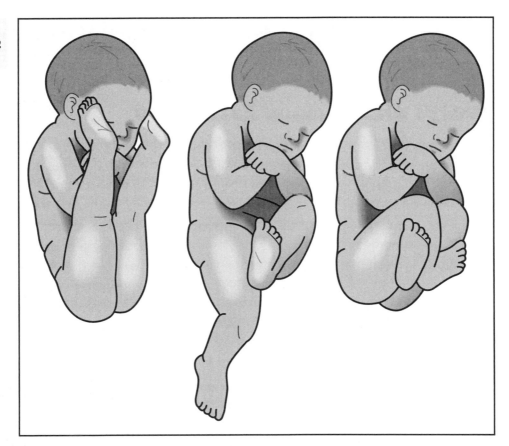

▲ The frank, incomplete, and complete breech positions.

A vaginal breech birth requires an experienced practitioner who has delivered breech babies successfully before. Ask your doctor or midwife what her personal success rate is with vaginal breech births. Even with the expertise of a good provider, risks to the fetus still exist. In a breech birth, the head is not leading the way to stretch the perineum and birth canal, a process which also molds the still-malleable fetal skull for easier passage. As a result, there's a possibility the fetal head can become stuck and your provider will need to use forceps or vacuum extraction to help your baby out.

Fetal injury is also a risk. Clinical studies have found that overall fetal mortality is higher with planned vaginal breech birth than with planned cesarean breech birth; the American College of Obstetricians and Gynecologists recommends that a fetus that is breech be delivered by planned cesarean whenever possible.

Forceps and Vacuum Extraction

If your baby needs assistance emerging from the birth canal, forceps or vacuum extraction may be recommended. Forceps, which are similar in appearance to a large set of tongs, are placed into the birth canal and locked into position around the baby's head. Your provider will gently pull the head out in tandem with your pushes. This application of forceps is referred to as "low forceps use." Low forceps may also be used to reposition a baby who is in a poor position for delivery. The other type of forceps use—"outlet forceps"—is employed in cases where the baby is right at the perineum and only needs to be lifted up and out. Your doctor may suggest an episiotomy if he thinks forceps use is indicated.

QUESTION?

The doctor used forceps to deliver my child and she has red marks on her head. Will they go away?

It's common for babies delivered with forceps to sport bruises or red marks on their heads after birth. Likewise, babies born with the assistance of vacuum extraction can have a bruised, swollen appearance. Your newborn should be back to normal in a few days.

Your provider may also opt for vacuum extraction. A vacuum extractor is a metal or soft plastic cup attached to a chain or long handle. An attached suction device enables the cup to attach to the fetal head. After the cup has been attached, the provider pulls on the cup as you push your baby out with contractions. The provider controls the level of suction, and the cup is designed to automatically detach if excessive pressure builds up. Once the head is delivered, the cup is removed. An injection of anesthetic block may be administered into the perineal area to ease your discomfort before forceps or a vacuum extractor is used.

Possible complications of vacuum extraction include lacerations of the fetal scalp and, less commonly but more serious, intracranial hemorrhage (bleeding within the baby's skull). Forceps use carries a slight risk of fetal brain injury as well as risk of injury to the perineal tissues of the mother.

Episiotomy

Episiotomy is the surgical incision of the perineum—the area between your vagina and your anus—in order to facilitate the passage of your baby's head during the final pushing stage of birth. The perineum, however, is an amazingly pliable piece of tissue, and the majority of women find it can stretch to accommodate their babies' heads without the need of episiotomy.

FACT

Several studies have shown a dramatic drop in episiotomy rates since the early 1980s, yet episiotomy continues to be one of the most frequently performed surgical procedures that women undergo. The ACOG does not endorse the practice of "routine episiotomy" without valid medical indications.

Types of Episiotomy

The midline episiotomy involves an incision from the vagina out toward the anus. The mediolateral episiotomy uses an incision that starts at the vagina but extends out diagonally instead of directly toward the anus to avoid rectal tearing.

The size of both episiotomy incisions and perineal tears are referred to in degrees to indicate their severity. A first-degree tear would be the most superficial, and a fourth-degree the most severe. See the following table for more information.

Degrees of Perineal Incision and Tear		
Degree	Perineal Tear	Episiotomy Incision
First degree	Vaginal mucosa and connective tissue	N/A
Second degree	Vaginal mucosa, connective tissue, and muscle	Through the vaginal mucosa extending halfway between vagina and rectum.
Third degree	Tear through the anal sphincter	Through the vaginal mucosa to anus.
Fourth degree	Tear of the rectal mucosa	Extends from the vagina through the rectum.

Preventing Perineal Tears

The use of warm (not hot) compresses on the perineum and perineal massage in the final weeks of pregnancy can help the stretching process along and avoid perineal tears. Controlled pushing during the second stage of labor can also keep your perineum intact, as can provider support of the head and perineal tissues if the baby is crowning too quickly. If you don't want an episiotomy, talk to your provider about your wishes and include that point in your birth plan.

Before birth, you can help prepare your perineum for the big day by massaging the perineal area with oils or lubricant and by practicing kegel exercises. Kegels exercise the pelvic floor muscles and can help you with more controlled pushing during the birth. They also help to avoid urinary incontinence. To do kegels, repeatedly tighten and relax the muscles you use to start and stop urine flow.

One of the common misconceptions about episiotomy is that it prevents urinary and/or fecal incontinence later in life. However, the truth is that the routine use of episiotomy can actually increase the chance of that complication. A 2003 metanalysis of the episiotomy literature in the journal *Urology* found that routine midline episiotomy increases the risk of serious perineal lacerations, which may lead to fecal incontinence, and routine mediolateral episiotomy does nothing to prevent urinary incontinence (UI) or severe perineal tears.

There may be some situations in which an episiotomy is unavoidable, such as when a forceps or vacuum extraction delivery is medically required or your baby is in distress and needs to be delivered quickly.

ALERT!

A 2002 study in the journal *Birth* that reviewed national birth data from the National Center for Health Statistics found that episiotomies are more likely to develop into more severe lacerations (that is, third and fourth degree) than natural tears of the perineum in women who don't have the procedure, which are usually first or second degree.

If an episiotomy is done, or if tearing does occur, you will receive stitches after the birth to close up the lacerations. An anesthetic block will be injected first if you haven't already had one. You may also receive postpartum antibiotic therapy depending on the degree of the tear or incision.

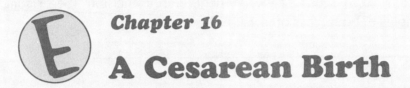

Chapter 16

A Cesarean Birth

Meeting your baby in an operating room may not be what you had planned for your ideal birth experience, but it is a possibility. You may have many weeks to get used to the idea of a cesarean birth, or only minutes. Either way, knowing what to expect before, during, and after a C-section can help make the emotional adjustment, and your physical recovery, much quicker.

Cesarean Section: The Procedure

A standard C-section involves two horizontal incisions right above your pubic bone—one through the skin and abdominal tissues, and the second through the muscle of the uterine wall. While this "low-transverse" incision is now common practice, prior to the 1990s many women having a cesarean were routinely given a "classic," or vertical, uterine incision. (See **FIGURE 16.1** for examples of both types of incisions.)

FIGURE 16.1

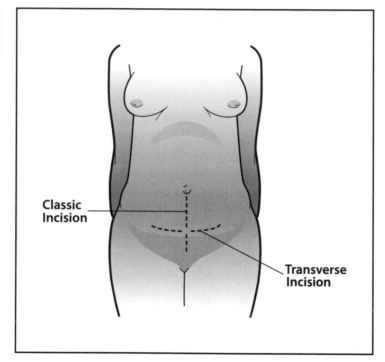

◀ Transverse and classic cesarean incisions

The classical incision has been largely abandoned because of the high rate of uterine rupture associated with it during any subsequent pregnancy and labor, as well as greater blood loss and increased healing time. However, there a classic incision may be sometimes be necessary, such as preterm birth; cases in which the fetus is in a transverse lie (sideways) position with his back down; or in instances of placenta previa, which means the placenta is implanted at or near the birth canal and a transverse incision may cause hemorrhaging. It may also be used if excessive scar tissue or tumors make a transverse incision undesirable.

Getting Ready

Before the cesarean procedure begins, you'll be prepped for surgery. The area around your bikini line will be cleaned and may be shaved at and around the area where the incision will be made. Shaving may be linked to an increased risk of skin infections with cesarean, so obstetricians have different preferences on whether to shave or not. The nurse will insert an intravenous line into your arm so you can receive fluids as needed and pain medication once the procedure is complete. A urinary catheter will also be necessary, since the anesthetic block will relax your control over the muscles that stop and start urine flow.

FACT

The insertion of a urinary catheter (called a Foley catheter) can be uncomfortable and potentially painful. While such glamorous tasks as catheter insertion are usually left to the nurse who preps you, you can ask your provider if your catheter can be inserted in the operating room after the anesthetic block has been administered.

Because you are required to lie still on your back for an extended period of time, which can lower your blood pressure and get your stomach churning, nausea is not uncommon during a cesarean. Due to the potential for vomiting, part of surgical prep involves drinking an antacid solution called sodium citrate. The sodium citrate will neutralize your stomach acid. If you throw up and aspirate the vomit into your lungs, the neutralized stomach acid will not injure your delicate lung tissue.

Once you are prepped, you will be wheeled into the operating room, accompanied by your partner. This is where the big event will happen. Among the masked men and women of your surgical team will be an anesthesiologist, who will be responsible for starting the anesthetic block (or, in rare cases, putting you under general anesthesia).

In the Operating Room

After the spinal catheter is in place, you will lie flat on your back with your arms straight out to your sides on boards that extend from the operating table. A curtain a foot or two high will be placed at your chest to keep the surgical field sterile. Your arms may be loosely tethered to the table with Velcro straps or a similar restraint as a gentle reminder to keep your hands down and away from the surgical field.

Lying prone will cause your heavy uterus to press down on your inferior vena cava, the artery that returns blood to the right atrium of your heart, which can cause your blood pressure to drop. The spinal block itself can also have a hypotensive effect. The surgical team will keep a close eye on your vital signs, and they may administer ephedrine or another medication to push your blood pressure back up to an acceptable level.

Nausea is not uncommon on the operating table. If you feel your stomach rumbling, let your partner or support person know right away so someone can be ready to help. Unfortunately, once everything is in place and the procedure has started, there is little you can do except turn your head and aim for the plastic tray. Your support person or a nurse can be your hands for you. Let yourself be comforted and cleaned up and know that the feeling will soon pass.

After your belly is draped and swabbed with an antibacterial/antimicrobial solution to ensure sterility, the surgery can begin. While you will be completely numb to any pain from the waist down, as the doctor makes the incision you may feel an odd sensation that some women liken to being "unzipped." Shortly after the incisions are made, you may experience pressure in your abdomen as the doctor maneuvers your uterus and prepares your baby for his departure, followed by a pulling sensation as she assists your baby out of the womb head-first or feet-first, depending on his position in the womb. The entire "birth" portion of the procedure—from incision to exit—will take only a few minutes.

Once the baby is out, his mouth and nose will be suctioned to assist him in getting acclimated to his nonwatery environment. The umbilical cord is cut—either by the physician or by your partner if arrangements have been made to do so. Then it's to your side for your first face-to-face.

Your meeting may be brief, as most hospitals require an assessment of the baby along with the usual postbirth tests right after delivery. If the area where they care for your newborn is not in the operating room itself, it will be in an adjoining room. Your partner can accompany your new addition to his first checkup if you wish.

Recovery

After removing and examining the placenta, the doctor will suture your incisions closed. From start to finish, the entire cesarean procedure will take anywhere from thirty to sixty minutes. Once the stitches are in place, you'll be wheeled into a surgical recovery area where your heart rate, blood oxygen level, and blood pressure will be monitored and a recovery-room nurse will keep a close eye on you. In most cases, your infant will join you here, and you and your partner can spend some time getting to know this new little person. If you have chosen to breastfeed, this is a perfect time to give it your first try.

The length of time you will spend in recovery is variable—from an hour or so to the better part of a day. Typically it's no longer than one to three hours. Things like the type of anesthesia used, the normalcy of your vital signs, and your pain level may impact how quickly you're ready to move into a postpartum room. In a particularly busy hospital with a high-traffic maternity ward, you may have to wait for a room to open up and be cleaned and prepped for your arrival.

FACT

The United States has the highest rate of cesarean birth in the world, with nearly a quarter of the roughly 4 million annual births being delivered surgically by C-section. In 2001, more than 978,000 C-sections were performed in the United States, a record 24.4 percent of all births that year.

Planned Cesarean

The technological evolution of diagnostic tests and imaging devices means that women find out earlier than ever before about the possibility of birth complications. It may also have the unintended effect of making women feel resigned to a C-section early in their pregnancy, even when a vaginal birth may be possible and even preferred as the due date draws closer.

So who has cesarean section delivery? There are some conditions that will definitely require a C-section, and others that are not so clear. Factors that commonly lead to a recommendation (or requirement) for planned C-section include these:

- **HIV-positive status.** In order to minimize the chances of transmitting HIV to an infant, the ACOG recommends (as of early 2004) that women who are HIV-positive deliver by C-section at thirty-eight weeks gestation. However, HIV medications and the mother's health picture at the time of birth may have an influence on how the birth proceeds. Women with HIV should consult with their perinatologist about their need for a cesarean.
- **Other specific, chronic, maternal health problems.** Certain cardiovascular diseases, prior vaginal surgery, tumors or genital human papilloma virus (HPV) warts that block the birth canal, and active genital herpes lesions in the mother at the time of birth are just a few health problems that may require a planned C-section.
- **Previous classical uterine incision.** If you had a previous C-section or other surgery such as removal of uterine fibroids that required a classical (vertical) incision, you are at a high risk for uterine rupture in labor and will require a C-section.
- **Placenta previa.** If your placenta is attached near or over the cervix, effectively blocking the birth canal, a C-section delivery will be required.
- **Fetal position.** If your baby is in a breech (feet- or buttocks-first) or transverse (sideways) position, your provider may suggest a cesarean. Keep in mind, however, that some breech babies can and have been successfully delivered vaginally.
- **Fetal size.** If ultrasound indicates that your baby may weigh ten pounds or more, a C-section may be recommended. Women with diabetes or gestational diabetes who are unable to maintain good blood-glucose control during pregnancy sometimes encounter this problem.

Educating Yourself

When your childbirth educator starts discussing cesarean section, don't pick that time to slip out for a bathroom break or quick snack. In the world of pregnancy and childbirth, anything is possible, so pay attention in order to be able to make informed decisions if you need to.

A cesarean procedure is major abdominal surgery. It involves the same risks as any surgical procedure—including hemorrhage, infection, and embolism—plus possible complications from anesthesia. (See Chapter 14 for more on anesthesia.) There is also a much longer recovery period involved with cesarean section than with vaginal birth, lasting up to six weeks.

Still, there are some perks to a planned cesarean. Your delivery date becomes a firm commitment, not the vague promise it is with regular labor and vaginal delivery. Your baby will also emerge with a perfectly round head, unlike the slightly cone-shaped version most vaginally delivered newborns have.

QUESTION?

I'm having twins, and my doctor wants me to have a cesarean. Is that my only option?

Assuming yours is a normal, healthy, and term pregnancy, the question of whether your twins can be delivered vaginally depends on their presentation (how they are situated in the womb). If both twins are vertex, or head down, vaginal birth shouldn't be a problem. If the twins are transverse or breech, however, a C-section may be indicated. Talk to your doctor about your twins' presentation and why he is encouraging cesarean, and remember that even twins may change position in the final weeks of pregnancy. For more on twins, see Chapter 17.

Birth Intervention Choices

While it's true that hospital rules and regulations will govern your birth experience to a certain extent, you do have some options. Things like surgical prep procedures and recovery room protocol are largely nonnegotiable, but there are a few things you can have some say in, including the following:

- **Support person.** Unless your C-section is a sudden emergency, you should be able to have your partner or another support person present in the operating room with you.
- **Cord-cutting.** Your physician may allow your partner to cut the umbilical cord if you request it in advance.
- **Baby bonding.** If you want to be able to hold your baby before she's taken away for a cleanup and checkup, you should discuss it with your doctor as early as possible. The intravenous lines and surgical screen may make prolonged cuddling difficult, but asking that you and your partner be able to hold your baby while your incision is being closed is not unreasonable.

Unplanned and Emergency Cesarean

Sometimes a cesarean becomes an option at the end of a long labor that isn't progressing. In other cases, sudden fetal or maternal distress makes an immediate emergency C-section a necessity. Either way, learning about the procedure and the risks and benefits now will help you make that critical decision later when seconds count.

Some problems that can occur in labor and may indicate the need for a cesarean section instead of a vaginal delivery include these:

- **Placental abruption.** If the placenta has completely or partially detached from the uterine wall, there is a danger of massive blood hemorrhage, and an immediate C-section delivery is required.
- **Cord prolapse or cord compression.** If the umbilical cord is pushed into the birth canal ahead of your baby, or if the cord becomes entangled around the baby's neck or compressed in some other fashion that could cut off blood and oxygen flow, a C-section will be necessary.
- **Fetal distress.** It's hard work finding your way out of the womb and down the birth canal, so some fetal stress (clinically known as "reassuring" or "reactive") is to be expected during labor. But when fetal monitoring of the baby's heartbeat and scalp pH level indicate that he is getting insufficient oxygen, an immediate C-section delivery may be indicated.
- **Eclampsia.** Women with preeclampsia who develop eclampsia (which is defined by the presence of seizures in addition to other preeclampsia

symptoms) and who are at least twenty-four weeks along will require an immediate cesarean delivery.

- **Failure to progress.** If your labor "stalls" to the point that your cervix has stopped dilating and/or your baby has stopped descending down the birth canal, a cesarean may become an option. This situation is referred to clinically as "dystocia."

Dystocia: When the Choice Isn't Clear

Greek for "difficult labor," dystocia is a catch-all term for labor that isn't progressing as it should. Some cases of dystocia are caused by factors beyond your control, which may make C-section the only choice. If your provider says you have cephalopelvic disproportion (CPD), where your pelvis is literally too small to accommodate your baby's head, this means you are facing a structural difficulty that only C-section will solve.

FACT

Cesarean section is not the only intervention available when your labor fails to progress in a timely fashion. Your physician may suggest a Pitocin drip to strengthen contractions if you haven't already tried it. For more on labor and birth interventions, see Chapter 15.

However, some labor may be labeled dystocia simply because it's slow going. Don't let your provider's impatience color your perception. As long as the fetus isn't exhibiting any abnormal distress and you have the energy and determination to keep going, it should be your call whether or not to continue laboring or to go the C-section route.

Your Partner's Presence

Emergency C-section may require the use of a general anesthetic if time is tight and you don't already have an epidural line in place. In such a situation, it's quite possible your partner will be asked to remain outside of the OR. Talk to your doctor about special circumstances during childbirth and your wishes about having your partner with you to see what can be arranged.

Anesthesia for C-Section

In most cases, you'll receive an epidural or spinal block for surgical anesthetic that will numb you from the waist down. However, if you have an emergency cesarean and time is of the essence, your physician may opt for a general anesthesia. If you have general anesthesia, you will be unconscious for the birth.

If your C-section is planned, you will most likely receive a spinal block, which will be administered in the operating room itself. The anesthesiologist will need access to the base of your spine, so she will ask you to lay on your side with your knees pulled toward your chest, or sit on the edge of the table with your feet hanging off the end so your lower back is exposed. Once the area is swabbed with an antimicrobial/antibacterial agent such as Betadine, a fine needle is inserted between your vertebrae into the cerebrospinal fluid sac cushioning the bundle of nerves that are your spinal cord. The spinal block (which may be lidocaine or some other -caine anesthetic agent) is injected through the needle.

In those cases in which a woman has already undergone a trial of labor and she and her provider have agreed that a cesarean is necessary to safely deliver the baby, and an epidural catheter is already in place from labor, anesthesia may be delivered directly through the same catheter, with no spinal block injection.

Morphine can cause excessive itchiness, which may reach maddening levels once your anesthetic block wears off completely. Benadryl or other antihistamines given intravenously may provide some relief, so if you do get a skin-crawling case of the itchies, let your nurse know.

The anesthesiologist may give you morphine or another painkiller via your intravenous line to take the edge of the pain once the spinal or epidural anesthetic has worn off. Patient-controlled analgesia (PCA) is commonly used for postpartum pain control. If you receive PCA, an infusion pump device will be hooked up to your intravenous line. When you start feeling uncomfortable, you can press a button to get the unit to release a measured dose of pain medication (called a bolus dose) into your intravenous line. The pump may also be programmed to deliver a low, continuous flow of pain medication (called basal infusion). The PCA unit has safeguards in place to prevent it from delivering too much medication if the button is pressed too frequently. Once the postsurgical pain has reached a manageable level (usually by day one or two postpartum), pain medication may be given as needed by mouth.

VBAC or Repeat C-Section?

The old adage "Once a cesarean, always a cesarean" was put out to pasture long ago. Today, vaginal birth after cesarean (VBAC) is not only commonplace, it is encouraged by the ACOG in women with previous transverse incision C-sections. And up to 80 percent of women who attempt a VBAC deliver successfully.

Still, not every woman wants a VBAC, even those with the odds in their favor. Some may have had a particularly difficult or long labor during their first attempt at vaginal birth, which may have left them physically and/or emotionally unwilling to try again. Others have concerns about the risk of uterine rupture. (According to studies done by the U.S. Centers for Disease Control (CDC), this risk is less than 1 percent for women with one previous transverse C-section.)

FACT

Approximately one-third of all cesarean procedures in the United States each year are repeat performances. Elective repeat cesarean is on the rise in America due to malpractice concerns and patient fears of uterine rupture and other VBAC complications. In 2002, only 12.6 percent of U.S. women with a previous cesarean section gave birth vaginally.

For women who have had two or more previous C-sections, there is a lower (although still fairly impressive) overall success rate with VBAC (an estimated 75 percent), and the risk of uterine rupture is higher than in women with a single previous C-section. The reason for the previous cesarean section can have an impact on your chances of a successful VBAC. Talk to your provider about your past history and how it may impact a VBAC attempt.

Making the Choice

In the end, the decision over whether or not to give VBAC a try is up to you. Talk to your doctor or midwife about the risks and benefits of both repeat cesarean and VBAC, and weigh them carefully. A good provider will present you with the full range of facts as they relate to your pregnancy and let you and your partner make the decision on your own.

Some providers may encourage repeat cesarean because of liability or safety concerns with VBAC. Don't feel pressured by a physician who pushes (or even strongly suggests) a repeat cesarean, and, conversely, don't be bullied into VBAC by a midwife who "can't understand why any woman who is given the opportunity to try a vaginal birth wouldn't choose to take it." Again—it's your decision, your choice, and your birth.

If you decide VBAC is best for you, your provider may require that you give birth in a hospital setting so that surgical facilities are close at hand in case the trial of labor is unsuccessful. If you have strong feelings about having a home or birth center birth, talk to your provider about your potential options.

Fear of Failure

Even the most rational and well-adjusted woman who ends up having a cesarean section may initially feel that she's somehow "failed" at childbirth. When a VBAC is unsuccessful, the resulting depression and anxiety may be even more pronounced. While a vaginal birth can be an extremely fulfilling experience, the most important thing to remember is the end result—your beautiful new baby. As long as she has entered the world safely, be it through the birth canal or out the escape hatch in your abdomen, you have achieved the ultimate goal and reward of childbirth.

Postpartum Issues

The average cesarean hospital stay is three to four days, but complete physical recovery can take up to six weeks. Things like heavy lifting and driving will be off limits, and you'll require plenty of rest to get back up to speed. Just taking care of baby will be a full-time job for you and your partner, so recruit a network of supportive friends and family to help out.

In-Hospital Recovery

After you're settled in a postpartum room, the nursing staff will make regular checks of your incision and vital signs. Getting your gastrointestinal system moving again will be a primary goal, so expect your nurse to quiz you regularly on your flatulence habits. Once you pass gas, it's a signal everything is up and running, and you will probably be allowed to enjoy solid food again if you're ready. Some physicians may agree to food earlier if surgery was uncomplicated.

FACT

Heavy vaginal bleeding is normal after a cesarean as your uterus sheds its lining. You'll be using a lot of sanitary napkins for the first week or so. Even though the hospital will provide these, you may feel more comfortable with a supply of your own brand. Pack plenty of extra underwear as well. Expect vaginal bleeding similar to your menstrual period for two to six weeks. This bleeding should not be excessive and should start to taper slowly.

The nursing staff will encourage you to get up and move around as soon as possible, most likely on the second day of your recovery, which is the day after the procedure is performed. Your IV line and catheter will probably be taken out at this point as well, which will make getting around a little easier. It's common to experience dizziness the first time you attempt to stand; make sure your partner or a nurse is within arm's reach to lean on if needed.

When you are discharged, you'll receive instructions on incision care and a prescription for pain medication to take as needed. Most doctors ask you to schedule a two-week postpartum appointment so they can check your incision and make sure it's healing properly.

Breastfeeding After C-Section

Your incision will be tender after your cesarean, and because you won't have much control over your abdominal muscles for a while, you'll need some support to bring yourself to a sitting position. Fortunately, this is one of the things those adjustable Craftmatic-style hospital beds are made for.

In addition to getting your bed in an upright position, you'll need to support your incision to properly hold and position your baby for breastfeeding and to minimize discomfort. There are nursing pillows on the market that are made specifically for supporting your baby while breastfeeding, but while you're spending most of your time in a hospital bed, a towel and an extra pillow or two across the incision area will do the job just as well. Your nurse can help you get adjusted until you have the hang of it.

You may also have some concerns about the potential for pain medication to be passed from you to baby through your breast milk. The clinical consensus is that the benefits of breastfeeding your baby early and often are greater than any risks from the minute traces of pain medication that may be passed to baby. Managing your pain effectively is an important part of your early recovery from C-section. It allows you to get much-needed rest and improves the quality of the time you spend getting to know your newborn. Your baby is drinking very small amounts of colostrum (the nutrient-rich precursor to breast milk—see Chapter 19) in the early postpartum days when the most pain medication may be required, so any transmission of pain medication is really very minimal.

Chapter 17

Multiple Choices: Choosing a Birth for Twins or More

Multiples pregnancy is full of surprises—from the moment you get the news that there's a stowaway (or two, or three) on board, to the day when they decide to disembark and meet their mom. Labor and delivery is no exception. Your twins, triplets, or more will require some special considerations and handling as they make the birth journey and join your family.

Making Preparations

Multiple births are increasing as a result of assisted reproductive technology (ART) and infertility treatments, but few women are prepared for the news that two or more babies are coming into their life when they were expecting only one. It's natural to feel apprehensive upon receiving the news of a multiples pregnancy. In addition to the emotional adjustments and practical considerations of things like finances, long-term child care, and housing, there is the knowledge that with multiples come certain inherent pregnancy and birth risks.

Multiples Childbirth Education

Many hospitals and birth centers offer childbirth education classes designed specifically for parents-to-be of multiples. These courses are a great way to get more information on the special issues that multiples moms face in birth and after, such as the possibility of preterm labor, the decision between vaginal and cesarean birth, and the logistics of breastfeeding. They can also plug you into a powerful support network for multiples moms.

FACT

It's a good idea to sign up for multiples education courses early in your pregnancy, since multiples have a shorter average length of gestation. Early education also gives you the opportunity to draft a well-considered birth plan in advance of a potential preterm birth.

Birth Plans

Once you have been through childbirth education and have had an in-depth discussion with your provider about your birth options, you should sit down with your partner and put your preferences on paper.

You'll be doing a lot of planning for alternate scenarios that could occur right up to birth, such as a shift of fetal positions, for example, if twin A is vertex, and twin B is breech. (Fetal positions of twins will be discussed in more detail later in this chapter) Leave leeway for the unexpected, and be sure to plan a follow-up visit with your provider dedicated solely to reviewing your birth plan and expectations. Chapter 5 and Appendix A will help you with the birth-plan basics.

Special Handling

The birth of two, three, or more carries some unique challenges. The position and size of your babies, the timing of labor, and the structure of both the amniotic sacs and the placenta(s) will all play a part in how your birth experience unfolds.

Some of these factors, such as details about the placenta and amniotic sac, you may know about early in your pregnancy, but fetal positions can change right up until birth. And just over half of all twin pregnancies result in preterm labor at or before the end of thirty-seven weeks, with numbers increasing dramatically with each additional fetus. If preterm labor is caught early enough, measures can be taken to stop its progress until you've reached a safer point in your pregnancy to deliver.

Women with multiples pregnancies face other possible problems in pregnancy, such as anemia and fetal problems including potential umbilical cord knotting and intrauterine growth retardation. *The Everything® Pregnancy Book, Second Edition* (Adams Media, 2003) by this author discusses in detail the issues multiples moms-to-be face, and is a good resource for information on multiples prenatal care and pregnancy in general.

Preterm Labor Risks

The more passengers you have on board, the quicker your uterus stretches to capacity. While the ultimate goal is to achieve a full-term pregnancy of thirty-seven to forty weeks, the average gestational age at delivery in the United States in 2002 was thirty-five weeks for twins, thirty-two weeks for triplets, and thirty weeks for quads, meaning that most multiple gestations come into the world prematurely.

Mothers-to-be of multiples should acquaint themselves with the signs and symptoms of labor early in their pregnancy so they can seek medical assistance if preterm labor should occur. (See Chapter 2 for a review of common labor signs.) If preterm labor is detected, and your cervix is less than four centimeters dilated, your health-care provider can sometimes stop it with one or more of these possible interventions:

- **Bed rest.** Staying off your feet will keep the pressure off your cervix, a common prescription for women at risk for or showing signs of premature labor. You may either be sent to your bedroom at home or asked to stay in the hospital.
- **Trendelenburg position.** Your provider may recommend that you spend some time on a tilted bed that elevates your feet and lowers your head so that the pressure is off your cervix completely.
- **Fluids.** Intravenous fluids may be administered to keep you hydrated.
- **Antibiotics.** Women who have had preterm premature rupture of membranes (called PPROM) will require antibiotic therapy. Antibiotics are used as a prophylaxis against maternal infection, and they have also been associated with a delay in the start of labor. (Any woman with PPROM who develops an infection needs to be delivered as soon as possible.)
- **Tocolytic medications.** Magnesium sulfate, calcium channel blockers, and terbutaline may be administered to stop contractions. Tocolytic drugs cannot be used if delivery is indicated due to fetal or maternal distress.
- **Cerclage.** Cerclage involves suturing the cervix closed if it is not yet significantly dilated, and may be performed on women with a short cervix (twenty-five mm or less at twenty-four weeks of gestation). Studies are inconclusive to its effectiveness.

If you're giving birth to multiples in a hospital setting, you may be required to deliver in an operating room or surgical suite, even if you plan on a vaginal birth. The rationale is that if one or more babies ends up having to be delivered via cesarean, a quick transition will be important.

Early Arrival

Despite your best efforts and your provider's preventative measures, sometimes multiples must arrive preterm. If you are close to thirty-five weeks, sometimes an amniocentesis is performed to determine whether or not each fetus's lungs are mature. If they are mature, labor can proceed.

FACT

According to the National Center for Health Statistics, 52 percent of twins arrived preterm in 2002, while 92 percent of triplets were preemies. The prematurity rate for singleton births in 2002 was 10 percent.

The amnio is performed by inserting a needle into each amniotic sac and drawing out a fluid sample, which also contains fetal cells, into a syringe. The fluid will be tested for the level of surfactant, the substance that coats the alveoli (or air sacs) of mature lungs and helps maintain lung pressure during exhalation. A nontoxic blue dye is injected into each sac after the fluid sample is extracted. If your provider mistakenly tests the same fetal amniotic sac twice, thinking it belongs to another fetus, he'll recognize the error from the color of the fluid. Fetal lung maturity can vary from fetus to fetus, so testing all amniotic sacs whenever possible is essential.

If the amniocentesis shows that the lungs are developed enough to breathe in the outside world, then vaginal or cesarean birth can proceed immediately. In cases in which the fluid sample shows that the fetal lungs are still immature and haven't developed an adequate level of surfactant, injections of corticosteroids are given to the mother while labor is delayed as long as possible in an attempt to boost surfactant levels before delivery. Steroid injections are often started earlier, as soon as symptoms of preterm labor first began.

Babies born without an adequate level of lung surfactant are at risk for respiratory distress syndrome (RDS), which may be treated with animal-derived or synthetic surfactants or with continuous positive airway pressure (CPAP)—an oxygen therapy that forces the alveoli of the lungs open.

Delivering Multiples Vaginally

Cesarean is not always a necessity with multiples. Many women successfully manage a vaginal birth of twins and even triplets. (However, the ACOG recommends that triplets and other higher order multiples be delivered via C-section. In the case of twins, if both are in the vertex position (head down) and there are no signs of fetal distress, a vaginal birth is quite achievable. Approximately 43 percent of twins are in a vertex/vertex position at the time of birth. (**FIGURE 17.1** shows the various twin position combinations.)

Fetal Position and Delivery

Breech position with at least one multiple is a common circumstance, and it is not at all surprising considering the cramped quarters your little ones are in. If the first baby to be delivered is vertex, but the second remains breech (either feet or buttocks first), then a vaginal birth is still possible for the first twin and may be possible for the second as well.

Sometimes the force of contractions and the departure of his sibling will cause the second twin to drop down into vertex position on his own. However, if the second twin doesn't turn during labor, he may have to be either a) coerced into turning through external version, b) delivered breech, or c) delivered via cesarean section (a vaginal/abdominal birth). For more on version and breech birth, see Chapter 15.

If the second baby is breech and version is either not an option or unsuccessful, then vaginal breech birth is possible if the baby is not in distress and meets weight requirements. Because multiples babies are typically smaller than singletons, and the first twin should widen the birth canal for the second, a breech delivery of a second twin may be easier than a singleton breech birth. Your provider may suggest a full or partial breech extraction of the second twin (pulling the baby out of the uterus feet first once dilation is complete) if he does not descend in a timely manner.

Not all doctors will agree to a vaginal delivery for twins or more, no matter what the presentation. You should speak with your doctor early in your pregnancy if vaginal delivery is important to you. If he will only do a C-section, you can arrange for alternative care if need be. Because midwifery is centered around the idea of birth as a natural process, you probably won't

FIGURE 17.1

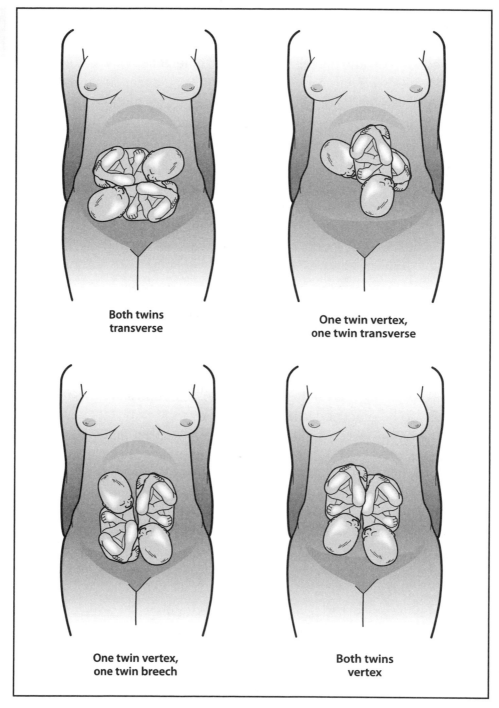

Both twins
transverse

One twin vertex,
one twin transverse

One twin vertex,
one twin breech

Both twins
vertex

▲ Twin positions in utero

have trouble finding a midwife who will offer her assistance at a vaginal birth of multiples, either at a birthing center or even at a home birth if you're considered low risk and are relatively close to emergency care should it be required. Midwives who care for women in multiples pregnancies usually have an ob/gyn available for consultation during pregnancy and birth in case complications do arise.

The ACOG recommends that women giving birth to multiples undergo continuous fetal monitoring. If you're having a hospital birth with twins or more, and you really want to be able to walk and move while in labor, talk to your provider now about your options.

You may find that the midwives in your area have experience with breech births. If you are having twins and want to deliver vaginally, speak with your doctor or midwife about their breech-delivery success rate so you can be sure you'll be getting skilled care. A perinatologist, an obstetrician who specializes in high-risk births, may also be an option since this type of doctor is likely to be practiced in multiples delivery.

Women who want to attempt a VBAC with a multiples pregnancy may have a more difficult time finding a provider who will meet their needs. Sometimes a doctor or midwife will agree to a trial of labor—usually in a hospital setting in case complications arise—to see how your body and your babies respond.

A Two-Part Performance

When giving vaginal birth to twins, you'll experience two pushing phases, or second stages, of labor. After the first baby is delivered, your provider may perform a quick ultrasound to check on the position of the second. Most physicians like to deliver the second twin within thirty minutes of the first to minimize the chance of potential complications, such as placental separation and the cervix reclosing. However, even when the second baby is breech, given that the fetal heart rate is good and mom and baby are doing fine, there is no reason to perform any interventions this early as long as progress is being made and a regular delivery is possible within an hour of the first birth. Some providers may even allow a longer lag between births as long as there is no fetal or maternal distress.

FACT

Interval delivery, also called delayed delivery, is a birth method used rarely for twins to delay birth of subsequent fetuses when preterm birth of the first is inevitable. It is usually achieved with the same methods used to stop preterm labor—tocolyctic drugs, bed rest, antibiotics, and steroid therapy to encourage development of the remaining babies' lungs—and may delay delivery of the remaining babies for several days to several weeks.

Just as breastfeeding a singleton baby right after her birth can assist in expelling the placenta, nursing your first twin while your second is still inside may help along the birth process by stimulating the production of oxytocin, which strengthens contractions.

Indications for C-Section

Approximately half of all twins are born via cesarean section. This statistic rises considerably when there are three or more babies involved. Cesarean is not always a given for twin births, but there are circumstances where C-section is the safest method of delivery for you and your babies. Cesarean is *always* preferred over vaginal delivery when any of the following cases occurs:

- The first baby in line to be delivered is breech and the second is vertex (because of the risk of fetal heads interlocking as the first baby is delivered, also known as locked twins).
- Both babies are in a transverse (sideways) position.
- Twins are monoamniotic, or share an amniotic fluid sac.
- Cord prolapse (the umbilical cord dropping out of the vagina) occurs.
- One or more multiples show signs of fetal distress.
- The birth is of more than three fetuses.

Cesarean *may* be preferred when any of the following is true:

- The birth is of triplets.
- A second twin is in breech position and is significantly larger than the first.
- Twins are known to be monochorionic (sharing a chorion membrane and a placenta). Monochorionic twins may have separate fluid sacs (diamniotic) or share a common fluid sac (monoamniotic).

ALERT!

Monoamniotic twins—or twins that share an amniotic sac—are at an increased risk for umbilical cord entanglement and compression, which can cut off the blood supply to one or both fetuses. For this reason, your provider will probably suggest that monoamniotic twins be delivered by cesarean at or before thirty-four weeks.

Home Birth: Risks Versus Benefits

With a dedicated and experienced provider, good prenatal care, and some fetal cooperation, a home birth is achievable with a low-risk twin birth. Comfort, freedom, and prevention of unnecessary interventions are just a few of the reasons women choose home birth. On your own turf, you are used to calling the shots and free to do whatever it takes to comfort yourself and facilitate the birth. Your home is also the cradle of your family, and welcoming a baby into these surroundings just seems natural. These benefits may be even more appealing when your birth experience will involve not just one, but two new lives.

However, with the increased chance of preterm delivery and potential for cesarean that multiples entail, there are also real risks to both mother and children associated with home birth that need to be considered when making the decision on where to give birth to your twins. There are many factors to take into account, including the following:

- **Fetal position.** Both babies in vertex position is the safest scenario for a home birth, although delivering the second baby breech may be achievable with a skilled midwife.

- **Age of gestation.** A preterm birth should take place in a hospital setting where your babies have immediate access to appropriate care.
- **Proximity to emergency care.** Make sure you can get to a hospital or emergency care facility in a timely manner should problems arise at the birth.
- **Tools and equipment of your midwife.** Does your midwife carry resuscitation equipment? Is she licensed to administer potentially necessary drugs?
- **Provider experience.** Does your midwife have sufficient experience delivering twins? Find out her success rate and her transport rate (that is, the percent of multiples mothers that ultimately had to deliver at a hospital).

There is also the risk of uncontrolled maternal bleeding following the delivery. This is called postpartum hemorrhage and can happen if the overstretched uterine muscles aren't contracting effectively following the birth. An injection of Pitocin (oxytocin) can help stimulate contractions again. Depending on state law, however, your midwife may be prohibited from administering Pitocin, which is considered a prescription drug.

Depending on where you reside, state law may even prohibit home births of multiples (or of the midwife attendance of multiple home-birth, which is in effect the same thing). Check with the state board of health if you have questions about regulations in your area.

As mentioned previously, finding a physician who will attend a home birth of multiples will be a difficult, if not impossible, proposition. If you are committed to home birth and aren't seeing a midwife already, it will pay to investigate that option now. Chapter 3 has more information on finding a health-care provider who fits your needs. If you do plan a home birth of your twins, aggressive prenatal care—including ultrasounds near your due date to determine the position and size of your babies—is a must.

Most providers will agree that because of the increased chance of cesarean and incidence of prematurity with higher order multiples (that is, triplets, quads, or more), these types of births are safer in a hospital setting or a birth center with close proximity to a hospital.

Extended Hospital Stays

Because of the high incidence of prematurity and associated health issues among multiples, it isn't uncommon for twins, triplets, or other higher-order multiples to have to remain in the hospital even after mom is discharged.

Premature babies are cared for in a neonatal intensive-care unit, or NICU. A level-three NICU is considered the state of the art for preterm infant care. It's a good idea to find out more about the neonatal care facilities at your local hospitals before the birth so you can ensure the very best care for your multiples should it be needed.

Premature babies seem so very fragile, but like any other newborn they need, and will thrive on, their parents' touch. Because very premature babies may require some special handling, the NICU staff and neonatal physical therapists can help you develop positive and nurturing methods of skin-to-skin contact with your newborn children.

FACT

A neonatologist is a physician who specializes in newborn and preemie care. Multiples are at a greater risk for prematurity and the health conditions that often accompany early birth, so even if your pregnancy is going well and you don't anticipate any problems, it may be a good idea to talk to your provider about referring you for a neonatologist consultation so you can have the information you need to make informed decisions at birth.

As long as other medical problems are not present, most premature babies will be able to leave the NICU for home once they have reached a weight goal of about 2,000 grams (or 4 pounds, 6 ounces) and are thirty-five weeks "corrected" age (from mom's last menstrual period). They also need to be able to feed, breathe, and stay warm on their own. Each NICU will have its own criteria for discharge, however, so talk to your babies' doctor about their specific situation.

After Birth Issues

Don't try to be a one-woman dynamo when you do bring your babies home. You and your spouse will have your hands full with diapers, feedings, baby care, and more. Get grandparents, friends, and family members in on the act; take neighbors up on their offers to pick up groceries, run errands, and whatever else they can help you with.

For women without adequate support at home to manage the hectic pace of two or more newborns in the house, a postpartum doula may be a good idea. For more on doulas, see Chapter 3. Mothers-of-multiples groups can also be a great resource for emotional support and parenting tips. If possible, try to tap into these organizations before your birth so you can tap other women's expertise on the birth experience itself with multiples. Appendix B lists resources for parents and parents-to-be of multiples. If you decide to breastfeed your multiples (an achievable goal), La Leche League can also be a great source of support and instruction.

Chapter 18

For Fathers

Birth represents your chance to finally get personal access to that little person your partner has been so close to for almost ten months. You will play a big role in the success of this birth experience. In many cases, you will be your partner's primary emotional support, her advocate and mediator, and a source of physical comfort. Being prepared for the job and knowing what's ahead will make the birth itself more fulfilling for all involved.

Preparing for the Birth

So are you up to the task? Many men (and women) never feel like they've been fully prepared for childbirth, despite having graduated from classes designed to do just that. Although you can learn a lot about the basic mechanics of how the whole thing should occur, every birth is unmapped territory, which is intrinsic to its joy and its drama.

Exactly what "getting ready" for birth involves depends on the childbirth setting and philosophy you and your partner have decided to pursue. If you're keen on the Bradley Method, for example, you'll be playing a fairly central role in helping your partner through the birth, while a method like HypnoBirthing may require you to step a little further into the background. Chapters 6 through 11 of this book can provide more background on the different childbirth methods available and what type of support role they involve—or, for a quick overview, see the chart on page 141. No matter what your *modus operandi*, you'll find educating yourself as much as possible to be essential to a successful and fulfilling experience.

Going to School

Prepared childbirth classes are important, even if they can't really prepare you for everything. They can help a clueless dad (or even a dad with some knowledge of these matters) get the lay of the land, and they also provide a great opportunity to meet other couples going through the same experience.

There are a few good reasons for second-time parents to go back to school. From a practical standpoint, most classes provide both a tour of the maternity area and important information on preregistration and parking—details you will need to know about if you're going to a different facility than last time. Refreshing your knowledge and skills is always a good idea, especially since accepted birth practices and procedures may have changed since your first child was born.

To get the most out of childbirth class, make sure the class you and your partner choose correlates with your birth needs. (If you're having a planned C-section, a Lamaze-focused class may not be the way to go.) And don't be shy about asking questions in class. The adage about there being no such thing as a stupid question especially holds true in childbirth class, where virtually everyone's a rookie. Chances are at least one other dad in the room has the same query in mind. If you need help deciding which class is right for you, check out Chapter 12, where childbirth education is discussed in more detail.

The Birth Plan

If you aren't one to stop and ask for directions, and if you generally prefer to assemble before reading the instruction manual, listen up. Making it up as you go along is not a good idea in this case. So even if you like to rely on instinct and spontaneity, try to quell the urge to wing it, and participate in the creation of a birth plan.

Chapter 5 discusses exactly what a birth plan is, and isn't, in detail. You should read it (yes, the whole thing) before you and your partner get your heads together to write one. But the condensed version is that a birth plan specifies exactly what your ideal birth experience will entail—including the place, the people attending, the pain-relief methods, and so on. And while it is prescriptive in nature, a good birth plan uses suggestive language rather than demands, and gives your provider room to maneuver should unforeseen complications arise during the labor and birth.

The birth plan that you and your partner put together is not an expendable item. Why be so particular when you just read above that birth is an unpredictable event? The act of designing the birth plan with your partner, and then refining it with her health-care provider, helps you discover what both of you want out of the experience and gives you time to settle any potential disagreements. It also allows you to carefully consider and research your options now instead of having to make a rushed judgment later should things not go smoothly.

Avoid the temptation to just "let her handle it." Your partner is not psychic, and you may find yourself feeling left out in the delivery room if the birth you had directed in your mind's eye is a far stretch from reality. For fathers who have strong feelings about cutting (or not cutting) the cord, catching (or not catching) the baby, or other aspects of the birth experience, discussing these with your partner now and getting them in writing in your birth plan is essential.

There may be circumstances under which a dad isn't able to be involved in the birth. Due dates are notoriously unreliable, and circumstances such as travel or job responsibilities can place you far from home when your baby decides to make his debut. A flu bug or other illness may also put you on the bench. If it's conceivable that this may happen, make sure you and your partner decide on a backup support person who can be your pinch hitter.

Finding a Comfortable Role

Many dads spend a great deal of their partner's pregnancy feeling "out of the loop" and isolated from their baby-to-be. Even if you're present at every ultrasound, were at the head of your childbirth class, and have had your hands on your partner's belly so much she's started to refer to you as "the leech," you've been unable to share that immediate physical and emotional connection to your baby that his mother has enjoyed.

So now, finally, you'll be able to see and touch the little person that you could only imagine for so long. What role will you play in the birth experience? Sit down with your partner and talk about her needs and your wishes.

Use Your Strengths

Capitalize on the personality traits that drive success in other aspects of your life—especially those attributes that your partner appreciates. Do you have a great sense of humor but tend to be hopelessly unorganized? Use laughter to keep your significant other's spirits up, but leave things like coordinating your other children's carpool schedules to a trusted designated friend or family member.

You will need to get used to being a follower rather than a leader in childbirth, responding to your partner's needs rather than directing the action. Even if this feels counterintuitive to you, go with it. Your baby is the one who is ultimately in charge here. No matter how detailed your birth plan, the baby isn't going by your plans. Instead, you and your partner are following her lead.

Talk openly with your partner about how you feel you can best help out and enjoy the birth while giving her the support she needs. There's nothing wrong with taking a pass on cutting the umbilical cord, for example, if it just isn't your cup of tea. But it's better to air your feelings now than it is to create an awkward moment later on.

Don't Go It Alone

As the saying goes, no man is an island. Talking to other guys who have been through birth (and lived to tell about it) can lessen any anxieties and give you a sense of the role you're about to take on. Keep in mind that each birth is unique and filtered through the eye of the beholder, so one guy's horror story may be another man's badge of honor.

If you have fears or reservations about your role in the birth, talk to your partner about them. And, of course, keep an open line of communication with your partner, and support each other as you prepare for birth.

Participation and Support

Labor support does not come naturally to all men. It is a complete role-reversal of the traditional view of men as the physical-labor half of a couple and women as emotional caregivers. If you are feeling anxious about your role in the birth, realize that it's perfectly natural to have some doubts. Your partner is feeling them as well, and she has the heavy work to contend with. However, if you're tense and apprehensive during labor, your spouse will sense your discomfort. Anxiety can be contagious, so the best way to ensure that you're at least marginally relaxed on the big day is to get comfortable now with how you'll carry out your role. Remember birth is a difficult job for her—both physically and emotionally—and she'll need support to focus completely on the task at hand.

These simple pointers can help you handle your role more effectively:

- **Learn to listen.** Hear her requests and carry them out to the best of your ability. If you can anticipate some of her needs and retrieve an extra blanket if the room is cold or give a back rub if she complains of soreness, by all means do so, but ask before you act in case you're off base.
- **Be her voice.** She needs to concentrate completely on getting through contractions and introducing this baby to the world. Take responsibility for asking questions for her, getting staff to respond if needed, and keeping friends and family updated.
- **Don't take it personally.** Any harsh words said in the heat of labor should not be held against her, nor should they be taken as a signal you aren't wanted in the room (unless she says directly: "You aren't wanted in the room," in which case you should probably take five outside the door).
- **Keep your cool.** Seeing your significant other in substantial pain may have you on emotional edge and quick to bark at anyone who seems to be holding up her relief. Stay calm, and if you do have to rattle some cages to get her needs met, make sure you step outside of her room (with her permission) to do it.
- **Stick with the plan.** This is where the birth plan can be your savior. Even if your emotional state has you forgetful and on edge, the printed word is there to guide you. Make sure the staff has a copy in the chart, and be alert for any unintended deviations.

QUESTION?

My wife is having a C-section. Can I, and should I, be present?
Yes! Fathers can play a very important role in cesarean birth, providing much-needed emotional support to their partners during what can be a scary and anxious time. They can also facilitate baby's first meeting with mom, and will oversee baby's first checkup as mom gets stitched up. If you think you may be queasy at the site of your significant other's internal organs, don't worry. The surgical screen placed at her chest will block her view and most of your view of the action, as long as you are seated.

In cases where you truly think you'll be more of a hindrance than a help to the process—if, for example, you're known to faint at the site of blood—think positive and give it a trial run, but have someone acceptable to your partner on standby to take your place if needed. A fainting father is not a good morale booster for the laboring mom.

Extra Support for Her (and You)

Birth can be emotionally draining for dads as well. Concern about your partner's health and the pain she is experiencing, anxiety about the well-being of the baby, fears about the "what ifs," stress over whether or not you will remember all you learned in childbirth preparation class, and the anticipation of actually meeting your child are all competing for your attention, and quite possibly making you the proverbial nervous wreck.

One way to ensure that you'll keep your cool and stay focused on helping your partner through childbirth is to hire a doula. A doula is there solely to provide emotional and physical comfort to the laboring woman and her family. She isn't a licensed medical professional (although many doulas are certified as professional birth attendants), but she does have expertise in making labor go more smoothly. A good doula with many births under her belt will have a wide variety of suggestions for comfort measures and coping techniques.

Dads and Doulas

Because a doula provides support to the entire family, she can be a great addition to your birth team. Dads who have the aid of a doula usually find her presence, and experience, invaluable—almost like having the childbirth educator in the delivery room with you. She isn't there to replace your role as partner and father but rather to supplement it. A doula can do things like provide a hands-on demonstration of ways to apply counterpressure to ease your partner's pain in back labor, and she can retrieve a nurse or midwife if needed so you don't have to leave your partner's side. She will provide support in whatever capacity you need—from fetching refreshments and phoning family members to suggesting more comfortable labor positions and providing massage pointers. Most fathers find that once labor begins, any doubts they had about sharing support duties with a doula quickly fade.

Communication

You'll be talking a lot as the birth unfolds—to your partner, to health-care providers present, and to the outside world. Given the range of emotions you'll be feeling—from delight to dread—it's possible for your psychological state to start to encroach on effective communication.

Your significant other needs a direct line to your empathy, understanding, and responsiveness as you communicate—both verbally and through your actions—throughout labor and birth. But when it comes to dialogue with health-care providers and other friends and family members who may be in the labor room or nearby, calm but firm is the key.

Being an Advocate

Advocating for your partner and your baby simply means looking out for what is in their best interests. That means you should never be afraid to ask questions about procedures, medications, or other medical treatments being proposed for or performed on your partner. If the explanation you receive is too technical, ask for it again in laymen's language.

FACT

If you run into any difficulties in a hospital setting, be aware that many hospitals have a patient advocate on staff responsible for addressing patient complaints and mediating any disagreements between staff and patients. Don't hesitate to call an advocate in if you don't seem to be making any headway.

The best way to resolve conflict is to leave emotions by the wayside and speak to the staff about your common wish for a healthy outcome and a positive birth experience. In most cases, you should be able to reach middle ground on your concerns without breaking hospital policy or burying your birth plan.

Family Guy

Conflicts can arise with those close to you and your partner as well. You may find yourself trying to deal with your mom, who wonders what's taking so long and just wants to spend a few minutes in the labor room with her daughter-in-law (who has no interest in seeing anyone at the moment), or the sister who lives halfway around the world but phones the birthing center hourly just in case you forgot to let her know the baby had arrived.

Thus, you may also take on the role of labor bouncer if friends or family get too intrusive. Keep the attendees to only those that your partner has indicated are welcome, and keep everyone else updated from a distance. If phone calls get to be a problem, give the birth center or hospital staff permission to intercept calls and announce your unavailability. If you're having a home birth, simply taking the phone off the hook will do the trick. Do keep in mind that even the most annoying relative has your best interests at heart. Designating someone to make all the official birth calls once it happens can take the time pressure off you and allow you to follow up at your own pace.

If labor is long, you may need sustenance to keep your strength up. But unless you have her explicit approval, don't eat in front of a laboring mom. The sight and smell of food could trigger nausea or worse. Leaving her side for a trip to the hospital cafeteria isn't such a good idea either. Instead, pack some nonperishable, quick foods like energy bars, juice boxes, crackers, and trail mix, and grab a bite or two just outside the room when you can.

First Impressions

Love at first sight pretty aptly describes that initial meeting with your new son or daughter. Pink and fragile, but tough enough to push out into the world, this tiny child is simply astonishing. Don't be afraid to hold your new baby right away.

Your partner may want to spend part of these early hours trying out breast-feeding—another amazing display of human instinct at work. Be sure to get your share of hands-on time with the baby too. Even if you've had little infant experience, jump right in and hold her, rock her, and do whatever else she seems to enjoy. You'll find in the coming weeks that she'll become attuned to the differences between her mommy's and daddy's ways of doing things and will enjoy the diversity of parenting styles.

This time the three of you share following the birth is something you'll treasure always, so be protective of it. Tell friends and family that you'll be spending time bonding before making the requisite phone calls, so they know to expect a delay. Ask the staff at your birth facility to delay any non-essential tests or procedures, or at least to allow you to be present for them if they are required within a certain timeframe. Making these wishes part of your birth plan will encourage you to make advance arrangements so you aren't distracted during this important time.

FACT

The term "engrossment" describes the special state of deep fascination and bonding that a new father undergoes with his baby. It was coined by researchers Martin Greenberg and Norman Morris, who wrote about it in their 1974 study, "Engrossment: The Newborn's Impact upon the Father."

Birth and Your Partner

As you witness your partner giving birth, you'll also get acquainted with a whole new side of her persona. Most fathers leave the birth experience awed by the sense of physical strength, endurance, and natural instinct their significant others display during labor and birth.

The dynamic of your relationship may change during the postpartum period. Suddenly your mate is a mother, and her attention is focused not on you but on the new member of the family. If she's nursing your newborn, she's spending even more one-on-one time with baby. While jealousy may be over-stating it, you probably are feeling a bit like the odd man out. The remedy?

Jump in and get your hands dirty. While you can't stand in for mom at mealtime (unless you're bottle-feeding), you can diaper, bathe, burp, walk, and play with your little one. Your partner will appreciate the respite, and you will deepen your dad-to-baby bonding experience.

From Lover to Mother

Keep in mind that new motherhood is an exhausting occupation. Couple that with your partner's physical recovery from pregnancy and childbirth and the sleep deprivation both of you are probably experiencing as baby imposes his new schedule on your lives, and it should be obvious why your sex life is lagging. In addition, most health-care providers recommend abstaining from intercourse for four to six weeks after birth anyway. This will benefit you both in the long run by enabling your partner to recover physically and your new family life to settle into a more comfortable and less exhausting groove.

Issues like postpartum depression, vaginal dryness related to hormone changes, and ongoing pain from perineal sutures can make sex uncomfortable or undesirable for your partner. Help is available, so if she's having ongoing problems with any of these issues, encourage her to see her health-care provider.

Even without the exhaustion factor, some women may experience conflicting feelings about getting intimate again. If they're nursing, they may feel awkward about treating their breasts as anything but a source of nutrition right now. Or they may feel uncomfortable with their postpartum bodies.

Once you get clearance from her doctor (usually at six weeks postpartum), the best way to ease back into a sexual relationship you both will enjoy is to talk openly about it. Ask her how she feels about it, and take any delays not as a personal rejection of you, but as what they are—part of her recovery. Spend time on building intimacy in other ways—a tired mom will appreciate a nice, long snuggle or a good massage.

Do Your Part

You can also help take the load off her by assuming some of the household and child-care duties or hiring someone to help her out. If she has time to rest, to exercise, and to take care of your child without being overwhelmed by other responsibilities, she'll feel better about herself and will see herself as more desirable to you. And many a new mom finds that a man who brings her a reasonably clean kitchen and does the laundry without being asked is infinitely more thoughtful and romantic than a guy who sends mere diamonds (although both are nice). Being able to get the baby back to sleep when it's three A.M. and she's tried everything will earn you "sexiest man alive" status. Work through it together, and, above all, communicate your feelings to each other, and your relationship will be as close as ever in no time.

Chapter 19

After Birth: Welcome to the World

Once your baby emerges from your body, the physical act of birth winds to completion. But the emotional genesis of your mother-child relationship has just begun. The time immediately following birth is critical for bonding and attachment, establishing breastfeeding, and laying the foundation for your new family and new life. Most birth facilities have standard medical practices that follow delivery of your baby. Learn about these in advance so you can coordinate the necessary procedures with the necessary bonding time.

Cutting the Cord

One snip of the surgical scissors marks your official physical separation from this tiny life you've nurtured for almost ten months. Cutting the umbilical cord is a ritual that is fraught with both emotional significance and cultural tradition. Because it is such a symbolic event, many women choose to either cut the cord themselves or designate a special person to do it rather than leaving it to their provider.

The umbilical cord is comprised of one vein and two arteries sheathed in a layer of gelatinous tissue called Wharton's jelly. The cord is surprisingly strong, and it sometimes takes a little elbow grease to slice through.

Whoever is chosen to cut the cord may be asked to don sterile surgical gloves before the procedure to minimize the chance of infection to the baby. Before cutting, the umbilical cord is clamped about an inch from the site of the baby's soon-to-be navel to prevent bleeding once the cut is made. A second clamp is applied a few inches away, toward the placenta. The cut is made between the two clamps with sterile scissors (**FIGURE 19.1**).

There are some integrated clamp-and-cut devices on the market that sever and clamp the cord in one step. Your designated cord-cutter may also be instructed to use these with a provider's guidance.

FIGURE 19.1

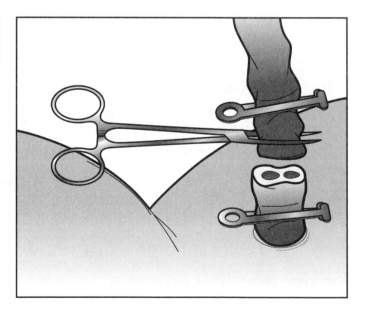

◀ Clamping and cutting the umbilical cord

Doing the Honors

If you're looking forward to cutting the cord yourself, or if you're delegating it to another family member, talk to your provider in advance just to confirm his or her policy on this procedure. Barring an emergency situation in childbirth, there's really no good reason you or a person of your choice shouldn't be able to take part in this important ritual.

You may assume that your partner or spouse should do the honors. Have a talk about his feelings on the subject and make sure it's something he is both comfortable with emotionally and can handle on a physical level. Guys who can spend the afternoon watching bones snap and blood flow during professional sporting events can go white at the thought of wielding the scissors.

Even if you have made prior arrangements with your provider for a special person to cut the cord, if you or your baby needs immediate medical attention after birth, it's likely that the cord will be quickly snipped by the attending doctor or midwife instead.

If you decide to give your new baby's sibling the privilege of cutting the cord, make sure that you a) clear it with your provider and b) have a backup in mind in case your child changes hers. Depending on your child's age and personality, cord-cutting may or may not be a feasible idea. Young children may be able to cut with a parent's assistance, but she may also be frightened by the sight of blood or the notion that the cut is somehow painful to mom or the new baby. Even an older child who is excited by the prospect of having such an important role in the birth may find the birth experience, or the sight of blood, so overwhelming that she opts out in the eleventh hour. Sit down and discuss the possibilities, and above all make sure she understands that whatever she decides is okay with you—it won't be fun for either of you if she feels pressured into doing something she isn't comfortable with.

Delayed Cord-Cutting

Exactly when the umbilical cord should be severed is a matter of some debate in childbirth circles. While the standard practice in hospital settings for many years has been to clamp and cut the cord immediately after birth, many providers now believe that delaying the cut until after the umbilical cord has stopped pulsating with blood is healthier for both baby and mom.

Clinical studies have shown that the practice of clamping the cord immediately after delivery lowers both blood pressure and hematocrit and hemoglobin levels in newborns by reducing the amount of placental blood that ends up in baby's circulation by up to 25 percent. Delaying cord clamping may also improve outcomes for preterm babies by reducing their need for transfusions.

FACT

Between 1995 and 2002, the ACOG officially sanctioned the practice of immediate cord-clamping in their Practice Bulletin #216, which called for immediate clamping in order to obtain newborn arterial pH levels. Although this bulletin was withdrawn in February 2002, many physicians still follow the practice, so it's a good idea to talk to your provider about his philosophy on when to clamp the cord, and the scientific basis behind it.

Cord-Blood Banking

Some women choose to have their child's umbilical cord blood cryogenically stored in the event that either their child or someone in their family needs treatment for a medical condition later in life.

Why umbilical cord blood? Both cord blood and blood that is drained from the placenta contains stem cells, the raw "unprogrammed" cells from which all organs and tissues are created. These stem cells have proved to be effective therapy for some cancers and other related blood diseases. In addition, they have scores of other promising applications in the rapidly evolving field of stem-cell research.

If you decide to bank your child's cord blood, it will be collected right after the cord is cut and placed in a collection kit. Collection can be done by any provider in any birth setting and virtually any circumstance—from a midwife-supervised home birth to an obstetrician-performed C-section in the operating room. A medical courier service will fly the blood to your chosen banking facility where it is frozen and stored. An initial banking fee and a monthly storage fee will be required, which may make it cost-prohibitive for some families. However, women who have a history of health problems in their family tree may find the peace of mind that banked cord blood provides well worth the expense.

There are a number of cord-blood banking services advertising in the United States. The American Association of Blood Banks (AABB) gives accreditation to blood banks with operational systems and procedures in place that have met strict quality and safety standards defined by the AABB. These banks also comply with federal guidelines for blood banking.

Delivering the Placenta

After your baby is born, your contractions will continue until the placenta is delivered, which is actually considered the third and final stage of labor. Again, you'll be instructed to push to help deliver the placenta. Your provider may assist by pressing down on your abdomen and gently tugging on the umbilical cord. If contractions wane, you may be given an injection of Pitocin to strengthen them until the placenta emerges.

Your provider will examine your placenta thoroughly to ensure that it is intact and no portions are missing. It's essential that the entire placenta be delivered, which is why your provider will examine it thoroughly. If placental fragments are left in the uterus, the uterus will not contract or shrink back down to normal size, and you run the risk of a life-threatening postpartum hemorrhage. This is one reason why you'll find maternity nurses and other caregivers frequently checking the progress of your uterus in the hours following your child's birth. Your provider may perform manual inspection of your uterus if she believes you have retained placental fragments.

Your provider may also administer some Pitocin via an intravenous line or intramuscular injection after the delivery of the placenta to increase uterine contractions and decrease uterine bleeding postpartum. Most providers will massage the uterus following delivery of the placenta to help the uterus contract and decrease blood loss.

FACT

If you require an episiotomy or experience perineal tearing during childbirth, your doctor or midwife will put in any required stitches after the placenta is delivered. A local anesthetic will be injected into the perineal area if you aren't already anesthetized from an epidural or other block.

Attachment and Bonding

Those first few hours with your newborn are a precious time. Usually, your infant is in a state of awareness known as "quiet alertness," in which he is calm but attentive, taking in his environment and new family.

Not only is baby getting adjusted to life outside the womb, but you are continuing and strengthening the mother-child relationship that began in the womb. Talk to your baby, and he will respond to your voice, recognizing it from his many long months inside your body. Immediately after birth is also a good time to start breastfeeding if you have chosen to do so. You'll find that baby instinctively knows what to do, even if you've never done this before.

Skin-to-skin contact with your newborn, also referred to as kangaroo care, facilitates bonding and promotes early and longer breastfeeding practices. Because the internal "thermostat" of a newborn baby is still immature, the warmth of a mother's, or a father's, body can help ward off hypothermia as well as provide a fulfilling bonding experience for both baby and parent.

Baby's First Checkup

All hospitals and some birthing centers will have a laundry list of procedures they want to perform on your child immediately following birth. Barring medical complications with either baby or mom, there is no clinical reason why these tests and measurements can't be held off temporarily while you and baby have a chance to bond.

Tests and procedures typically performed on newborn infants include the following:

- **Suction.** Your baby's mouth and nose may be suctioned to remove mucus and fluid from his airway.
- **APGAR score.** An assessment of your newborn's health, reactivity, and appearance after birth; APGAR evaluates appearance (skin color), pulse, grimace (reflexes), activity, and respiration.
- **Weights and measures.** Your baby's length and head circumference will be measured, and he will be weighed.
- **Infant ID.** If you give birth in a hospital, your little one will receive hospital identification bands on the wrist and/or ankle that match yours. Your child's footprints may also be taken.
- **Eyedrops.** Antibiotic eyedrops or ointment may be administered to prevent infection. Since these will blur your baby's vision for a time, you might ask to have this treatment withheld until after you've had a little bonding time and visual contact with your child.
- **Heelstick.** Blood is drawn via a heelstick to test for PKU and hypothyroidism. If you have had gestational diabetes or your baby is otherwise at risk for low blood-glucose levels, this may be tested via a heelstick as well.
- **Vitamin K injection.** Vitamin K, which helps in blood clotting, is injected into the baby's thigh to prevent bleeding problems until he is able to manufacture the vitamin on his own.
- **Hepatitis B vaccine.** In some hospitals, a shot of this vaccine may be required.

Other tests and procedures may be performed, depending on your birth facility and your specific medical history. Talk to your provider about what tests are typical in your particular situation.

Breastfeeding Basics

Breast milk is the best food for your baby, hands down. Tailored specifically for his digestive and immune system, it is nutritionally perfect for his needs. However, the issue of whether or not to breastfeed encompasses much more than nutrition—emotional, social, cultural, and career concerns can all have an impact on whether or not breastfeeding is right for you.

If you give birth in a hospital, ask if they have a lactation consultant on staff. She can be invaluable in helping you get off on the right foot (or breast, as the case may be). Your midwife, doctor, or child's pediatrician can also provide you with a referral. Finally, the La Leche League is a great source of breastfeeding support. See Appendix B in the back of this book for information on getting in touch with a local chapter.

Making the Choice

Social pressures—both for and against breastfeeding—can be enormous on a new or soon-to-be-new mother trying to make a decision on whether or not nursing is right for her. Make sure you're basing your choice on *your* needs and not the preconceived notions of others. Don't assume bottle-feeding is your only option because you'll be back at work in six weeks and your best friend asserts that pumping at work is unprofessional, or because your great aunt tells you nursing will "ruin your figure." And don't let others convince you that you're a bad and insensitive mother if you decide that you're too physically and emotionally taxed to commit to breastfeeding.

If this is your first child and you just aren't sure which way to go, trying to nurse certainly can't hurt and will definitely help your child. Breastfeeding your child for even a few weeks will benefit him both physically and emotionally.

Here are some reasons why breast may be best:

- **Closeness.** This one-on-one time spent with your baby is priceless.
- **Convenience.** Your breast milk is always available and the perfect temperature. No rubber nipples, bottles, coolers, or can openers required.
- **Cost.** You can save a significant chunk of change by forgoing formula and all the feeding paraphernalia required with bottles.
- **Customization.** Even the best formula doesn't come close to providing the nutrition and antibodies that your breast milk does. It is your child's perfect food.

Reasons why a bottle may be more your style:

- **Sleep.** Your partner can give that three a.m. bottle once in a while.
- **Sovereignty.** Breastfeeding requires a commitment to relative closeness at all times (although a breast pump can provide enough freedom for many women). It also requires that you continue "sharing" your body with baby by watching the quality of your diet and avoiding alcohol and other harmful substances.
- **Self-consciousness.** Some women feel uncomfortable with the prospect of nursing in public.
- **Society.** Along the same lines, our society still has a long way to go in providing a comfortable and socially acceptable environment that supports breastfeeding in public.

ALERT!

There are some medical conditions that eliminate breastfeeding as an option. Some women who have undergone breast surgery may have difficulty producing sufficient milk for nursing. In addition, Women who are HIV-1 positive can transmit the virus to their infants via breast milk, and both the American Academy of Pediatrics and the U.S. Centers for Disease Control recommend that these women abstain from breastfeeding.

Whatever you decide, make sure it's right for both you and your baby. If you are in a situation in which you are already emotionally and physically overtaxed with work, family, and/or health concerns, pushing yourself further by being pressured into breastfeeding will do more harm than good to both you and baby.

On the other hand, women who are supported at home, healthy, and don't have excessive demands on their time should consider breastfeeding—even if they feel a little awkward or uncomfortable about the prospect. Often those feelings quickly disappear as a mother gains expertise in breastfeeding and experiences the special bond that breastfeeding builds.

First Feeding

For several days before your milk comes in, your breasts will produce a yellowish sticky substance called colostrum. Colostrum contains antibodies that help to strengthen the infant immune system. Low in carbohydrates and high in protein, this precursor to breast milk is gentle on baby's immature digestive system and helps to establish intestinal flora (a beneficial bacteria) in your baby's gastrointestinal tract.

Approximately three days after birth, your milk will come in. You'll know when it happens—the milk ducts (alveoli) in your breasts will become engorged with milk and your breasts will feel hard and sore to the touch. Nursing your baby will relieve some of this initial discomfort, as will warm compresses and massage. Rest assured that the soreness is only temporary. With regular nursing you shouldn't feel uncomfortably full, and if you are away from baby for a time and become engorged, expressing milk with a breast pump or by hand can relieve the pressure.

If you choose to bottle feed instead of breastfeed, cold packs, mild analgesics, and a very supportive bra can help ease the discomfort of engorgement. Expressing milk to relieve the pressure will only stimulate your breasts to produce more milk and should be avoided.

There are a number of ways you can hold your baby when nursing. The general rule is to make it comfortable, and keep baby's body (not just her head) facing yours. If you've had a C-section, make sure you support your incision when nursing.

Ensure that your baby is getting your entire nipple and most of the areola in her mouth when she latches on. You can help her along by cupping your breast and offering the nipple out to her. Stroke her bottom lip with your nipple to get her to open wide, a reflex known as "rooting." Listen for sounds of swallowing.

You'll find your baby nursing often the first few weeks—up to twelve times a day. The frequent feedings help establish your milk supply, and she will gradually start lengthening the time between feedings as she grows older. Some new moms worry that this endless snacking means their child is not getting enough to eat. As long as she is making six to eight wet diapers and about three dirty diapers daily, she's getting plenty.

Babies who are born prematurely or have health issues at birth may not be able to latch or suck effectively enough to breastfeed. A breast pump can help mom keep up her milk supply until baby is able to nurse again.

While instinct certainly plays a role, persistence and patience are factors just as critical, if not more, in successful breastfeeding. It may not just "come naturally" at first, particularly if you don't have the guidance of a lactation consultant or other mentor to help you get your technique down, and the anxiety and stress that result from imperfect results can further sabotage your breastfeeding efforts. Get support, and remember it will come with practice.

When Baby Needs Special Care

If your newborn is born prematurely or encounters medical problems, he may spend some time in the neonatal intensive care unit (NICU). It's normal to feel frightened, vulnerable, and helpless as you see your newborn infant lying in a glass incubator, lost in a tangle of wires and tubes. But it's important to remember that your baby is benefiting from your presence and your physical touch, even if he can't be held or nursed yet.

Premature babies with no other serious medical problems are usually discharged when they can maintain their body temperature, feed and breathe well on their own, and achieve a weight of approximately 4.4 pounds (2000 grams). Infants also usually need to reach an age of thirty-five weeks from the date of their mother's last menstrual period.

The NICU staff can coach you on ways of touching your baby that will provide nurturing without overstimulation. Remember that your baby knows your voice, and talk to him often. Get involved with any care and feeding that you can, and learn about any special medical requirements your child may have early on while you have the benefit of an expert staff around you. Feel empowered by the fact that the presence of you and your partner is probably doing just as much, if not more, for your child's recovery as all the technology around him.

Rooming In or Going Home

Looking forward to taking your new addition home soon after she arrives? In a birthing-center environment, barring any unforeseen medical problems, you'll be able to introduce your newborn to her new digs just hours after the birth is complete. In a hospital, your stay is a bit longer; however, that doesn't mean that you'll be separated from your baby or confined to your hospital bed. Make sure "rooming in" is available at your birth facility of choice, and you can spend your hospital stay in the same room as your baby. For more on rooming in, see Chapter 4.

Getting Acquainted

Your baby will spend a great deal of time sleeping the first few days and weeks. The time just after she awakens, when she is both quiet and alert, is perfect for playtime. Babies see best at a distance of about nine to twelve inches, and will focus on the edges of your face because they see better with their peripheral vision, so keep that in mind as you interact.

While you're at the hospital, even if you're rooming in, don't be afraid to tap the expertise of the nurses if you're having the trouble getting the hang of diaper changes or other essential baby-care skills. That's what they're there for. And if you're exhausted and just need some uninterrupted sleep, don't feel guilty about sending your baby down to the nursery for a few hours if your partner isn't around to care for her. Birth is a physically exhausting experience, and getting your rest and recuperation now will ensure that you're ready to meet the many challenges your little one will put before you in the coming weeks and months.

Chapter 20

The Postpartum Experience

The birth is over, you've met your baby, and you're now settling into the new routine of motherhood. While you've waited months, or perhaps years, for this, things may not be falling into place exactly as you planned. Be patient with yourself. Great mothers, and families, are made—not born. Cherish this postpartum time as a learning experience while you, your partner, and your baby get to know one another.

The Postpartum Body

While you will lose between ten and fifteen pounds at birth in the form of baby, amniotic fluid, placenta, and lochia fluids, it will take some time before your body reverts to prepregnancy weight. Remember that you didn't gain it overnight, so don't expect it to disappear that quickly either.

Your uterus will shrink steadily from the time of birth so that by the tenth day postpartum, it should be approximately one-twentieth of the size it was at the peak of your pregnancy, and you will no longer be able to feel the fundus (or top) when pressing on your abdomen. The cervix will close itself, but your vaginal canal may remain somewhat loose. Kegel exercises can help firm things up again. (See Chapter 15 for more on kegels.)

Bleeding, which is actually lochia—a mixture of blood, mucus, and tissue from the placental implantation site—will continue for several weeks. Lochia flow is generally heavy and bright red at first, but should slow significantly by two weeks after delivery. Some discharge, usually of a brown or pinkish nature, is normal for up to six weeks after birth.

ALERT!

If you have sudden heavy or bright-red bleeding after a period of light lochia flow, you may be overexerting or stressing yourself. Slow down, and see if things return to normal. Always consult your health-care provider if you experience any abnormal or prolonged heavy bleeding requiring more than one sanitary pad in an hour.

Because your body is no longer supporting the cardiovascular needs of two, your blood volume will decrease. Hormonal changes are also in full swing once again. The resulting fatigue from all these physical changes can be exacerbated by your baby's erratic sleeping schedule. It's important to stay well nourished and well hydrated during this time, particularly if you're breastfeeding, and to rest whenever you can.

The Recovery Period

The length of time to fully recover from the physical strains of childbirth will vary by birth experience and individual. In a normal, uncomplicated vaginal birth with no tearing, you can expect some perineal swelling and tenderness for about a week, although in some cases discomfort may persist a bit longer. Women who undergo cesarean, perineal tearing, or episiotomy incisions will of course need time for their bodies to heal. A second-degree episiotomy or perineal tear, the most common type, can take up to two months to heal, while third and fourth-degree lacerations may remain painful for three months or longer.

If you aren't breastfeeding, your menstrual period will resume anywhere from three to eight weeks after birth. For women who are breastfeeding, the return of your period will depend on your particular cycle and on how much your baby is nursing. Most health-care professionals advise that you wait six weeks before resuming sexual activity to reduce the risk of infection and ensure that you're adequately healed. Speak with your health-care provider at your postpartum visit about contraception options. (For more on postpartum contraception, see "Family Planning" later in this chapter.)

After Vaginal Birth

Some perineal discomfort is common after vaginal birth, especially if you've had an episiotomy. Your provider may recommend a hip or sitz bath, which involves sitting in a shallow (hip-deep) tub of warm water to soak your perineal area. Visiting the bathroom may be particularly difficult; a stool softener can help make passing a bowel movement easier, and a warm-water rinse will keep any stitches clean and soothe the area. An ointment may also be prescribed to promote healing of an episiotomy. Remember to check with your provider before taking any medication if you are breastfeeding.

If you find sitting for extended periods painful, try a foam donut on your chair. Foam donuts are relatively inexpensive and can be purchased from a medical supply store. If you can't locate one in your area, a thick piece of foam rubber from your local craft store with a hole cut in the middle will do just as well. Also an acceptable substitute is a large, circular nursing pillow.

After Cesarean

In addition to dealing with the normal adjustments of having a new baby in the house, moms who have had C-sections also have postsurgical pain and physical limitations to cope with. Cesarean section is major surgery, and you will need to slow your pace and have adequate support around your household to ensure a quick and complete recovery.

Six weeks is the typical rest and recuperation period for women after cesarean. Things like heavy lifting (if it's heavier than the baby, don't try it), driving, and strenuous activity will be off limits. Your doctor may prescribe pain medication to ease your discomfort and help you get adequate rest. Women who choose to breastfeed should talk with their doctor about the potential impact of any medication on their baby.

Your incision will be sore and your abdomen quite tender during those first postpartum weeks. In fact, sitting up or standing from a prone position will be a major chore. Push yourself up with your arms or help from your partner, not with your abdominal muscles. And always support your incision with a towel or pillow when you hold and breastfeed your baby.

FACT

Before you leave the hospital, your provider will instruct you on proper incision care. She will also give you a list of warning signs to be aware of—such as fever, incision redness, excessive warmth, oozing, swelling, or bleeding—that may indicate infection or another problem. If you experience any of these symptoms, contact your health-care provider immediately.

Emotional Upheavals

Your body may be easing back toward its prepregnancy state, but your life will never be the same. The change from childless to primary caregiver is a radical one, and it's normal to feel overwhelmed and unsure of yourself. Stress and self-doubt may have you on an emotional rollercoaster, with postpartum hormonal changes contributing to the ups and downs. You're also feeling the brunt of too little sleep as you try to adjust to the new way of life.

In these first few months, your baby will be sleeping about eighteen hours a day—and waking up several times each night to be fed.

A good night's sleep is a distant memory for most new moms. You've probably heard the advice "Sleep when the baby sleeps," but are you following it? The laundry, dishes, and other household tasks can wait. You need your rest right now to stay healthy. If you just can't stand the mess, consider bringing in a cleaning service to help out, or enlist the help of friends and family.

Postpartum Depression

With sleep at a minimum, your body undergoing such radical changes, the discomfort of postpartum recovery, and typical new-mother jitters about your baby's health and your parenting skills, it's normal to feel emotionally drained. In fact, up to 85 percent of women experience some level of mild depression after birth—sometimes referred to as "the baby blues." Usually time, rest, and growing self-confidence in your own abilities will have you feeling more emotionally balanced within a few days to a few weeks.

However, if feelings of depression drag on, and they reach the point where they are interfering with your ability to effectively function and your enjoyment of life and your new baby, you might have postpartum depression, or PPD. Be aware of signs that you may be experiencing PPD, such as these:

- You don't take any pleasure in things that you used to enjoy.
- You are sad for no well-defined reason, and cry with little to no provocation.
- You have trouble concentrating on tasks.
- You obsess over what might be wrong or go wrong with the baby (beyond the normal new-parent anxieties).
- You have little to no interest in the new baby.
- You feel worthless and have little to no self-esteem.
- Your appetite is gone.
- You feel that you might hurt yourself or the baby.

If you're experiencing any of the above symptoms, contact your provider for a referral to a mental-health-care professional. Don't try to tough it out on your own. PPD can be treated successfully with counseling, antidepressant medications, or a combination of the two. Some women may feel embarrassed or stigmatized by the need for help and their emotional misery during a time that they "should be" happy and enjoying their newborn. Realize that an estimated 10 percent of new mothers experience PPD, so you are not alone.

Women who breastfeed should talk to their providers before taking any antidepressant medication to weigh the risks versus the benefits of its use. On one hand, there are currently no long-term studies on possible long-range effects and safety of these medications on nursing infants. On the other, it is known that left untreated, chronic postpartum depression can have a detrimental effect on the children of depressed mothers. Follow-up studies have linked PPD to delayed cognitive development, learning disabilities, and behavioral and emotional problems.

ALERT!

Women who are depressed postpartum and are also experiencing additional symptoms, such as hallucinations, delusions, extreme mood swings, and thoughts of hurting themselves or others, may have postpartum psychosis (also known as puerperal psychosis). The condition is relatively rare (only one in 1,000 women experience it) and highly treatable, but it is a serious emergency that requires immediate medical attention.

Even with the unknowns surrounding antidepressant use with breastfeeding, there are some antidepressant medications that are thought to be potentially safer than others for the nursing baby. Sertraline (Zoloft) passes into breast milk, but studies have demonstrated that it reaches a nursing baby in such clinically insignificant levels that it often can't be detected in standard lab tests. Sertraline is a member of the selective serotonin reuptake inhibitor (SSRI) class of antidepressant drugs; another SSRI, paroxetine (Paxil) and the tricyclic antidepressant nortriptyline (Pamelor) have also been found to have no adverse affects on nursing infants in clinical studies. Estrogen treatment for PPD has also had some promising results in clinical studies, although further research on hormone therapy is needed.

Embracing Your Birth Story

For women who ended up with a birth that wasn't exactly what they had envisioned, coming to terms with missed expectations can be difficult. Know that ending up with a cesarean, forceps delivery, or pain medication when you had expected otherwise does not make your achievement—a new life that you have wrought and brought into the world—any less miraculous.

If something did "go wrong" during your birth experience, don't torture yourself second-guessing your own decisions. You can use the information to make things go better the next time you give birth, if that's in your future. Even if it isn't, appreciating your successes instead of dwelling on "what might have been" is key to really appreciating your birth experience, no matter what it was.

Your birth story, warts and all, is uniquely yours and your child's. Even the roughest labors and deliveries have their bright spots—most notably, the first time you hold your brand-new child. Take the time to write down your thoughts about the birth and how it progressed now that you have had some time for it to all sink in. Recording these memories can be therapeutic, and it may reveal the beauty of your birth experience to you in the process. Your child will also enjoy hearing about all the details at some point in the future.

Your Baby and You

Getting settled into this new life, routine, and relationship takes time. Having someone so utterly dependant on you, first for life and now for continuous care, shelter, and sustenance, can be a little daunting. But the joy you get from the unconditional love of your newborn will far outstrip any fears or anxieties about not being up to the challenge.

As you continue strengthening the bond you built in pregnancy while learning that delicate sense of balance among your various roles as mother, partner, breadwinner, and general household glue (the one that holds it all together), here are some cardinal rules to help you on your journey:

- **Great moms are made, not born.** Sure, maternal instinct gets a lot of press, but any mother can tell you that it's the trial and error of daily infant care and ongoing experience that make a greenhorn a pro.

- **Remember your childhood.** Be a kid again. Regress back to the songs, rhymes, and games of your childhood and learn to really play again. Your child will love you for it, and you'll find it's a great stress-buster as well.
- **Learn new shortcuts.** The day is about twelve hours too short for most new moms. Get some of that time back by making your "to do" list shorter. Have the groceries delivered instead of lugging all the baby gear to the store. Let an accountant do your taxes. Get a yard service to tend to your garden and mow the lawn. You'll find the extra time you have for yourself and your baby worth the added expense.
- **Set priorities.** Just because you've always taken on overtime projects at work or hosted all the family holidays at your house doesn't mean that you have to continue to do so. You have a lot more on your plate these days, so set priorities and stick to them. Delegate everything else that you don't have the time or inclination to handle to others.
- **Give yourself a time out.** Between diaper changes, feedings, the constant quest for sleep, and playing catch-up on housework, simply sitting back and having fun with your baby can get lost in the shuffle. You only get one chance to witness this baby's first smiles, words, and steps as she learns to navigate life. Drop everything, at least once in a while, and enjoy it with her.

Birth of a Family

Of course, your baby's arrival marks the beginning of a whole new family as well. Your partner is now a father, and he may be experiencing some of the same insecurities about his parenting skills that you are. Giving him one-on-one time with the new baby will enable him to gain confidence in his abilities and develop his own unique parenting style. Don't hover or judge; it would drive you crazy if someone were doing it to you. Your baby will actually learn to discern, and enjoy, the differences in the way mom and dad do things.

If this isn't your first baby, you now have new sibling relationships you will need to help define and nurture, and your role as mom just got a little larger. Depending on the age and personalities of your other children, you may be dealing with jealousy and resentments as they look for reassurance that they will continue to be just as important in your eyes as the new baby.

Remind your children of their special role as big brothers and sisters by involving them in the new baby's care. Even the smallest child can help out by retrieving a fresh diaper or holding a tiny hand. You can also ensure they feel less threatened by setting aside a block of time that is designated baby-free for the two of you each day.

Doing It Again?

Feeling like you never want to look at another pair of maternity pants again? With the aches and pains of pregnancy so fresh in your memory, getting back to your old body may be your number-one goal right now. But depending on your personal objectives, age, and health history, you might already be thinking about your next pregnancy.

If another baby is a short-term goal of yours, try to give your body enough time to recover before conceiving again. Healing completely and losing any extra pregnancy weight will make your next pregnancy, and postpartum period, a healthier experience. Waiting at least two years from birth to next conception will offer your body enough rest and recovery to provide a healthy environment for your future fetus. It will also allow you to give your newborn your undivided attention during these important early years.

FACT

Women who are planning on breastfeeding their newborn long-term through a next pregnancy should keep in mind that they will be nourishing two growing bodies at once (three if they count themselves). Many infants wean themselves by the fourth or fifth month of their mother's pregnancy as maternal milk supply naturally decreases at that point.

Family Planning

Women can and do get pregnant in the postpartum period, even if they are breastfeeding, so if you aren't interested in getting right back on the pregnancy train, choose a contraception method before you need it.

Nonhormonal barrier methods, such as condoms and copper intrauterine devices (IUDs), may be preferred by some women who are breastfeeding; combined estrogen and progestin birth control pills are not a good first option for contraception when breastfeeding because they can reduce both quality and quantity of breast milk. However, the progestin-only "minipill" is considered safe and effective for nursing mothers and babies. The ACOG recommends initiation of its use at two to three weeks postpartum. Other implantable and injectable progestin-only contraception methods are also available, so talk to your doctor about your options.

QUESTION?

I'm breastfeeding my baby. Do I need additional contraception?
Breastfeeding inhibits ovulation, so if you are nursing exclusively and have not had any postpartum menstruation or spotting, the lactational amenorrhea method (LAM) of birth control can be highly successful—more than 98 percent during the first six months postpartum. However, for LAM to be most effective, you should be nursing your baby at least every four hours during the day and six hours at night. If you don't meet all of the above criteria, you should be using supplemental birth control methods.

No Two Births Are Alike

For women who have had a difficult labor and birth experience, or a complicated pregnancy, contemplating another pregnancy may be an internal struggle. Keep in mind that in most respects, your next pregnancy and birth will be as unique as your children themselves will turn out to be. You will also have experience on your side the next time out, and perhaps a clearer picture of your own sense of purpose and place in relation to your birth choices. If you and your partner have dreams of more children, don't let fear prevent you from pursuing them.

Your New Life

Childbirth initiates a complex personal transformation that goes beyond motherhood. A woman who has given birth—no matter what the circumstances—is awakened to a previously untapped source of physical and emotional strength within herself. If you can manage to create this beautiful living being and bring it out into the world, life's biggest challenges start to look like a skinned knee by comparison. Don't forget that strength; carry it with you, and use it often.

While new motherhood is a time-intensive role, don't let it become an all-consuming one. You need time for adult pursuits, both solitary and social, so make your needs known to your spouse or others around you and make sure you get some downtime from childcare. It will make you a much more pleasant person to be around and a better mom as well.

The weeks and months following the birth of a new baby are an exciting and irreplaceable time, as unpredictable and thrilling as the childbirth experience itself. And while, like birth, they may not go exactly as your careful planning dictates, the journey itself—with all its grins and groans, anxieties and unabashed delight—is one to be treasured forever. Sit back and enjoy the ride.

Appendix A

Birth-Plan Checklist

Begin your birth plan with a brief note to your health-care provider and others who will be attending the birth. Explain your general wishes for a healthy and safe delivery, for joint decision-making with your provider should medical interventions be required, and for open communication throughout the birth process.

Birth-Plan Checklist

If you're having a home birth and attendees such as your children will be given specific duties such as announcing the sex of the baby, include a section outlining your wishes for this. Read Chapter 5 to learn more about birth plans, then use this checklist as a guide to assembling the basics and customizing your own.

1. Where will the birth take place?
   - ○ Hospital
   - ○ Birthing center
   - ○ Home
   - ○ Other

   _____

   _____

   _____

2. Who will be there for labor support?
   - ○ Husband or significant other
   - ○ Doula
   - ○ Friend
   - ○ Family member

3. Will any room modifications or equipment be required to increase your comfort mentally and physically?
   - ○ Objects from home (pictures, blanket, pillow)
   - ○ Lighting adjustments
   - ○ Music
   - ○ Video or photos of birth
   - ○ Other

   _____

   _____

   _____

4. Any special requests for labor prep procedures?
   - ○ Forego enema
   - ○ Self-administer the enema
   - ○ Forego shaving
   - ○ Shave self
   - ○ Heparin lock instead of routine IV line
   - ○ Other

5. Eating and drinking during labor
   - ○ Want access to a light snack
   - ○ Want access to water, sports drink, or other appropriate beverage
   - ○ Want ice chips
   - ○ Other

6. Do you want pain medication?
   - ○ Analgesic (Stadol, Demerol, other)
   - ○ Epidural (if so, is timing an issue?)
   - ○ Other

7. What nonpharmaceutical pain relief equipment might you want access to?
   - ○ Hydrotherapy (shower, whirlpool)
   - ○ Warm compresses
   - ○ Birth ball
   - ○ Massage aids
   - ○ Other

   _____
   _____
   _____
   _____

8. What interventions would you like to avoid unless deemed a medical necessity by your provider during labor? Specify your preferred alternatives.
   - ○ Episiotomy
   - ○ Forceps
   - ○ Internal fetal monitoring
   - ○ Continuous fetal monitoring
   - ○ Pitocin (Oxytocin)
   - ○ Other

   _____
   _____
   _____
   _____

9. What would you like your first face-to-face with baby to be like?
   - ○ Hold off on all nonessential treatment, evaluation, and tests for a specified time.
   - ○ If immediate tests and evaluation are necessary, mother, father, or another support person will accompany baby.
   - ○ Want to breastfeed immediately following birth.
   - ○ Would like family members to meet baby immediately following birth.
   - ○ Other

10. If a cesarean is required, what is important to you and your partner?
    - ○ Type of anesthesia (general, spinal block)
    - ○ Having partner or another support person present
    - ○ Spending time with baby immediately following procedure
    - ○ Bonding with baby in the recovery room
    - ○ Type of postoperative pain relief and nursing considerations
    - ○ Other

11. Do you have a preference for who cuts the cord and when the cut is performed?
    - ○ Mom
    - ○ Dad
    - ○ Provider
    - ○ Delay until cord stops pulsing
    - ○ Cord blood will be banked. Cut per banking guidelines.
    - ○ Cut at provider's discretion.
    - ○ Other

12. What kind of care will you and baby have at the hospital postpartum?
    - ○ Baby will room-in with mom.
    - ○ Baby will sleep in the nursery at nights.
    - ○ Baby will breastfeed.

continued . . .

○ Baby will bottle feed.
○ Don't feed baby any supplemental formula and/or glucose water.
○ Don't give baby a pacifier.
○ Other

_____

_____

_____

_____

13. Considerations for after discharge
    ○ Support and short-term care for siblings
    ○ Support after a cesarean
    ○ Maternity leave
    ○ Other

_____

_____

_____

_____

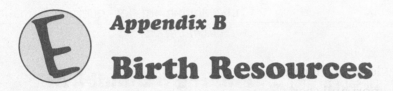

Appendix B

Birth Resources

Organizations, publications, and Web resources for finding more information about pregnancy, birth, and beyond.

General Pregnancy and Birth Resources

About Pregnancy and Childbirth
With Robin Elise Weiss, L.C.C.E.,
I.C.C.E.-C.P.E., C.D. (DONA)
✍ http://pregnancy.about.com

The Everything® Pregnancy Book, Second Edition
By Paula Ford-Martin with Dr. Elisabeth Aron
ISBN: 1-58062-808-7
Adams Media, 2003

Finding a Provider

American College of Nurse Midwives
✉ 818 Connecticut Avenue, NW
Suite 900
Washington, D.C. 20006
☎ 202-728-9860
✍ www.midwife.org

American College of Obstetricians and Gynecologists (ACOG)
✉ 409 12th Street S.W.
Washington, D.C. 20090-6920
☎ 202-863-2518
💻 E-mail: resources@acog.org
✍ www.acog.org

Doulas of North America (DONA)
✉ P.O. Box 626
Jasper, IN 47547
☎ 888-788-DONA
💻 E-mail: Referrals@dona.org
✍ www.dona.org

Midwives Alliance of North America (MANA)
✉ 4805 Lawrenceville Highway
Suite 116-279
Liburn, GA 30047
☎ 888-923-MANA
💻 E-mail: membership@mana.org (for referrals)
💻 info@mana.org (for general information)
✍ www.mana.org

Finding a Childbirth Educator

Association of Labor Assistants and Childbirth Educators (ALACE)
✉ P.O. Box 390436
Cambridge, MA 02139
☎ 888-222-5223
✍ www.alace.org

International Childbirth Education Association (ICEA)
✉ P.O. Box 20048
Minneapolis, MN 55420
☎ 952-854-8660
💻 E-mail: info@icea.org
✍ www.icea.org

The Bradley Method
The American Academy of Husband-Coached Childbirth
✉ Box 5224
Sherman Oaks, CA 91413-5224
☎ 800-4-A-BIRTH
✍ www.bradleybirth.org

HypnoBirthing
✉P.O. Box 810
  Epsom, NH 03234
💻E-mail: hypnobirthing@hypnobirthing.com
✏*www.hypnobirthing.com*

Lamaze International
✉2025 M Street
  Suite 800
  Washington, D.C. 20036-3309
☎800-368-4404
✏*www.lamaze.org*

Cesarean and VBAC Support

**Cesareans/Support Education
and Concern (C/SEC)**
Director of Client Services
✉22 Forest Road
  Framingham, MA 01701
☎508-877-8266

**International Cesarean
Awareness Network (ICAN)**
✉1304 Kingsdale Avenue
  Redondo Beach, CA 90278
☎310-542-6400
💻E-mail: info@ican-online.org
✏*www.ican-online.org*

VBAC.com
A place for "research-based information, resources, continuing education and support for VBAC (vaginal birth after cesarean)."
✏*www.vbac.com*

Fitness for Birth

The Everything® Pregnancy Fitness Book
By Robin Elise-Weiss, L.C.C.E.,
  I.C.C.E.-C.P.E., C.D. (DONA)
Adams Media, 2003

Home Birth Resources

*Birth Your Way: Choosing Birth at
Home or in a Birth Centre*
By Sheila Kitzinger
Dorling Kindersley, 2002

Childbirth at Home: A Labor of Love
Wholistic Midwifery School of
  Southern California
✏*www.socalbirth.org*

Joyous Birth League International
Support for Unassisted Home Birth
💻E-mail: members@jbli.org
✏*www.jbli.org*

Relaxation and Guided Imagery Resources

**Imagery and Meditations for Labor
and Birth Preparation (Audio CD)**
By Jennifer Bloome, MS OTR
Anji, Inc.
✏*www.anjionline.com*

*Pregnancy Relaxation: A Guide to
Peaceful Beginnings* **(Audio CD)**
By Dana Schardt, MS, RN, APNP
Audio CD with progressive-relaxation
  and guided-imagery exercises

Multiples Birth and Postpartum Support

About Multiples
With Pamela Prindle Fierro
✍*http://multiples.about.com*

Marvelous Multiples
✉P.O. Box 381164
   Birmingham, AL 35238
☎205-437-3575
💻E-mail: marvmult@aol.com
✍*www.marvelousmultiples.com*

Mothers of Supertwins (MOST)
✉P.O. Box 951
   Brentwood, NY 11717
☎631-859-1110
💻E-mail: info@MOSTonline.org
✍*www.mostonline.org*

National Organization of Mothers of Twins Clubs (NOMOTC)
Executive Office
✉P.O. Box 438
   Thompson Station, TN 37179-0438
☎800-243-2276
✍*www.nomotc.org*

Water Birth Information
Choosing Water Birth: Reclaiming the Sacred Power of Birth
By Lakshmi Bertram
Hampton Roads Publishing, 2001
ISBN: 1571741526

Waterbirth International
Global Maternal/Child Health Association, Inc.
✉P.O. Box 1400
   Wilsonville, OR 97070
☎800-641-2229
💻E-mail: info@waterbirth.org
✍*www.waterbirth.org*

Cord-Blood Banking Resources

National Marrow Donor Program
✉Suite 500
   3001 Broadway Street Northeast
   Minneapolis, MN 55413-1753
☎1-800-MARROW2
✍*www.marrow.org (cord blood FAQs)*

Viacord, Inc.
✉131 Clarendon St.
   Boston, MA 02116
☎1-866-668-4895
✍*www.viacord.com*

Special Issues
Depression After Delivery
✉91 East Somerset Street
   Raritan, NJ 08869
☎800-944-4773
✍*www.depressionafterdelivery.com*

Hygeia Foundation for Perinatal Loss, Inc.
✉P.O. Box 3943
   Amity Station
   New Haven, CT 06525
☎203-387-3589
✍*www.hygeia.org*

Appendix C

Glossary

Common clinical and layman's terminology associated with childbirth, and what it all means.

— A —

amniocentesis:

A diagnostic test in which a long needle is inserted through the abdomen into the amniotic sac to extract a fluid sample containing fetal cells. Amniocentesis is used for genetic testing and can also determine the lung maturity of a fetus.

amniotic sac:

The fluid-filled sac that a fetus develops within throughout pregnancy. Also known as "the bag of waters."

amniohook:

An instrument resembling a long crochet hook that is used to perform an amniotomy.

amniotomy:

Artificial rupture of the membranes or amniotic sac. Also called "AROM" and "breaking the bag of waters," amniotomy is performed in an effort to speed up labor.

APGAR score:

A test given to a newborn at one minute and five minutes after birth to assess appearance, pulse, grimace, activity level, and respiration.

— B —

birth center:

A facility that is freestanding from a hospital and is devoted exclusively to women's reproductive health care, where births take place in a home-like atmosphere, attended by midwives or physician staff members.

birth plan:

A written document that outlines the wishes a woman and her partner have for their upcoming birth and allows for open discussion with their provider.

bloody show:

The pink to brown mucous-like discharge that women may have at the start of labor. This discharge indicates that the cervix is ripening (thinning and widening).

buoyancy:

Weightlessness in water; one of the principals behind the effectiveness of water birth.

Bradley Method:

A method of childbirth education founded by Dr. Robert Bradley that focuses on deep relaxation for pain relief. Also called husband-coached childbirth because it teaches that a birth partner should coach a woman through her labor and birth experience.

Braxton-Hicks:

Painless, prelabor uterine contractions that can start as early as the twentieth week of pregnancy.

breech:

A fetus that is situated in any position other than a head-down (vertex) position. A breech fetus may be in transverse (sideways), bottom-down (complete or frank), or foot-first (footling) position, called breech presentation or breech position.

— C —

catecholamines:
Stress hormones, such as adrenaline and nor-adrenaline.

cephalopelvic disproportion:
A birth in which the baby's head is too large for the pelvic opening.

cervical ripening:
Effacement (thinning) and dilation (widening) of the opening of the cervix in preparation for birth.

cervix:
Latin for "neck," the cervix is the narrow opening in the lower half of the uterus. During pregnancy, the cervix is thick and closed, its opening plugged with a mucous substance (called a mucous plug). As labor progresses, it ripens in anticipation of childbirth.

colostrum:
The high-protein, antibody-rich liquid that is a precursor to breast milk.

contractions:
The muscular tightening of the uterus that is associated with labor.

cord-blood banking:
A process where umbilical cord blood is collected at birth, transported, and stored cryogenically for potential later use in stem cell therapy, transfusion, transplant, or other medical treatment.

cord compression:
Compression or squeezing of the umbilical cord, usually through pressure from the fetus, which impairs blood flow (and therefore, fetal oxygen supply) through the umbilical cord.

cord prolapse:
See prolapsed cord.

counterpressure:
A pain management technique involving applying firm pressure against the area of the body that is in pain. Can be used to relieve lower-back pain in labor.

crowning:
The appearance of the baby's head at the vaginal opening during childbirth.

— D —

dilation:
Widening of the cervical opening during labor. Measurements of dilation range from zero to ten centimeters.

doula:
A birth attendant who provides emotional and physical support for a laboring woman and her family.

doppler:
An ultrasound device used to listen to the fetal heartbeat.

dystocia:
Labor that fails to progress.

— E —

eclampsia:
A life-threatening condition involving seizures or convulsions that can occur when preeclampsia is not treated effectively.

effacement:
Thinning of the cervix.

electronic fetal monitoring:
A method of measuring the fetal heart rate that also measures the length and severity of contractions. Fetal monitoring may be intermittent, where only periodic checks are required, or continuous, where a permanent hook-up during labor is necessary.

endorphins:
Naturally produced neurotransmitters that relieve pain and, in large amounts, generate feelings of euphoria.

engagement:
See lightening.

epidural:
An anesthetic technique that involves injecting medication into the epidural space of the spinal canal to numb the body from the waist down.

episiotomy:
A surgical incision in the perineum for the purpose of making the vaginal opening larger for birth.

external cephalic version:
Used for a fetus in the breech position, ECV involves manually manipulating the mother's abdomen to turn the baby vertex (or head down).

— **F** —

fetoscope:
A stethoscope designed for listening to the fetal heartbeat.

forceps extraction:
Use of forceps, a tong-like surgical instrument, to extract the baby from the birth canal when medically indicated.

fundus:
The top of the uterus.

 — **G** —

general anesthesia:
Anesthetic that renders the patient unconscious; not commonly used in childbirth or cesarean section.

gestational diabetes:
Diabetes of pregnancy; characterized by high blood-glucose levels and insulin resistance caused by rising levels of pregnancy hormones.

guided imagery:
A technique of using mental pictures to visualize a positive birth experience, which is often used in tandem with relaxation techniques. Guided imagery is directed by a person or recording offering cues for the visualization.

— **H** —

heelstick:
The process of collecting blood for diagnostic testing from a newborn by sticking a surgical lance into his heel to start the blood flow.

HypnoBirthing:
A childbirth preparation technique based on self-hypnosis, relaxation, and guided imagery.

— I —

induction:
A method of starting labor either through medication (oxytocin, prostaglandins), manual manipulation (amniotomy, mechanical dilation, membrane stripping), herbs, or other methods (nipple stimulation, castor oil).

internal fetal monitoring:
A process of electronic fetal monitoring that uses a tiny spring-like wire inserted just under the skin of the baby's scalp. Internal monitoring is always continuous. (See also: electronic fetal monitoring).

— K —

kegels:
An exercise involving repeated tightening and relaxation of the pelvic floor muscles (the "hammock" of muscles that support the uterus and bladder) in order to tone them for birth and firm them postpartum.

— L —

labor-delivery-recovery room:
A hospital room in which a woman can spend her entire labor, birth, and immediate postpartum period. Also called an LDR room.

Lamaze:
A prepared childbirth method created by French physician Fernand Lamaze that emphasizes a woman's "inner wisdom" in her ability to give birth.

Leboyer bath:
A warm postpartum bath given to an infant shortly after birth that is designed to re-create the fluid environment of the womb and lessen the stress of the birth experience.

lightening:
Also known as engagement or the baby dropping, lightening is when the fetus descends, or engages, into the mother's pelvis.

lithotomy:
A childbirth position in which the mother is flat on her back with legs raised.

lochia:
Blood and tissue that is discharged from the vagina in the postpartum period. Similar to menstrual flow.

low-lying placenta:
A placenta that is implanted near the cervix, but not close enough to be considered placenta previa.

— M —

McRobert's position:
Supine (lying down) position with knees bent and pulled up close to the chest. This birth position is sometimes used to widen the pelvic outlet in cases of shoulder dystocia.

meconium:
An infant's first bowel movement; may appear in the amniotic fluid of a fetus in distress or a post-term pregnancy. There is a risk of aspiration (inhalation) of the dark, tarry meconium by the fetus if it is present in the amniotic fluid.

monoamniotic twins:
Twins that share a common amniotic sac.

— **N** —

neonatal intensive care unit:
A hospital unit with trained staff and special equipment intended specifically for the medical care of premature, low birth-weight, and critically ill infants. Also called the NICU.

NPO:
Abbreviation for the Latin *nil per os*, or nothing by mouth. If NPO orders are given for a laboring woman, or for a woman giving birth by cesarean, it means she is not permitted to eat or drink while the order stands. NPO may be ordered in certain situations where aspiration is thought to be a risk.

nuchal cord:
An umbilical cord that is wrapped around the baby's neck.

— **O** —

occiput position:
A face-up, or posterior, position of the newborn at birth (as opposed to the typical anterior, or face-down position) that can cause the lower back discomfort referred to as back labor. Sometimes referred to as "sunny side up."

os:
The cervical opening.

oxytocin:
A hormone secreted by the pituitary gland of the hypothalamus. Oxytocin stimulates contractions of the smooth muscles of the uterus in labor, and it also stimulates the milk-ejection reflex for breastfeeding.

— **P** —

patient advocate:
A hospital employee who is responsible for advocating for patient's rights and who acts as a liaison between a patient and the hospital staff and/or administration.

pelvic outlet:
The opening of the pelvic girdle that the baby passes through at birth.

perinatologist:
Also called a maternal fetal medicine specialist. A physician who specializes in caring for high-risk pregnancies and births.

perineum:
The tissue between the vaginal opening and the anus that stretches to accommodate the baby's head in childbirth.

phenylketonuria:
Also called PKU. A genetic disorder that impairs the body's ability to metabolize the protein phenylalanine from food and causes the protein to reach toxic levels in the bloodstream. If left untreated, PKU can cause mental retardation; PKU screening is a standard component of newborn testing, but must be performed twenty-four hours after birth to be accurate.

Pitocin:
The trade name for the synthetic form of oxytocin that is used for inducing labor and sometimes

injected either before or after the third stage of labor (expulsion of the placenta).

placenta:
A round, flat vascular organ that attaches to the uterine wall and provides nutrition and oxygen to the fetus through pregnancy via the umbilical cord. Delivery of the placenta is considered the third stage of labor.

placenta accreta:
A condition in which the placenta implants itself into the myometrium, or uterine muscle, instead of the endometrium, or uterine lining. Placental separation during the third stage of delivery can cause hemorrhage, or uncontrolled blood loss.

placenta previa:
A placental implantation over or near the cervical opening. Cesarean delivery may be required for some cases of placenta previa because of the risk of hemorrhage.

placental abruption:
A life-threatening condition for fetus and mother in which the placenta begins to separate from the uterine wall prematurely.

posterior position:
See occiput position.

postpartum:
Occurring after the birth.

postpartum depression:
A period of extreme sadness following birth that occurs in an estimated one out of ten women. Symptoms can include an inability to enjoy things that once brought pleasure, feelings of worthlessness, difficulty concentrating, anxiety, and unexplained irritability. Also called PPD.

postpartum psychosis:
A more extreme and rare variation of PPD that involves hallucinations and delusions. Postpartum psychosis is a medical emergency.

PPROM:
Preterm premature rupture of membranes; when the amniotic sac ruptures spontaneously before the due date.

preeclampsia:
A prenatal condition also known as toxemia that is characterized by high blood pressure, swelling of the hands and/or feet, protein in the urine, blurred vision, abdominal pain, and headache. Without proper treatment, preeclampsia may develop into eclampsia. (See also: eclampsia.)

premature labor:
Labor that begins before thirty-seven weeks of pregnancy. Also called preterm labor.

premature baby:
A baby that is born before thirty-seven weeks of pregnancy. Also called preterm or preemie. Premature infants may need specialized medical care in a neonatal intensive care unit.

prenatal:
Occurring before birth and during pregnancy.

progressive relaxation:
A method of achieving deep physical relaxation by tightening and then releasing tension in specific muscle groups. When used in childbirth

education, it is with the goal of being able to achieve relaxation quickly and easily when labor begins.

prolapsed cord:
An umbilical cord that drops out of the vagina before the baby emerges, or that is visible when the amniotic sac is ruptured. Because of the risk for cutting off the flow of blood and oxygen to the fetus, a prolapsed cord is a medical emergency.

psychoprophylaxis:
The basis of the Lamaze method. The use of relaxation and other mental exercises to control pain in labor and childbirth.

prostaglandins:
A hormone-like fatty-acid derivative. Synthetic prostaglandins in gel or suppository form are sometimes applied to the cervix to promote cervical ripening. (See also: cervical ripening.) Prostaglandins can also stimulate uterine contractions.

pudendal block:
An injection of a local anesthetic in the wall of the vagina that numbs the perineum and may be given when an episiotomy is anticipated.

— R —

regional anesthetic:
An anesthetic agent and/or procedure that deadens sensation in a certain part of the body. Unlike general anesthesia, regional anesthesia does not cause loss of consciousness.

relaxin:
A naturally produced hormone that promotes relaxation of the pelvic joints and ligaments to accommodate a growing uterus in pregnancy and the passage of the fetus at birth.

ring of fire:
Burning or stinging pain on the part of the perineum that surrounds the vaginal opening, which may occur as the baby crowns.

rooming in:
A postpartum hospital arrangement where an infant remains in his mother's room under her care instead of in a communal nursery.

— S —

saddle block:
An anesthetic block that numbs the perineum, vagina, and buttocks (the areas of the body that would have contact with a saddle if one were sitting on a horse).

shoulder dystocia:
A complication of birth where the baby's head has emerged but her shoulders are stuck or wedged behind the symphysis pubis (the joint where the front of the pelvic bones meet) in the birth canal.

silver nitrate:
A preparation that may be applied to an infant's eyes shortly after birth as a prophylactic against infection. Not as commonly used as other antibiotic agents today.

sitz bath:
Also called hip bath. Soaking the perineal area

in a shallow tub of warm water to ease discomfort. Often used after episiotomy.

spinal block:
An anesthesia technique that deadens all sensation from the waist down.

stress hormones:
See catechnolamines.

surges:
What HypnoBirthing practitioners call uterine contractions.

squat:
A labor and birth position that widens the pelvic outlet and uses gravity to its advantage.

— **T** —

toxemia:
See preeclampsia.

transition:
The last phase of the first stage of labor, in which the cervix achieves full dilation.

transverse:
A fetus that is positioned sideways in the uterus; also called a transverse lie.

— **U** —

ultrasound:
A diagnostic test that uses sound waves to create a visual representation of your uterus and fetus. Ultrasound may be used in pregnancy to assess the growth and health of a fetus, or at or near labor to determine the position of singleton or multiple fetuses.

— **V** —

vaginal birth after cesarean:
A birth that occurs through the birth canal and vagina in a woman with a previous cesarean section (as opposed to a repeat cesarean). Also called VBAC.

vacuum extraction:
An alternative to forceps extraction that uses a vacuum device to attach a suction cup to the baby's head, which is attached to a chain that the provider slowly pulls on to extract the baby from the birth canal (See also: forceps extraction.)

vernix:
The white, waxy substance that covers a fetus to protect his skin from constant exposure to amniotic fluid and is still present on a newborn at birth. The full Latin term, vernix caseosa, translates to "cheese-like varnish."

— **W** —

water birth:
A birth that takes place with the mother immersed in a tub or pool of warm water. The newborn is brought to the surface immediately after emerging from the birth canal.

womb:
The uterus.

Index

THE EVERYTHING SERIES!

BUSINESS

Everything® Business Planning Book
Everything® Coaching and Mentoring Book
Everything® Fundraising Book
Everything® Home-Based Business Book
Everything® Landlording Book
Everything® Leadership Book
Everything® Managing People Book
Everything® Negotiating Book
Everything® Online Business Book
Everything® Project Management Book
Everything® Robert's Rules Book, $7.95
Everything® Selling Book
Everything® Start Your Own Business Book
Everything® Time Management Book

COMPUTERS

Everything® Computer Book

COOKBOOKS

Everything® Barbecue Cookbook
Everything® Bartender's Book, $9.95
Everything® Chinese Cookbook
Everything® Chocolate Cookbook
Everything® Cookbook
Everything® Dessert Cookbook
Everything® Diabetes Cookbook
Everything® Fondue Cookbook
Everything® Grilling Cookbook
Everything® Holiday Cookbook
Everything® Indian Cookbook
Everything® Low-Carb Cookbook
Everything® Low-Fat High-Flavor Cookbook
Everything® Low-Salt Cookbook
Everything® Mediterranean Cookbook
Everything® Mexican Cookbook
Everything® One-Pot Cookbook
Everything® Pasta Cookbook
Everything® Quick Meals Cookbook
Everything® Slow Cooker Cookbook
Everything® Soup Cookbook

Everything® Thai Cookbook
Everything® Vegetarian Cookbook
Everything® Wine Book

HEALTH

Everything® Alzheimer's Book
Everything® Anti-Aging Book
Everything® Diabetes Book
Everything® Dieting Book
Everything® Hypnosis Book
Everything® Low Cholesterol Book
Everything® Massage Book
Everything® Menopause Book
Everything® Nutrition Book
Everything® Reflexology Book
Everything® Reiki Book
Everything® Stress Management Book
Everything® Vitamins, Minerals, and
    Nutritional Supplements Book

HISTORY

Everything® American Government Book
Everything® American History Book
Everything® Civil War Book
Everything® Irish History & Heritage Book
Everything® Mafia Book
Everything® Middle East Book

HOBBIES & GAMES

Everything® Bridge Book
Everything® Candlemaking Book
Everything® Card Games Book
Everything® Cartooning Book
Everything® Casino Gambling Book, 2nd Ed.
Everything® Chess Basics Book
Everything® Crossword and Puzzle Book
Everything® Crossword Challenge Book
Everything® Drawing Book
Everything® Digital Photography Book
Everything® Easy Crosswords Book
Everything® Family Tree Book

Everything® Games Book
Everything® Knitting Book
Everything® Magic Book
Everything® Motorcycle Book
Everything® Online Genealogy Book
Everything® Photography Book
Everything® Poker Strategy Book
Everything® Pool & Billiards Book
Everything® Quilting Book
Everything® Scrapbooking Book
Everything® Sewing Book
Everything® Soapmaking Book

HOME IMPROVEMENT

Everything® Feng Shui Book
Everything® Feng Shui Decluttering Book, $9.95
Everything® Fix-It Book
Everything® Homebuilding Book
Everything® Home Decorating Book
Everything® Landscaping Book
Everything® Lawn Care Book
Everything® Organize Your Home Book

EVERYTHING® KIDS' BOOKS

All titles are $6.95

Everything® Kids' Baseball Book, 3rd Ed.
Everything® Kids' Bible Trivia Book
Everything® Kids' Bugs Book
Everything® Kids' Christmas Puzzle
    & Activity Book
Everything® Kids' Cookbook
Everything® Kids' Halloween Puzzle
    & Activity Book
Everything® Kids' Hidden Pictures Book
    Everything® Kids' Joke Book
Everything® Kids' Knock Knock Book
Everything® Kids' Math Puzzles Book
Everything® Kids' Mazes Book
Everything® Kids' Money Book

All Everything® books are priced at $12.95 or $14.95, unless otherwise stated. Prices subject to change without notice.

Everything® Kids' Monsters Book
Everything® Kids' Nature Book
Everything® Kids' Puzzle Book
Everything® Kids' Riddles & Brain Teasers Book
Everything® Kids' Science Experiments Book
Everything® Kids' Soccer Book
Everything® Kids' Travel Activity Book

KIDS' STORY BOOKS

Everything® Bedtime Story Book
Everything® Bible Stories Book
Everything® Fairy Tales Book

LANGUAGE

Everything® Conversational Japanese Book
  (with CD), $19.95
Everything® Inglés Book
Everything® French Phrase Book, $9.95
Everything® Learning French Book
Everything® Learning German Book
Everything® Learning Italian Book
Everything® Learning Latin Book
Everything® Learning Spanish Book
Everything® Sign Language Book
Everything® Spanish Phrase Book, $9.95
Everything® Spanish Verb Book, $9.95

MUSIC

Everything® Drums Book (with CD), $19.95
Everything® Guitar Book
Everything® Home Recording Book
Everything® Playing Piano and Keyboards Book
Everything® Rock & Blues Guitar Book
  (with CD), $19.95
Everything® Songwriting Book

NEW AGE

Everything® Astrology Book
Everything® Dreams Book
Everything® Ghost Book
Everything® Love Signs Book, $9.95
Everything® Meditation Book
Everything® Numerology Book
Everything® Paganism Book
Everything® Palmistry Book
Everything® Psychic Book
Everything® Spells & Charms Book
Everything® Tarot Book
Everything® Wicca and Witchcraft Book

PARENTING

Everything® Baby Names Book
Everything® Baby Shower Book
Everything® Baby's First Food Book
Everything® Baby's First Year Book
Everything® Birthing Book
Everything® Breastfeeding Book
Everything® Father-to-Be Book
Everything® Get Ready for Baby Book
Everything® Getting Pregnant Book
Everything® Homeschooling Book
Everything® Parent's Guide to Children
  with Asperger's Syndrome
Everything® Parent's Guide to Children
  with Autism
Everything® Parent's Guide to Children
  with Dyslexia
Everything® Parent's Guide to Positive Discipline
Everything® Parent's Guide to Raising a
  Successful Child
Everything® Parenting a Teenager Book
Everything® Potty Training Book, $9.95
Everything® Pregnancy Book, 2nd Ed.
Everything® Pregnancy Fitness Book
Everything® Pregnancy Nutrition Book
Everything® Pregnancy Organizer, $15.00
Everything® Toddler Book
Everything® Tween Book

PERSONAL FINANCE

Everything® Budgeting Book
Everything® Get Out of Debt Book
Everything® Homebuying Book, 2nd Ed.
Everything® Homeselling Book
Everything® Investing Book
Everything® Online Business Book
Everything® Personal Finance Book
Everything® Personal Finance in Your
  20s & 30s Book
Everything® Real Estate Investing Book
Everything® Wills & Estate Planning Book

PETS

Everything® Cat Book
Everything® Dog Book
Everything® Dog Training and Tricks Book
Everything® Golden Retriever Book
Everything® Horse Book
Everything® Labrador Retriever Book
Everything® Poodle Book

Everything® Puppy Book
Everything® Rottweiler Book
Everything® Tropical Fish Book

REFERENCE

Everything® Car Care Book
Everything® Classical Mythology Book
Everything® Einstein Book
Everything® Etiquette Book
Everything® Great Thinkers Book
Everything® Philosophy Book
Everything® Psychology Book
Everything® Shakespeare Book
Everything® Toasts Book

RELIGION

Everything® Angels Book
Everything® Bible Book
Everything® Buddhism Book
Everything® Catholicism Book
Everything® Christianity Book
Everything® Jewish History & Heritage Book
Everything® Judaism Book
Everything® Koran Book
Everything® Prayer Book
Everything® Saints Book
Everything® Understanding Islam Book
Everything® World's Religions Book
Everything® Zen Book

SCHOOL & CAREERS

Everything® After College Book
Everything® Alternative Careers Book
Everything® College Survival Book
Everything® Cover Letter Book
Everything® Get-a-Job Book
Everything® Job Interview Book
Everything® New Teacher Book
Everything® Online Job Search Book
Everything® Personal Finance Book
Everything® Practice Interview Book
Everything® Resume Book, 2nd Ed.
Everything® Study Book

SELF-HELP/
RELATIONSHIPS

Everything® Dating Book
Everything® Divorce Book
Everything® Great Sex Book

All Everything® books are priced at $12.95 or $14.95, unless otherwise stated. Prices subject to change without notice.

Everything® Kama Sutra Book
Everything® Self-Esteem Book

SPORTS & FITNESS

Everything® Body Shaping Book
Everything® Fishing Book
Everything® Fly-Fishing Book
Everything® Golf Book
Everything® Golf Instruction Book
Everything® Knots Book
Everything® Pilates Book
Everything® Running Book
Everything® T'ai Chi and QiGong Book
Everything® Total Fitness Book
Everything® Weight Training Book
Everything® Yoga Book

TRAVEL

Everything® Family Guide to Hawaii
Everything® Family Guide to New York City,
    2nd Ed.

Everything® Family Guide to Washington D.C.,
    2nd Ed.
Everything® Family Guide to the Walt Disney
    World Resort®, Universal Studios®,
    and Greater Orlando, 4th Ed.
Everything® Guide to Las Vegas
Everything® Guide to New England
Everything® Travel Guide to the Disneyland
    Resort®, California Adventure®,
    Universal Studios®, and the
    Anaheim Area

WEDDINGS

Everything® Bachelorette Party Book, $9.95
Everything® Bridesmaid Book, $9.95
Everything® Creative Wedding Ideas Book
Everything® Elopement Book, $9.95
Everything® Father of the Bride Book, $9.95
Everything® Groom Book, $9.95
Everything® Jewish Wedding Book
Everything® Mother of the Bride Book, $9.95
Everything® Wedding Book, 3rd Ed.

Everything® Wedding Checklist, $7.95
Everything® Wedding Etiquette Book, $7.95
Everything® Wedding Organizer, $15.00
Everything® Wedding Shower Book, $7.95
Everything® Wedding Vows Book, $7.95
Everything® Weddings on a Budget Book, $9.95

WRITING

Everything® Creative Writing Book
Everything® Get Published Book
Everything® Grammar and Style Book
Everything® Grant Writing Book
Everything® Guide to Writing a Novel
Everything® Guide to Writing Children's Books
Everything® Screenwriting Book
Everything® Writing Well Book

Introducing an exceptional new line of beginner craft books from the *Everything*® series!

EVERYTHING
C·R·A·F·T·S

All titles are $14.95.

Everything® Crafts—Create Your Own Greeting Cards
1-59337-226-4
Everything® Crafts—Polymer Clay for Beginners
1-59337-230-2

Everything® Crafts—Rubberstamping Made Easy
1-59337-229-9
Everything® Crafts—Wedding Decorations
and Keepsakes
1-59337-227-2

Available wherever books are sold!
To order, call 800-872-5627, or visit us at *www.everything.com*
Everything® and everything.com® are registered trademarks of F+W Publications, Inc.